ANIMAL TEXTILE

ANIMAL TEXTILE

By

Meenakshi Rastogi

SONALI PUBLICATIONS
NEW DELHI-110002

First Published-2009

ISBN 978-81-8411-214-6

Published by

SONALI PUBLICATIONS

4228/1, Ansari Road,
New Delhi-110 002 (India)
Phone: 23266109, 23279245
Fax: 91-11-23253475
E-mail: sonalipub@yahoo.co.in

Printed at:

Sachin Printers, Delhi-

Preface

Textiles can be made from many materials. These materials come from four main sources: animal, plant, mineral, and synthetic. In the past, all textiles were made from natural fibres, including plant, animal, and mineral sources. In the 20th century, these were supplemented by artificial fibres made from petroleum.

Textiles are made in various strengths and degrees of durability, from the finest gossamer to the sturdiest canvas. The relative thickness of fibres in cloth is measured in deniers. Microfibre refers to fibres made of strands thinner than one denier.

Animal fibers generally comprise proteins; examples include silk, wool, angora, mohair and alpaca. **Animal fibers** are natural fibers that consist largely of particular proteins. Instances are silk, hair/fur (including wool) and feathers. The most commonly used type of animal fiber is hair.

Not all animal fibers have the same properties. Alpaca fiber is known for its softness, and silk for its sheen and strength. Even within a species the fiber is not consistent. Merino is a very soft, fine wool, while Cotswold is coarser, and yet both merino and Cotswold are types of sheep. This comparison can be continued on the microscopic level, comparing the diameter and structure of the fiber.

Wool provides warm, comfortable fabrics for dresses, suits, and sweaters. Silk comes from cocoons spun by silkworms. Workers unwind the cocoons to obtain long, natural filaments. Fabrics made from silk fibers have great luster and softness and can be dyed brilliant colors. Silk is especially popular for scarfs and neckties.

With animal fibers, and natural fibers in general, the individual fibers look different, whereas all animal fibers look the same. This provides an easy way to differentiate between natural and animal fibers under a microscope. The animal fibers used most commonly both in the manufacturing world as well as by the hand spinners are wool and silk.

Animal Textile plays an important role in our collection of technical apparel. Garments made with animal yarns are comfortable, adaptable, lightweight and dry quickly. Synthetic fleece keeps you warm and dry in the winter while synthetic base layer keeps you cool and dry in the summer. However, animal fabrics do require natural resources to produce. That's why whenever possible we source animal fabrics that contain recycled content.

Textile industry in India has started gaining prominence in the national agenda right from early years of the independence. India has vast picturesque locations, age-old cultures and traditions, architectural heritage as well as large and relatively inexpensive manpower resources (skilled and Unskilled) suitable for deployment in this industry; yet, these resources – natural and Manpower – have not been exploited optimally in India. There is enormous potential for growth in the industry leading to significant socio-economic benefits for the population.

"One hundred years of chemical fibers, and of these more than fifty years of synthetic fibers, do demand an inventory of the required technologies. While there is literature for the chemistry of the chemical and animal fibers, as well as for the processes and the textile testing technology, it is hardly possible to find comprehensive descriptions from installation, equipment and machinery manufacture through production of synthetic fibers and filaments and the manipulation of their properties..."

The objective of this book is to provide the whole knowledge about what kind of animal textiles are and in which form they exists, by which user can understand all the aspects of this book. We hope that the discussion made in this book will help the readers to understand and learnt about the different aspects of "Animal Textile" in a most comprehensive way to face the present and future challenges which are occured in this field.

Thanks

Contents

1

Introduction of Textile

A **textile** is a flexible material consisting of a network of natural or artificial fibres often referred to as thread or yarn. Yarn is produced by spinning raw wool fibres, linen, cotton, or other material on a spinning wheel to produce long strands known as yarn. Textiles are formed by weaving, knitting, crocheting, knotting, or pressing fibres together (felt).

The term 'Textile' is a Latin word originating from the word 'texere' which means 'to weave'. Textile refers to a flexible material comprising of a network of natural or artificial fibres, known as yarn. Textiles are formed by weaving, knitting, crocheting, knotting and pressing fibres together. Textile Museum is that specialized category of museum which primarily preserves different types of textile and textile products.

The words *'fabric'* and *cloth* are used in textile assembly trades (such as tailoring and dressmaking) as synonyms for *textile*. However, there are subtle differences in these terms. *Textile* refers to any material made of interlacing fibres. *Fabric* refers to any material made through weaving, knitting, crocheting, or bonding. *Cloth* refers to a finished piece of fabric that can be used for a purpose such as covering a bed.

History of Textile

The History of textile is almost as old as that of human civilization and as time moves on, the history of textile has further enriched itself. In the 6th and 7th century BC, the oldest recorded indication of using fibre comes with the invention of flax and wool fabric at the excavation of Swiss lake inhabitants. In India the culture of silk was introduced in 400AD, while spinning of cotton traces back to 3000BC. In China, the discovery and consequent development of sericulture and spin silk methods got initiated at 2640 BC while in Egypt the art of spinning linen and weaving developed in 3400 BC. The discovery of machines and their widespread application in processing natural fibres was a direct outcome of the industrial revolution of the 18th and 19th centuries. The discoveries of various synthetic fibres like nylon created a wider market for textile products and gradually led to the invention of new and improved sources of natural fibre. The development of transportation and communication facilities facilitated the path of transaction of localized skills and textile art among various countries.

Textile History of Various Countries: India

Indian textile enjoys a rich heritage and the origin of textiles in India traces back to the Indus Valley Civilization where people used home spun cotton for weaving their clothes. Rigveda, the earliest of the Veda contains the literary information about textiles and it refers to weaving. Ramayana and Mahabharata, the eminent Indian epics depict the existence of wide variety of fabrics in ancient India. These epics refer both to rich and stylized garment worn by the aristocrats and ordinary simple clothes worn by the common people. The contemporary Indian textile not only reflects the splendid past but also cater to the requirements of the modern times.

Japan

In 1869 the capital of Japan was shifted from Kyoto to Tokyo and from this time onwards the Nishijin weaving tradition seemed threatened with extinction. The industry again started to grow along with Japan's new capitalist economy by 1890 when the Nishijin weavers embraced and applied modern technology to their own ancient and original textile art. The textile art of Japan particularly reached an epitome of excellence by exhibiting a cultural distinction and remarkable artistic skill in the Edo and succeeding Meiji periods (1868 - 1912).

China

Chinese textiles enjoy an excellent heritage in textile sector and occupy a prominent position in the global textile market. Chinese textiles are world famous and extraordinary for their fine quality and profound symbolic meanings. Textiles in China often form an integral aspect of its heritage and symbolically reflect its tradition and culture. In China, textile is often closely associated with prosperity and involved in the process of elaborate rituals. Parents' spontaneous love for their children is most visibly reflected through the excellent clothes they provide on festive occasions to their children. These clothes are made up of expensive materials and excellent craftsmanship.

Africa

In the ancient times the most important aspect of textiles or more precisely cloth in Africa was that cloth was used as form of money. The width of cloth strip was usually standardized in each region of Africa and therefore there used to be a regular number of such standard length cloth strips required to make a woman's wrapper cloth. This would then be used to serve as the unit of value. Cloth was a convenient form of money primarily because it was used by everybody, fairly durable and easily sub dividable.

The weavers, dyers and other textile artists of Africa together makes an active contribution in creating exquisite and amazing range of textiles. African usually embody a great variety of styles.

Adinkara, kente and bogolan are some of the African textiles which are becoming increasingly popular while some others like Yoruba, Ase-oke and Adire are equally beautiful but less well known.

The textile industry, with its extremely long and rich history, has had a massive impact on the world economy and the very evolution of modern society. Weaving is believed to be one of the oldest surviving crafts in the world today, the actual origins of which are thought to date back to Neolithic times 12,000 years ago. Even before that time, the same principle was used to interlace branches and twigs to form protective fences, shelters and baskets. Once the practicality of interlacing these kinds of materials was understood, further experimentation with other natural materials probably produced the first basic fabrics and clothes.

Uses

Textiles have an assortment of uses, the most common of which are for clothing and containers such as bags and baskets. In the household, they are used in carpeting, upholstered furnishings, window shades, towels, covering for tables, beds, and other flat surfaces, and in art. In the workplace, they are used in industrial and scientific processes such as filtering. Miscellaneous uses include flags, backpacks, tents, nets, cleaning devices, such as handkerchiefs; transportation devices such as balloons, kites, sails, and parachutes; and strengthening in composite materials such as fibre glass and industrial geotextiles. Textiles can be used for educational purposes. Textiles can be used as a material for children to use and explore in their classrooms as another element of learning. Children can manipulate and come up with creative uses for textiles such as collage materials, art materials and so on.

Textiles used for industrial purposes, and chosen for characteristics other than their appearance, are commonly referred to as *technical textiles.* Technical textiles include textile structures for automotive applications, medical textiles (e.g. implants), geotextiles (reinforcement of embankments), agrotextiles (textiles for crop protection), protective clothing (e.g. against heat and radiation for fire fighter clothing, against molten metals for welders, stab protection, and bullet proof vests. In all these applications stringent performance requirements must be met. Woven of threads coated with zinc oxide nanowires, laboratory fabric has been shown capable of "self-powering nanosystems" using vibrations created by everyday actions like wind or body movements.

Sources and Types

Textiles can be made from many materials. These materials come from four main sources: animal, plant, mineral, and synthetic. In the past, all textiles were made from natural fibres, including plant, animal, and mineral sources. In the 20th century, these were supplemented by artificial fibres made from petroleum.

Textiles are made in various strengths and degrees of durability, from the finest gossamer to the sturdiest canvas. The relative thickness of fibres in cloth is measured in deniers. Microfibre refers to fibres made of strands thinner than one denier.

Animal textiles

Animal textiles are commonly made from hair or fur.

Wool refers to the hair of the domestic goat or sheep, which is distinguished from other types of animal hair. That the individual strands are coated with scales and tightly crimped, and the wool as a whole is coated with an oil known as lanolin, which is waterproof and dirtproof. Woollen refers to a bulkier yarn produced from carded, non-parallel fibre, while worsted refers to a finer yarn which is spun from longer fibres which have been combed to be parallel. Wool is commonly used for warm clothing. Cashmere, the hair of the Indian Cashmere goat, and Mohair, the hair of the North African angora goat, are types of wool known for their softness.

Other animal textiles which are made from hair or fur are alpaca wool, vicuna wool, llama wool, and camel hair, generally used in the production of coats, jackets, ponchos, blankets, and other warm coverings. Angora refers to the long, thick, soft hair of the angora rabbit.

Wadmal is a coarse cloth made of wool, produced in Scandinavia, mostly 1000-1500.

Silk is an animal textile made from the fibres of the cocoon of the Chinese silkworm. This is spun into a smooth, shiny fabric prized for its sleek texture.

Plant textiles

Grass, rush, hemp, and sisal are all used in making rope. In the first two, the entire plant is used for this purpose, while in the last two, only fibres from the plant are utilized. Coir (coconut fibre) is used in making twine, and also in floormats, doormats, brushes, mattresses, floor tiles, and sacking.

Straw and bamboo are both used to make hats. Straw, a dried form of grass, is also used for stuffing, as is kapok.

Fibres from pulpwood trees, cotton, rice, hemp, and nettle are used in making paper.

Cotton, flax, jute, hemp and modal are all used in clothing. Pina (pineapple fibre) and ramie are also fibres used in clothing, generally with a blend of other fabrics such as cotton.

Acetate is used to increase the shininess of certain fabrics such as silks, velvets, and taffetas.

Seaweed is used in the production of textiles. A water-soluble fibre known as Alginate is produced and is used as a holding fibre; when the cloth is finished, the alginate is dissolved, leaving an open area

Tencel is a man-made fabric derived from wood pulp. It is often described as a man-made silk equivalent and is a tough fabric which is often blended with other fabrics - cotton for example.

Mineral Textiles

Asbestos and basalt fibre are used for vinyl tiles, sheeting, and adhesives, "transite" panels and siding, acoustical ceilings, stage curtains, and fire blankets.

Glass Fibre is used in the production of spacesuits, ironing board and mattress covers, ropes and cables, reinforcement fibre for composite materials, insect netting, flame-retardant and protective fabric, soundproof, fireproof, and insulating fibres. Metal fibre, metal foil, and metal wire have a variety of uses, including the production of cloth-of-gold and Jewellery. Hardware cloth is a coarse weave of steel wire, used in construction.

Synthetic textiles

A variety of contemporary fabrics. From the left: even weave cotton, velvet, printed cotton, calico, felt, satin, silk, hessian, polycotton. All synthetic textiles are used primarily in the production of clothing.

Polyester fibre is used in all types of clothing, either alone or blended with fibres such as cotton.

Aramid fibre (e.g. Twaron) is used for flame-retardant clothing, cut-protection, and armor.

Acrylic is a fibre used to imitate wools, including cashmere, and is often used in replacement of them.

Nylon is a fibre used to imitate silk; it is used in the production of pantyhose. Thicker nylon fibres are used in rope and outdoor clothing.

Spandex (trade name *Lycra*) is a polyurethane fibre that stretches easily and can be made tight-fitting without impeding movement. It is used to make activewear and swimsuits.

Olefin fibre is a fibre used in activewear, linings, and warm clothing. Olefins are hydrophobic, allowing them to dry quickly. A sintered felt of olefin fibres is sold under the trade name Tyvek.

Ingeo is a polylactide fibre blended with other fibres such as cotton and used in clothing. It is more hydrophilic than most other synthetics, allowing it to wick away perspiration.

Lurex is a metallic fibre used in clothing embellishment.

Types of Fibre

Fibres is a class of hair-like materials that are continuous filaments or are in discrete elongated pieces, similar to pieces of thread. They can be spun into filaments, thread, or rope. They can be used as a component of composite materials. They can also be matted into sheets to make products such as paper or felt. Fibres are of two types: **natural fibre** and **man made** or **synthetic fibre**.

Natural Fibres

Natural fibres include those made from plant, animal and mineral sources. Natural fibres can be classified according to their origin.

Vegetable fibres

Vegetable fibres are generally comprised mainly of cellulose: examples include cotton, jute, flax, ramie, sisal, and hemp. Cellulose fibres serve in the manufacture of paper and cloth.

COTTON- Cotton is a soft, staple fibre that grows in a form known as a boll around the seeds of the cotton plant (*Gossypium* sp.), a shrub native to tropical and subtropical regions around the world, including the America, India and Africa. The fibre most often is spun into yarn or thread and used to make a soft, breathable textile, which is the most widely used natural-fibre cloth in clothing today.

JUTE-Jute is a long, soft, shiny vegetable fibre that can be spun into coarse, strong threads. It is produced from plants in the genus *Corchorus*, family Tiliaceae.

Jute is one of the cheapest natural fibres and is second only to cotton in amount produced and variety of uses. Jute fibres are composed primarily of the plant materials cellulose (major component of plant fibre) and lignin (major components wood fibre). It is thus a ligno-cellulosic fibre that is partially a textile fibre and partially wood. It falls into the bast fibre category (fibre collected from bast or skin of the plant) along with kenaf, industrial hemp, flax (linen), ramie, etc. The industrial term for jute fibre is *raw jute*. The fibres are off-white to brown, and 1–4 meters (3–12 feet) long.

Jute fibre is often called hessian; jute fabrics are also called hessian cloth and jute sacks are called gunny bags in some European countries. The fabric made from jute is popularly known as burlap in North America.

FLAX- Flax (also known as **common flax** or **linseed)** (binomial name: ***Linum usitatissimum***) is a member of the genus *Linum* in the family Linaceae. It is native to the region extending from the eastern Mediterranean to India and was probably first domesticated in the Fertile Crescent. This is called as Jawas/Javas or Alashi in Marathi. Flax was extensively cultivated in ancient Egypt. (NewZealand flax is not related to flax, but was named after it as both plants are used to produce fibres.)

Flax is an erect annual plant growing to 1.2 m tall, with slender stems. The leaves are glaucous green, slender lanceolate, 20–40 mm long and 3 mm broad. The flowers are pure pale blue, 15–25 mm diameter, with five petals; they can also be bright red. The fruit is a round, dry capsule 5–9 mm diameter, containing several glossy brown seeds shaped like an apple pip, 4–7 mm long.

In addition to referring to the plant itself, "flax" may refer to the unspun fibres of the flax plant.

Uses- Flax is grown both for its seeds and for its fibres. Various parts of the plant have been used to make fabric, dye, paper, medicines, fishing nets and soap. It is also grown as an ornamental plant in gardens.

RAMIE- Ramie (*Boehmeria nivea*) is a flowering plant in the nettle family Urticaceae, native to eastern Asia. It is a herbaceous perennial growing to 1 - 2.5 m tall; the leaves are heart-shaped, 7-15 cm long and 6-12 cm broad, and white on the underside with dense small hairs - this gives it a silvery appearance; unlike nettles, the hairs do not sting. The true Ramie or China Grass also called Chinese plant or white Ramie is the Chinese cultivated plant. A second type, is known as green Ramie or Rhea and is believed to have originated in the Malay Peninsula. This type has smaller leaves which are green on the underside, and it appears to be better suited to tropical conditions.

SISAL- Sisal is an agave. *Agave sisalana* that yields a stiff fibre traditionally used in making twine and rope. (The term may refer either to the plant or the fibre, depending on context.) It is sometimes been incorrectly referred to as *sisal hemp* because hemp was for centuries a major source of fibre, so other fibres were sometimes named after it.

The plant originated in the Yucatan Peninsula of Mexico. In the 19th century, Sisal cultivation spread to Florida, the Caribbean islands and Brazil, as well as to countries in Africa, notably Tanzania and Kenya, and Asia. The first commercial plantings in Brazil were made in the late 1930's and the first Sisal fibre exports from there were made in 1948. It was not until the 1960,s that Brazilian production really accelerated and the first of many spinning mills were established. Today, Brazil is the major world producer of Sisal. There are both positive and negative environmental impacts from Sisal growing. Traditionally used for rope and twine, sisal has many uses, including paper, cloth, wall coverings and carpets.

HEMP- Hemp (from Old English *hænep*, see cannabis (etymology)) is the common name for plants of the entire genus *Cannabis*, although the term is often used to refer only to *Cannabis* strains cultivated for industrial (non-drug) use.

Industrial. Hemp has many uses, including paper, textiles, biodegradable plastics, health food, and fuel. It is one of the fastest growing biomasses known, and one of the earliest domesticated plants known. It also runs parallel with the "Green Future" objectives that are becoming increasingly popular. Hemp requires little to no pesticides, no herbicides, controls erosion of the topsoil, and produces oxygen. Furthermore, Hemp can be used to replace many potentially harmful products, such as tree paper (the processing of which uses bleaches and other toxic chemicals, and contributes to deforestation), cosmetics, and plastics, most of which are petroleum-based and do not decompose easily. The major difference between the two types of plants is the appearance and the amount of–tetrahydrocannabinol (THC) secreted in a resinous mixture by epidermal hairs called Glandular Trichomes. Industrial Hemp is produced in many countries around the world.

This fibre can be further categorized into the following:

- Seed fibre: Fibres collected from seeds or seed cases. e.g. Cotton and Kapok
- Leaf fibre: Fibres collected from leaves. e.g. sisal and agave.
- Bast fibre or skin fibre: Fibres are collected from the skin or bast surrounding the stem of their respective plant. These fibres have higher tensile strength than other fibres. Therefore, these fibres are used for durable yarn, fabric, packaging, and paper. Some examples are flax, jute, kenaf, industrial hemp, ramie, rattan, soybean fibre, and even vine fibres and banana fibres.

- Fruit fibre: Fibres are collected from the fruit of the plant, e.g. coconut (coir) fibre.
- Stalk fibre: Fibres are actually the stalks of the plant. E.g. straws of wheat, rice, barley, and other crops including bamboo and grass. Tree wood is also such a fibre.

The most used natural fibres are cotton, flax and hemp, although sisal, jute, kenaf, and coconut are also widely used.

Hemp fibres are mainly used for ropes and aerofoils because of their high suppleness and resistance within an aggressive environment. Hemp fibres are, for example, currently used as a seal within the heating and sanitary industries.

Animal fibres : Animal fibres generally comprise proteins; examples include silk, wool, angora, mohair and alpaca.

- Animal hair (wool or hairs): Fibre or wool taken from animals or hairy mammals. e.g. sheep's wool, goat hair (cashmere, mohair), alpaca hair, horse hair, etc.
- Silk fibre: Fibre collected from dried saliva of bugs or insects during the preparation of cocoons, Examples include silk.
- Avian fibre: Fibres from birds, e.g. feathers and feather fibre.

Industrial use of natural fibres

After World War II, the build-up of synthetic .fibres significantly decreased the use of natural fibres. Now, with the increase of oil prices and environmental considerations, there has been a revival of natural fibre use within the textile, building, plastic and automotive industries. This interest is reinforced by the developmental perspectives on the agro-industrial market and local productions, allowing economic development and independence versus imported materials.

France remains the greatest European Hemp fibre producer with 50,000 tons yearly (EU 100,000 tons). France also produces the largest range of industrial seeds worldwide. China and Russia are also important producers, but the statistics in that field are not available. In the industrial domain, the consortium DAIFA group SAS have reached a leading position in Europe in the automotive plastics market. They specialize in injection and thermopress plastics reinforced with natural fibres.

The use of natural fibres at the industrial level improves the environmental sustainability of the parts being constructed, especially within the automotive market. Within the building industry, the interest in natural fibres is mostly economical and technical; natural fibres allow insulation properties higher than current materials.

Synthetic Fibre

Synthetic fibres are the result of extensive research by scientists to improve upon naturally occurring animal and plant. In general, synthetic fibres are created by forcing, usually through extrusion, fibre forming materials through holes (called spinnerets) into the air, forming a thread. Before Synthetic fibres were developed, artificially manufactured fibres were made from cellulose, which comes from plants.

The first artificial fibre, known as artificial silk from 1799 onwards, became known as Viscose around 1894, and finally Rayon in 1924. A similar product known as Cellulose Acetate was discovered in 1865. Rayon and Acetate are both artificial fibres, but not truly synthetic, being made from wood. Although these artificial fibres were discovered in the mid-nineteenth century, successful modern manufacture began much later (see the dates below).

Nylon, the first synthetic fibre, made its debut in the United States as a replacement for silk, just in time for World War II rationing. Its nobel use as a material for women's stockings overshadowed more practical uses, such as a replacement for the silk in parachutes and other military uses.

Common Synthetic fibres include:

- Rayon (1910) (artificial, not synthetic)
- Acetate (1924) (artificial, not synthetic)
- Nylon (1939)
- Modacrylic (1949)
- Olefin (1949)
- Acrylic (ORLON)(1950)

- Polyester (1953)
- PLA (2002)

Speciality Synthetic fibres include:

- Vinyon (1939)
- Saran (1941)
- Spandex (1959)
- Vinalon (1939)
- Aramids (1961) - known as Nomex, Kevlar and Twaron
- PBI (Polybenzimidazole fibre) (1983)
- Sulfar (1983)
- Lyocell (1992)
- Zylon (PBO fibre)

Modern fibres that are made from older artificial materials include:

- Glass Fibre is used for:
    - o industrial, automotive, and home insulation (Fibreglass)
    - o reinforcement of composite and plastics
    - o specialty papers in battery separators and filtration
- Metallic fibre (1946) is used for:
    - o adding metallic properties to clothing for the purpose of fashion (usually made with composite plastic and metal foils)
    - o elimination and prevention of static charge build-up
    - o conducting electricity to transmit information
    - o conduction of heat

➛ **Rayon** is a manufactured regenerated cellulosic fibre. Because it is produced from naturally occurring polymers, it is neither a truly synthetic fibre nor a natural fibre; it is a semi-synthetic fibre. Rayon is known by the names *viscose rayon* and *art silk* in the textile industry. It usually has a high lustre quality giving it a bright shine. Rayon contains the chemical elements carbon, hydrogen, and oxygen.

➛ **Cellulose acetate**, first prepared in 1865, is the acetate ester of cellulose. Cellulose acetate is used as a film base in photography, and as a component in some adhesives; it is also used as a Synthetic fibre

Acetate fibre and Triacetate fibre

Acetate and Triacetate are mistakenly referred to as the same fibre; although they are similar, their chemical compounds differ. Triacetate is known as a generic description or primary acetate containing no hydroxyl group. Acetate fibre is known as modified or secondary acetate having a few hydroxyl groups. Triacetate fibres, although no longer produced in the United States, contain a higher ratio of acetate-to-cellulose than to acetate fibres.

- **Nylon** is a generic designation for a family of synthetic polymers known generically as polyamides and first produced on February 28, 1935 by Wallace Carothers at DuPont. Nylon is one of the most commonly used polymers.

Nylon is a thermoplastic silky material, first used commercially in a nylon-bristled toothbrush (1938), followed more famously by women's stockings ("nylons"; 1940). It is made of repeating units linked by peptide bonds (another name for amide bonds) and is frequently referred to as *polyamide* (PA). Nylon was the first commercially successful polymer and the first synthetic fibre to be made entirely from coal, water, and air. These are formed into monomers of intermediate molecular weight, which are then reacted to form long polymer chains.

Nylon was intended to be a synthetic replacement for silk and substituted for it in many different products after silk became scarce during World War II. It replaced silk in military applications such as parachutes and flak vests, and was used in many types of vehicle tires.

Nylon fibres are used in many applications, including fabrics, bridal veils, carpets, musical strings, and rope.

Solid nylon is used for mechanical parts such as machine screws, gears and other low-to medium-stress components previously cast in metal. Engineering-grade nylon is processed by extrusion, casting, and injection molding. Solid nylon is used in hair combs. Type 6/6 Nylon 101 is the most common commercial grade of nylon, and Nylon 6 is the most common commercial grade of molded nylon. Nylon is available in glass-filled variants which increase structural and impact strength and rigidity, and molybdenum sulfide-filled variants which increase lubricity.

Aramids are another type of polyamide with quite different chain structures which include aromatic groups in the main chain. Such polymers make excellent ballistic fibres.

Nylon fibre

The Federal Trade Commission's definition for Nylon Fibre: "A manufactured fibre in which the fibre forming substance is a long-chain synthetic polyamide in which less than 85% of the amide-linkages are attached directly (-CO-NH-) to two aliphatic groups."

- A synthetic thermoplastic fibre (Nylon melts/glazes easily at relatively low temperatures)
- Round, smooth, and shiny filament fibres
- Cross sections can be either
    - trilobal to imitate silk
    - multilobal to increase staple like appearance and hand
- Its most widely used structures are multifilament, monofilament, staple or tow and is available as partially drawn or as finished filaments.
- Regular nylon has a round cross section and is perfectly uniform. The filaments are generally completely transparent unless they have been delustered or solution dyed. Thus, they are microscopically recognized as glass rods.
- Molecular chains of nylon are long and straight variations but have no side chains or linkages.
    - Cold drawing can align the chains so they are oriented with the lengthwise direction and are highly crystalline.
- Nylon is related chemically to the protein fibres, silk and wool.
    - They both have similar dye sites but nylon has many fewer dye sites than wool.

➛ **A Modacrylic** is a synthetic co-polymer. Modacrylics are soft, strong, resilient, and dimensionally stable. They can be easily dyed, show good press and shape retention, and are quick to dry. They have outstanding resistance to chemicals and solvents, are not attacked by moths or mildew, and are nonallergenic. Among their uses are in apparel linings, furlike outerwear, paint-roller covers, scatter rugs, carpets, and work clothing and as hair in wigs.

Commercial production of Modacrylic fibre began in 1949 by Union Carbide Corporation in the United States . Modacrylic and acrylic fibres are similar in composition and at one time were in the same category. In 1960 the Federal Trade Commission decided to separate the two fibres and establish a category for each.

The Federal Trade Commission defines Modacrylic fibres as manufactured fibres in which the fibre-forming substance is any long-chain synthetic polymer composed of less than 85%, but at least 35% weight of acrylonitrile units except when the polymer qualifies as rubber.

Modacrylic fibres are modified acrylic fibres made from acrylonitriles, but larger amounts of other polymers are added to make the copolymers.

The Modacrylic fibres are produced by polymerizing the components, dissolving the copolymer in acetone, pumping the solution into the column of warm air (dry-spun), and stretching while it is hot.

Modacrylics are creamy or white and are produced in tow and staple form. If looked at in cross section views, they have an irregular shape. Modacrylic fibres are also produced in many different lengths, crimp levels, deniers and they can have various shrinkage potentials.

Current modacrylic fibre producers include Solutia Inc. in the U.S. and Kaneka Corporation in Japan.

Properties : A Modacrylic has properties that are similar to an Acrylic. However, modacrylics are flame retardant and do not combust. The fibres are difficult to ignite and are self-extinguish. In addition to a modacrylic's flame retardant properties it has a relatively high durability that is comparable to wool. Modacrylic fibres have a moderate resistance to abrasion and a very low tenacity.

Modacrylics are poor conductors of heat. The fabrics are soft, warm and resilient but are prone to pilling and matting.

Modacrylics display high performance when it comes to appearance retention. The fibres are quite resilient and will not wrinkle. They also have great dimensional stability and high elastic recovery, which gives them the ability to hold their shape.

Care **:** Modacrylics are sensitive to loss of appearance due to improper care; therefore, it is important to know how to care for modacrylics. Modacrylics are resistant to acids, weak alkalis, and organic solvents. These fibres are also resistant to moths, mildew and sunlight. Modacrylic fabrics can be machine washed using warm water and tumble dried on a low setting. Modacrylic pieces can also be dry-cleaned, however, they should not be steamed and should only be tumbled on cold. Some fabrics may also be cleaned using the furrier method (a special non-immersion cleaning process). The fibres are heat sensitive and will shrink at 250 °F and will stiffen at temperatures over 300 °F.

Uses **:** Modacrylics are used primarily in applications where environmental resistance or flame retardancy is necessary or required. Modacrylics have the ability to combine flame retardancy with a relatively low density, meaning protective gear is not uncomfortably heavy (i.e. shirts and trousers worn by electrical linemen). The combination of flame retardancy and low density is also useful in furnishings, draperies, and outdoor fabrics.

Modacrylics are also commonly used in furlike fabrics, hairpieces, wigs and fleece type fabric. By mixing the various forms of fibres it is easy to create a realistic fur look. The fabrics can then be sheared or embossed to create a closer resemblance to fur. The heat-sensitivity of modacrylic also allows wigs and hairpiece to be curled and heat styled without damage.

Modacrylics are also used in fleece, knit-pile fabric backings, and non-woven fabrics. Other uses of modacrylics include paint rollers, industrial fabrics, stuffed toys and filters.

➛ **Olefin fibre** is a synthetic fibre made from alkenes. It is used in the manufacture of various textiles as well as clothing, upholstery, wallpaper, ropes, and vehicle interiors. Olefin is also referred to as polypropylene, polyethylene, or polyolefin. Olefin's advantages are its strength, colourfastness and comfort, stain, mildew, abrasion and sunlight resistance, and good bulk and cover.

Olefin fibres have great bulk and cover while having low specific gravity. This means "warmth without the weight." The fibres have low moisture absorption, but they can wick moisture and dry quickly. Olefin is abrasion, stain, sunlight, and chemical resistant. It does not dye well, but has the advantage of being colour fast. Since Olefin has a low melting point, textiles can be thermally bonded. The fibres have the lowest static of all manufactured fibres and a medium lustre. One of the most important properties of Olefin is its strength. It keeps its strength in wet or dry conditions and is very resilient. The fibre can be produced for strength of different properties.

Physical and Chemical Structure

Physical : Olefin fibres can be multi or monofilament and staple, tow or film yarns. The fibres are colourless and round in cross section. This cross section can be modified for different end uses. The physical characteristics are a waxy feel and colourless.

Chemical : There are two types of polymers that can be used in Olefin fibres. The first, Polyethylene, is a simple linear structure with repeating units. These fibres are used mainly for ropes, twines and utility fabrics.

The second type, Polypropylene, is a three dimensional structure with a backbone of carbon atoms. Methyl groups protrude from this backbone. Stereoselective polymerization orders these methyl groups to the same spatial placement. This creates a crystalline polypropylene polymer. The fibres made with these polymers can be used in apparel, furnishing and industrial products.

➛ **Acrylic fibres** are synthetic fibres made from a polymer (Polyacrylonitrile) with an average molecular weight of 100,000, about 1900 monomer units. To be called Acrylic in the U.S, the polymer must contain at least 85% acrylonitrile monomer. Typical comonomers are vinyl acetate or methyl acrylate. The Dupont Corporation created the first acrylic fibres in 1941 and trademarked them under the name "**Orlon**".

Acrylic is lightweight, soft, and warm, with a wool-like feel. It dyes very well and has excellent colourfastness. It is resilient, retains its shape, and resists shrinkage and wrinkles. Acrylic has recently been used in clothing as a less expensive alternative to cashmere, due to the similar feeling of the materials. The disadvantages of Acrylic are that it tends to fuzz (or pill) easily and that it does not insulate the wearer as well as cashmere. Many products like fake pashmina or cashmina use this fibre to create the illusion of cashmere to the consumer. Acrylic is resistant to moths, oils, and chemicals, and is very resistant to deterioration from sunlight exposure.

➛ **Polyester** is a category of polymers which contain the ester functional group in their main chain. Although there are many polyesters, the term "polyester" as a specific material most commonly refers to Polyethylene Terephthalate (PET). Polyesters include naturally-occurring chemicals, such as in the cutin of plant cuticles, as well as synthetics such as polycarbonate and polybutyrate. Polyesters aren't biodegradable.

Polyesters may be produced in numerous forms such as sheets and three-dimensional shapes. Polyesters as thermoplastics may change shape after the application of heat. While combustible at high temperatures, polyesters tend to shrink away from flames and self-extinguish upon ignition. Polyester fibres have high tenacity and E-modulus as well as low water absorption and minimal shrinkage in comparison with other industrial fibres.

Woven polyester fabrics are used in consumer apparel and home furnishings such as bedsheets, bedspreads, curtains and draperies. Similarly, industrial polyesters are used in tyre reinforcements, ropes, fabrics for conveyor belts, safety belts, coated fabrics and plastic reinforcements with high energy absorption. Polyester fibrefills are also used to stuff pillows, comforters and cushion padding.

Polyester fabrics are claimed to have a "less natural" feel when compared to similarly-woven fabrics made from natural fibres (i.e. cotton in textile uses). However, polyester fabrics may exhibit other advantages over natural fabrics, such as improved wrinkle resistance. As a result, polyester fibres are sometimes spun together with natural fibres to produce a cloth with blended properties.

Polyesters are also used to make bottles, films, tarpaulin, canoes, liquid crystal displays, holograms, filters, dielectric film for capacitors, film insulation for wire and insulating tapes.

Liquid crystalline polyesters are among the first industrially-used liquid crystalline polymers. They are used for their mechanical properties and heat-resistance. These traits are also important in their application as an abradable seal in jet engines.

Thermosetting polyesters are used as casting materials, and Chemosetting polyester resins are used as fibreglass laminating resins and non-metallic auto-body fillers. Fibreglass-reinforced unsaturated polyesters find wide application in bodies of yachts and as body parts of cars.

Polyesters are also widely used as a finish on high-quality wood products such as guitars, pianos and vehicle / yacht interiors. Cured polyesters can be sanded and polished to a high-gloss, durable finish.

Mechanical Properties

Energy absorption of chemical fibre reinforced plastics (impact, bending and tensile tests) Investigation of the practical requirements for measuring the energy absorption of composite materials, and development of a suitable method for carrying out such measurements. A number of dynamic testing methods for measuring the energy absorption of laminates are reviewed, including an impact bending test, repeated-impact tests, an impact tensile test, and a ram bending test. Also discussed are impact tests on plate laminates. Particular emphasis is placed in these studies on composites with a chemical fibre reinforcement. It is established that a relation exists between the quasi-static energy absorption of the fibres and the dynamic energy absorption of the composite. Composites with commercial polyester and polyamide fibres lead to the highest energy absorptions, in which the testing apparatus has a significant effect.

➛ **Polylactic acid** or **Polylactide (PLA)** is a biodegradable, thermoplastic, aliphatic polyester derived from renewable resources, such as corn starch (in the U.S.) or sugarcanes (in rest of the world). Although PLA has been known for more than a century, it has only been of commercial interest in recent years, in light of its biodegradability.

Chemical and Physical Properties

Due to the chiral nature of lactic acid, several distinct forms of polylactide exist: poly-L-lactide (**PLLA**) is the product resulting from polymerization of L,L-lactide (also known as L-lactide). PLLA has a crystallinity of around 37%, a glass transition temperature between 50-80 °C and a melting temperature between 173-178 °C.

Polylactic acid can be processed like most thermoplastics into fibre (for example using conventional melt spinning processes) and film. The melting temperature of PLLA can be increased 40-50 °C and its heat deflection temperature can be increased from approximately 60°C to up to 190 °C by physically blending the polymer with PDLA (poly-D-lactide). PDLA and PLLA form a highly regular stereocomplex with increased crystallinity. The temperature stability is maximised when a 50:50 blend is used, but even at lower concentrations of 3-10% of PDLA, there is still a substantial improvement. In the latter case, PDLA acts as a nucleating agent, thereby increasing the crystallization rate. Biodegradation of PDLA is slower than for PLA due to the higher crystallinity of PDLA. PDLA has the useful property of being optically transparent.

➔ **Vinyon** is a synthetic fibre made from Polyvinyl Chloride. In some countries other than the United States, Vinyon fibres are referred to as **polyvinyl chloride fibres**. It can bind non-woven fibres and fabrics. It was invented in 1939.

It has the same health problems associated with chlorinated polymers. In the past, Vinyon was used as a substitute for plant-based filters in tea bags.

Vinyon fibre characteristics :

- Doesn't flame, but softens at low temperatures (55 C)
- High resistance to chemicals

- Moisture absorption is less than 0.5% and moisture regained is less than 0.1%

Major vinyon fibre uses :

- Industrial applications as a bonding agent for non-woven fabrics and products.

➛ **Saran** is the trade name for a number of polymers made from Vinylidene Chloride (especially polyvinylidene chloride or **PVDC**), along with other monomers. The main advantage of Saran film is a very low permeability to water vapour, flavour and aroma molecules, and oxygen compared to other plastics. The barrier to oxygen prevents food spoilage, and the barrier to flavour and aroma molecules helps food retain its flavour and aroma.

Saran is best known for having been used in *Saran Wrap* — a thin, clingy plastic wrap that was sold in rolls and used primarily for wrapping food. Saran Wrap is now a brand of S. C. Johnson & Son. Environmental concerns with halogenated materials have led to the removal of PVDC from the Saran Wrap product which is now composed of polyethylene. With this change, Saran Wrap no longer provides the excellent oxygen barrier and therefore the food spoilage prevention benefit of the original product formulation. In some jurisdictions, the name Saran is a registered trademark of the Dow Chemical Company, while in others, it has lost trademark status and become a generic term for these polymers.

➛ **Spandex** or **elastane** is a synthetic fibre known for its exceptional elasticity. It is stronger and more durable than rubber, its major non-synthetic competitor. It was invented in 1959 by DuPont chemist Joseph Shivers. When first introduced, it revolutionized many areas of the clothing industry.

"Spandex" is a generic name and not derived from the chemical name of the fibre, which most manufactured fibres are, but an extension of the word *expand*. "Spandex" is the preferred name in North America; elsewhere it is referred to as "elastane".

The most famous brand name associated with Spandex is **Lycra**, a trademark of Invista (formerly part of DuPont). Such is the prominence of the Lycra brand that it has become a genericised trademark in many parts of the world, used to describe any kind of Spandex. Invista discourages such use, protecting its trademark vigorously.

Spandex fibres are produced in four different ways including melt extrusion, reaction spinning, solution dry spinning, and solution wet spinning. All of these methods include the initial step of reacting monomers to produce a prepolymer. Once the prepolymer is formed it is reacted further in various ways and drawn out to produce a long fibre. The solution dry spinning method is used to produce over 90% of the world's Spandex fibres.

➛ **Vinalon** is a synthetic fibre, produced from polyvinyl alcohol using anthracite and limestone as raw materials. Vinalon was first developed by the Korean scientist Ri Sung Gi at the Takatsuki Chemical Research Institute in 1939. The fibre was largely ignored until Ri defected to North Korea in 1950. Trial production began in 1954 and in 1961 the massive February 8 Vinalon Complex was built in Hamhung. Its success and widespread usage in North Korea is often pointed to in propaganda as an example of the success of the *juche* philosophy. Hamhung remains a major production centre for Vinalon; in 1998, a vinalon factory opened up in South Pyongan.

The factory complex also produces other chemicals. Some North Korean defectors have claimed that Dr. Lee Seung-ki was involved in chemical weapons research and that the complex was used to produce them.

Vinalon, also known as Juche fibre, has become the national fibre of North Korea and is used for the majority of textiles, outstripping fibre such as cotton or Nylon, which are only produced in small amounts in North Korea. Other than clothing, Vinalon is also used for canvas shoes, ropes and quilt wadding.

Vinalon is resistant to heat and chemicals but has numerous disadvantages: it is stiff, uncomfortable, shiny, prone to shrinking and difficult to dye. It is not produced outside of North Korea.

➛ **Aramid** fibres are a class of heat-resistant and strong synthetic fibres. They are used in aerospace and military applications, for ballistic rated body armor fabric, and as an asbestos substitute. The name is a shortened form of "aromatic polyamide". They are fibres in which the chain molecules are highly oriented along the fibre axis, so the strength of the chemical bond can be exploited.

Aramids are generally prepared by the reaction between an amine group and a carboxylic acid halide group. Simple AB homopolymers may look like:

nNH$_2$-Ar-COCl '! -(NH-Ar-CO)$_n$- + nHCl

The most well-known aramids (Nomex, Kevlar, Twaron and New Star) are AABB polymers. Nomex, New Star and Teijinconex contain predominantly the meta-linkage and are poly-*metaphenylene isophtalamide*s (MPIA). Kevlar and Twaron are both P-Phenylene Terephtalamides (PPTA), the simplest form of the AABB para-polyaramide. PPTA is a product of *p*-phenylene diamine (PPD) and terephtaloyl dichloride (TDC or TCl). Production of PPTA relies on a co-solvent with an ionic component (calcium chloride ($CaCl_2$)) to occupy the hydrogen bonds of the amide groups, and an organic component (N-methyl pyrrolidone (NMP)) to dissolve the aromatic polymer.

➛ **Polybenzimidazole** or **PBI** fibre (1983) is a synthetic fibre with an extremely high melting point that also does not ignite. Because of its exceptional thermal and chemical stability, it is often used by fire departments and space agencies.

PBI is prepared by step-growth polymerization from tetra-aminobiphenyl and diphenyl isophthalate spun via a dry spinning process using dimethyl acetamide as the solvent.

PBI fibre characteristics **:** The chemical formula of Poly[2,2'-(m-phenylen)-5,5' bibenzimidazol] (PBI) is believed to be: ([NH-C=CH-C=CH-CH=C-N=C-]$_2$-[C=CH-C=CH-CH=CH-])$_n$ OR ($C_{20}N_4H_{12}$)$_n$ of Molar mass 308.33608 ± 0.01764 g/mol.

- dyeable to dark shades with basic dyes following caustic pre-treatment
- resistant to most chemicals

➛ **(SULFUR) Polyphenylene sulfide** ("PPS") is an organic [polymer] consisting of aromatic rings linked with sulfides. Synthetic fibre and textiles derived from this polymer are known to resist chemical and thermal attack. PPS is used to make filter fabric for coal boilers, papermaking felts, electrical insulation, specialty membranes, gaskets, and packings. PPS is the precursor to a conducting polymer of the semi-flexible rod polymer family. The PPS, which is otherwise insulating, can be converted to the semiconducting form by oxidation or use of dopants.

Fibre Characteristics : PPS is one of the most important high temperature polymers because it exhibits a number of desirable properties. These properties include resistance to heat, acids and alkalies, and to mildew,to bleaches, aging, sunlight, and abrasion. It absorbs only small amounts of solvents and resists dyeing.

➛ **Lyocell** is a fibre made from wood pulp cellulose. It was first manufactured in 1987 by Courtaulds Fibres UK at their pilot plant S25. The only current manufacturer in the United States is Lenzing Inc, who market it under the trademarked brand name **Tencel**. There is another larger plant with over twice as much capacity at Grimsby in the United Kingdom.

The Federal Trade Commission defines Lyocell as "a cellulose fabric that is obtained by an organic solvent spinning process". It classifies the fibre as a sub-category of rayon.

The fibre is used in the production of many clothes, such as jeans, trousers and coats.

Major Properties

Lyocell was introduced to consumers in 1991 and originally marketed as a type of Rayon. The only current manufacturer in the United States is Lenzing Inc, who market it under the trademarked brand name Tencel. Lyocell is produced from wood pulp cellulose. Lyocell shares many properties with other cellulosic fibres such as cotton, linen, ramie and rayon. Some main characteristics of Lyocell fibres are that it is soft, absorbent, very strong when wet or dry, and resistant to wrinkles; it can be machine or hand-washed or drycleaned, it drapes well, and it can be dyed in many colours, as well as simulating a variety of textures like suede, leather, or silk. FibreSource

Production method : Lyocell is created through a process called solvent spinning. The wood pulp is dissolved in N-Methylmorpholine N-oxide, creating a solution called "dope." The dope is then pushed through a spinneret to form the individual fibres. After the dope has been spun into Lyocell fibres, it is washed and the chemicals are retrieved from the water, purified, and recycled.

➤ **Zylon** is a trademarked name for a range of thermoset polyurethane synthetic polymer materials manufactured by the Toyobo Corporation. Zylon was invented and developed by SRI International in the 1980s. Like Kevlar, Zylon is used in a number of applications that require very high strength with excellent thermal stability. Tennis racquets, table tennis blades, various medical applications, and some of the Martian rovers are some of the more well known instances.

IUPAC name: poly(p-phenylene-2,6-benzobisoxazole)

2

History of Textile

Since the beginning of mankind, human beings are different than other animals. Very early in the process of civilization man has invented some kind of fabric. From the Stone Age to this modern age the art of making textiles has come a long way.

Initially man used the skin of the dead animals to cover his body or used the fur of the animal to seek comfort from the bitter cold.

After the industrial revolution the production of textile has seen a vast change. But the main types of Textiles have remained almost the same.

The History of textile is almost as old as that of human civilization and as time moves on, the history of textile has further enriched itself. In the 6th and 7th century BC, the oldest recorded indication of using fibre comes with the invention of flax and wool fabric at the excavation of Swiss lake inhabitants. In India the culture of silk was introduced in 400AD, while spinning of cotton traces back to 3000BC. In China, the discovery and consequent development of sericulture and spin silk methods got initiated at

2640 BC while in Egypt the art of spinning linen and weaving developed in 3400 BC. The discovery of machines and their widespread application in processing natural fibres was a direct outcome of the industrial revolution of the 18th and 19th centuries. The discoveries of various synthetic fibres like nylon created a wider market for textile products and gradually led to the invention of new and improved sources of natural fibre. The development of transportation and communication facilities facilitated the path of transaction of localized skills and textile art among various countries.

Types of Textiles

The type of the textile depends on the material that is used to make it. Broadly textiles can be divided into two categories.

- Natural
- Manmade

Natural textiles are made up by using

- Animal textiles- animal hair or fur
- Plant textiles-grass, rush, sisal, Coir, straw, bamboo
- Mineral textiles-basalt fiber and asbestos ,glass fiber
- Synthetic textiles- they are primarily used to produce clothing.

Uses

Textiles have an assortment of uses, the most common of which are for clothing and containers such as bags and baskets. In the household, they are used in carpeting, upholstered furnishings, window shades, towels, covering for tables, beds, and other flat surfaces, and in art. In the workplace, they are used in industrial and scientific processes such as filtering. Miscellaneous uses include flags, backpacks, tents, nets, cleaning devices, such as handkerchiefs; transportation devices such as balloons, kites, sails, and parachutes; and strengthening in composite materials such as fibre glass and industrial geotextiles.

Textiles used for industrial purposes, and chosen for characteristics other than their appearance, are commonly referred to as *technical textiles.* Technical textiles include textile structures for automotive applications, medical textiles (e.g. implants), geotextiles (reinforcement of embankments), agrotextiles (textiles for crop protection), protective clothing (e.g. against heat and radiation for fire fighter clothing, against molten metals for welders, stab protection, and bullet proof vests.

Animal textiles

A filament or threadlike strand derived from animals that manufacturers use to produce clothes or other goods that require weaving, knitting or felting, which include silk, wool, mohair and other forms of animal hair. Animal textiles are commonly made from hair or fur.

All animal fibers are complex proteins. They are resistant to most organic acids and to certain powerful mineral acids such as sulfuric acid (H2SO 4). However, protein fibers are damaged by mild alkalies (basic substances) and may be dissolved by strong alkalies such as sodium hydroxide (NaOH). They can also be damaged by chlorine-based bleaches and undiluted liquid hypochloride bleach will dissolve wool or silk.

The principal component of silk is the protein fibroin. Silk is exuded in continuous filaments from the abdomens of various insects and spiders. It is the only natural filament that commonly reaches a length of more than 1000 m (more than 3300 ft). The only silk used in commercial textiles is produced from the cocoons of the silkworm. Several silk filaments can be gathered to produce textile yarn. However, silk is often produced and used in staple form to manufacture spun yarns.

The principal component of hair, wool, and fur is the protein keratin. Individual hairs may be as long as 91 cm (36 in) but are usually no more than 41 cm (16 in). Thus, fibers of hair and wool are not continuous and must be spun into yarn if they are to be woven or knitted into textile fabrics, or they must be made into felt. Any hair fiber can legally be marketed as wool or bear the common English name of the animal from which it was gathered—for example, camel's hair.

The principal hair fiber used to produce textile fabrics is sheep's wool. In wild sheep, the wool is a short, soft underlayer protected by longer, coarser hair. In domesticated sheep bred for their fleece, the wool is much longer. Yarns made of wool are classified as either woolen or worsted. Wool fibers less than 5 cm (less than 2 in) in length are made into fuzzy, soft woolen yarns. Longer fibers are used for the smoother and firmer worsted yarns. Naturally crimped wool fibers produce air-trapping yarns that are used for insulating materials.

Other animals used as sources of hair fibers for textiles include camels, llamas, alpacas, guanacos, vicuñas, rabbits, reindeer, Angora goats, and Kashmir (or cashmere) goats. Fur fibers from animals such as mink and beavers are sometimes blended with other hairs to spin luxury yarns but are most often found as fur pelts. Horsehair and cow's hair are used for felts and are sometimes spun as yarn, particularly for upholstery and other applications for which durability is important. Even human hair has been spun into yarn and used for textiles.

The main animal fiber used for textiles is wool. Another animal fiber, silk, produces one of the most luxurious fabrics. Sheep supply most of the wool, but members of the camel family and some goats also furnish wool. Wool provides warm, comfortable fabrics for dresses, suits, and sweaters. Silk comes from cocoons spun by silkworms. Workers unwind the cocoons to obtain long, natural filaments. Fabrics made from silk fibers have great luster and softness and can be dyed brilliant colors. Silk is especially popular for scarfs and neckties.

Wool refers to the hair of the domestic goat or sheep, which is distinguished from other types of animal hair in that the individual strands are coated with scales and tightly crimped, and the wool as a whole is coated with an oil known as lanolin, which is waterproof and dirtproof. Woolen refers to a bulkier yarn produced from carded, non-parallel fibre, while worsted refers to a finer yarn which is spun from longer fibres which have been combed to be parallel. Wool is commonly used for warm clothing. Cashmere, the hair of the Indian cashmere goat, and mohair, the hair of the North African angora goat, are types of wool known for their softness.

Wool is the fiber derived from the specialized skin cells, called follicles, of animals in the Caprinae family, principally sheep, but the hair of certain species of other mammals such as goats, llamas, rabbits and keeshonds may also be called wool. Wool has several qualities that distinguish it from hair or fur: it is crimped; it has a different texture or handle; it is elastic; and it grows in staples (clusters).

Other animal textiles which are made from hair or fur are alpaca wool, vicuña wool, llama wool, and camel hair, generally used in the production of coats, jackets, ponchos, blankets, and other warm coverings. Angora refers to the long, thick, soft hair of the angora rabbit.

Wadmal is a coarse cloth made of wool, produced in Scandinavia, mostly 1000~1500CE.

Silk is an animal textile made from the fibres of the cocoon of the Chinese silkworm. This is spun into a smooth, shiny fabric prized for its sleek texture.

Silk is a natural protein fiber, some forms of which can be woven into textiles. The best-known type of silk is obtained from cocoons made by the larvae of the mulberry silkworm *Bombyx mori* reared in captivity (sericulture). The shimmering appearance for which silk is prized comes from the fibers' triangular prism-like structure which allows silk cloth to refract incoming light at different angles.

Packaging of Animal Textile

Following fibre harvesting and preparation the packaging of the textile fibre into bales for transport to the processors is the next important task and one that must be done properly.

Packaging standards are a fundamental part of marketing and high standards must always be maintained when baling animal fibres for presentation to world markets. The packaging material (pack) used to form bales of animal fibre is unfortunately prone to damage because of the bales size, weight, coupled with the handling systems and transportation methods used. The pack material used must therefore be strong enough to withstand the handling methods used through the transport route.

Essential Requirements

The packaging of animal fibres has three essential requirements.

- The packs used must completely contain the contents and prevent the contents of the bale from being contaminated and must not in itself contribute to the contamination of the contents.
- The identification marks applied to each bale must be unique and be clearly and easily read.
- Pack into each bale only one category, grade or type of fibre.

To achieve the first of these requires

- the use of packs that completely contain the fibre, ie. no exposed fibre.
- the use of a pack material that is strong enough and is constructed in a manner that will withstand damage from the bale handling, transport and storage systems. This requires the setting of a detailed pack specification which specify minimum requirements of the fabric tensile strength, resistant fibrillation, selvage strength, construction, composition etc. The specifications must be set at levels of proven acceptable pack performance and only such packs should thereafter be used. Such specifications have been set in Australia, New Zealand and South Africa for use in the wool industry.

To achieve the second packaging objective, each bale should have the following clearly and easily readable marks applied, preferably using a stencil with a minimum letter, size of 50mm.

- Owner/seller identification mark(s)
- Lot number
- Individual bale number
- Description of the bale content
- Bale weight

The bale branding substance used should be scourable, as this will not contaminate the contents should some of the branding substance soak through the pack material onto the valuable fibre contained inside the bale.

Packaging Materials

Historically, jute sacks were the most widely used packaging material. Over more recent years, High Density Polyethylene (HDPE) has taken over as the packaging material in many fibre producing countries.

However, the world textile industry has repeatedly expressed serious concern at the levels of contamination from both jute and HDPE packs. They feel that this contamination issue is one of the biggest threats facing the animal fibre industry. This situation has focused attention on alternative packaging materials in recent years, and as a result, other materials have been identified. However, for a different pack material to gain widespread use requires the material to have equal or better performance properties, be non-contaminating and be comparatively priced. Multifilament nylon packs have been used to pack the very fine Merino wools with some success. These nylon packs meet the performance and non-contamination requirements, but they are considerably more expensive than HDPE. It is for this reason the use of nylon packs is limited to the finest and most expensive Merino wools.

Some use is now made of polyethylene film for use as an alternative to woven HDPE for the wrapping material which is placed around the bale and under the bands which hold the bale together. This type of package requires a high dense press with a minimum 200 tonne pressure. Polyethylene film used as a pack material has not proved successful to date in farm type wool presses as used in Australia, New Zealand and South Africa.

Because of the pack contamination concerns expressed by the textile industry, it is difficult to make clear recommendations as to what pack material animal fibre producers should use. Two things are clear however - previously used packs should not be used because of the increase in pack contamination that may occur and customer preference in packaging materials should be obtained. If possible, the fibre they purchase should be packed in their preferred material. It is also preferable that twine should not be used to sew up the top of the bale because the twine is a source of contamination. Processors have a clear preference for clips to be used instead of twines.

History of Fabrics

In music, craft architecture and fine arts India possessed a great—heritage. India's textile product is were in great demand over world India. In India the textiles produced were very fine and rich with beautiful artistic designs, harmonies and good colour schemes. Silks, brocades, and muslins in artistic creations were the stamp of individuality of craftsmen who produced it. Some of the textiles varieties from deverse parts of India are as under—

1. Muslins: In producing finest grade Dacca was the expertise. The value of muslins is estimated by number of warp threads in a given length as compared with its weight. 'Malmal Khas', the finest muslin was known to have 1000 to 1800 threads in warp. The weaver took five months to weave 1.0 yards of fabric. The weaving of muslin would be done only in rainy season due to its fineness. Some of the muslins are named as ab-i-ravan, Baft-hawa, and shabnam.

(a) *Dacca Sarees*: Till the beginning of 19th century Dacca saris were considered as most artistic specimen handlooms of Bengal women. They were gray, white, blue and black designs with silver and gold threads. Now they are available in all shades. The weaving pattern in flowers is called 'Tandani' The pallows are heavy as parders and rest of the saree is covered with bootie-s'. The flowers (boota) when spread allover is called' Bootedar I sari', when in diagonal lines is known as 'terchha' when there is network of flowers is known as jatar. When flowers are dustered like jewels, it is called , Panna hazari' .Other motifs used on pallows are 'mayura' 'hansa " animals and human figures.

(b) *Chanderi Sarees* : Chanderi is a place near Gwalior. Chanderi sarees are woven on pallavs and borders with gold threads. When silk and cotton threads are brought into use, it is known as 'Garbh reshmi' .The ground saree is checked with booties in each square, while pallows are worked with gold threads. The length is usually 9 yards which is much valued by Maharashtrian ladies.

2. Silks : Silk's cultivation is an ancient art which had its beginning in china. The empress si-ling-chi reared silk worms and spun silk thread and made a robe to present it to her husband. Chinese kept this knowledge to themselves for 3000 yrs. Then in 289 A. D. Japan and India received this knowledge. India exported much of silk textiles to western countries.

3. Baluchari : Near Murshidabad Baluchari is a town. In Baluchari saris the pallows are most exaggerate like Dacca saris with floral, bird and human figure designs. The fancied designs are Kalka, Torang, Guldasta etc. In olden times the human figures were dressed in Persian dress or European dress holding flowers or a wine glass. Still among Hindus the saris were famous.

4. Brocades : The brocades are the most gorgeous and highly ornamental of all Indian textiles. It is inter-weaving of silk threads and gold wires in beautiful colours and floral designs. It yields the most gorgeous, the most fascinating of India's silk fabrics. The designs are produced by warp and weft threads of different colours and materials suitable even today. Brocades are mainly produced in Aurangabad, Ahmedabad, Bhopal, Surat, Delhi, Banaras, Lucknow and Madras. But Banaras is their real home. A large range of textiles in Brocades are mainly done in western India. The various types of Brocades are Amru, Himru, Tanchoi, Surat Brocades and Jarnnagar Brocades. The Amrus of Hyderabad are pure silk brocades while the Himrus are brocaded silk with a mixture of wool or cotton. Gold wire was lavishly used in ancient days to work and delicate patterns on the kimkhabs which utilised to be manufactured chiefly in Banaras. Chief motifs seen in the design are bunch .of flowers, flying birds, and water wales. The heavier the brocade the more expensive it is considered.

The designs and colours used are varied. The three chief patterns are- 1. Beldar 2. Butidar 3. Shikar Ghar.

In Banarasi kimkhab, the famous hunting scene design and sun is the fines of them all. Some of the favourite motifs are the sacred geese and animal pattern. The Kalka or the flame design is also popular. The most traditional pattern is *Beldar* .

(a) ***Himru*** : These are the shawls done in Maharashtra. Him means snow. This fabric is utilised in winter. These shawls have an over all pattern.

Here warp and weft is silk and Buti is gold. No extra thread is seen at the back. Bigger shawls are used for dresses also. The Himru of Hyderabad is popular. Himru is an inferior kind of Brocade in which both silk and cotton threads are used to produce the several coloured designs. Today the Himrus are chiefly utilised for ladies blouses and cholies. Shervanies for man are also as furnishing fabric.

(b) ***Amru*** : Amru is commonly woven in Ahmedabad, Surat and Banaras: Silk thread is widely used for weaving.

(c) ***Tanchoi*** : These are chiefly done in western India. In tanchoi the and weft is in silk. Buties are in silk and gold both. Sometimes even silk'thread is seen. Tanchoi has no wasted material at the back that means warp and weft inserted in that makes the fabric. Heavier fabric is considered to be more beautiful. Tanchoi takes a lot of time while weaving. In a day one can weave just about 3-4" of tanchoi. Tanchoi designs are mainly parrots, birds, flowers, peacocks. Most of tanchoi have very heavy borders with rich colour and designs. Chiefly blue colour is used, buties are alone in silver and gold. Silver thread is very explicitly seen. Some of tanchoi sarees are just the combination of colour without any print on it. In olden periods some of tanchoi had very heavy effect of silver and gold so that one could hardly see any silk on it. Another kind of tanchoi is done in western India. For that, chief centre is Jarnnagar. This tanchoi was called Ghaghra tanchoi. These are looked only on border and is meant only for skirt and at times daint creepers along with tiny flowers are seen above border and below border . Different kinds of brocades are utilised in large quantities in and outside Banaras.

5. Orissa -Ikat : Ikat is an Indonesian word. It is the ancient technique of creating textiles in India. India is the home for Ikat. The so known as Ikat technique is another sort of tie-dye. It is the technique reverse to Bandhan in bandhani first resist method is applied and then the fabric is designed while in Ikat, yarns are tied and dyed before being woven, that is, in the making of these clothes the warp and the weft thread are dyed separately by the tie and dye process before weaving.

That are made in many parts of India. Moreover, the well-known patola marriage saree of Gujarat, notable instances are the cotton shawls of Orissa and telia rumals. The chief centres of Ikat are Surat, Gujarat, Rajkot, Pochampalli and Chiriala. Majority of the that are exported to Africa. There are three types of that—

1. Single Ikat-It has only warp tied and dyed.
2. Weft Ikat-It has only weft tied and dyed.
3. Double Ikat-In this both warp and weft are tied and dyed.

In chiriala a special sort of Rumals is utilised by Muslims and the fishermen. Most of these rumals are exported to Africa and are now named as Asian rumals. In Pochampali chiefly sarees are dyed.

These sarees have geometrical designs and are done on cotton and silk both utilising single weft and double weft. These sarees are famous as wedding Sarees. The weavers who produce wedding sarees are called selirec. Their main characteristic is thai any thing made by them done in cloth has stories. Half the Asian rumals would enact mythological stories. Just one piece would form the whole story or one piece of Mahabharat. The figures done on these rumals are not at all balanced. But the cotton contrast produces the colourful effect. In recent past it is done in Hyderabad. Here these are done particular on cotton lungies. But still Gujarat and Pochampalli are the only well-known centres of Ikat. Rajkot is the Ikat training centre to follow the technical way of weaving. Since the art of Ikat was beginning to die sometimes ago and Ikat is supposed to be one of the most conventional art pieces, but now it has revived again.

6. Kanthas of Bengal : This is a folk art of Bengal. It was almost a lost art unit a few years back when it started to be revived. The particular significance of the kanthas quilt is not only in its artistic elegance but its vivid narration of tales of heroism and legends. It is a domestic art of the use of waste material. It is a treasure preserved in every home. This embroidery is done by all classes of people and worked by women only.

Kanthas were made both in East and West Bengal. They were mainly done in Jessore, Faridpur, Khulna and Mymensing all in East Bengal. Now in Bangladesh the fabrics utilised for Kanthas are made even" today by women for their personal use. The fabric utilised for Kanthas are old sarees, dhoties, placed greatly together in layers in running stitches using white thread covering the whole field. The discarded old sarees are placed on top of each other. The edges are folded and tucked together. The field is filled in with fine quilt work by means of a white thread. The craftsmen embroider according to the imagination giving a pictorial account of ancient folklore in each Kantha piece.

There are five types of Kanthas. They are as given below:

1. ***Lep*** : This is a thick quilted wrap used in winter as a cover. To make it thick, a big number of saree layers are arranged one on top of the other. Designs on lep are geometrical and worked with the running stitch.

2. ***Sarlni*** : This is also a quilted wrap or cover and used for ceremonial purposes.

3. ***Voyton*** : It is utilised as wraps for valuables etc. In shape it is square. It has a central motif and 2 or 3 borders. The size is about 3 feet square. It has wide borders of human and animal figures, a lotus in the centre the comers being covered by trees, flowers or leaves. This Kanthas is meant to be carried during journeys or to be presented to relatives.

4. ***Oar*** : It is rectangular in shape about 2 feet by 1/2 feet in size. It is utilised for pillow cases. The designs used on this are trees and birds or a linear pattern. The embroidery is simple but decorative, probably only a series of broad lines of leaves and trees. Sometimes an extra boarder made by decorative stitch is sewn around the four sides.

5. ***Arsilata*** : It is utilised as a wrap for mirrors and combs. It has a wide border and in the centre lotuses, creepers or trees are used for motif. The women in Bengal generally wear white sarees. Hence the base material was always white for Kanthas. Today silks generally Kanchipuram, tussore or raw silk could be utilised as a base if they are to be discarded. The threads generally used are taken out from the borders of the discarded sarees which are utilised for the base. The colours of the threads used are blue, green, yellow, red and black. Today instead of thread drawn from

the border vividly coloured silk of bright embroidery stands are used.

Stitches used are darning, satin and chair. For border stem stitches are used most commonly and typical stitch being used are very short darning stitches providing dotted line. Even a large area may be covered with closely made lines of these stitches. Back stitches are also used for continuous lines. The outline of the design is commonly in dark blue filled with stitches of same colour or in contrasting colour. Sometimes the outlines and the areas enclosed by the outline are in blue, stitches are in red. After the design has been embroidered any area left are filled with stitches in white remaining parallel to the outline of the motifs.

Kanthas is utilised during festivals and rituals where the house-wife ants to fulfil her vows. In each case, one has special religious designs like Mandala and Kalasa. Applique work is also seen on the Kanthas. Their two kind are found-one is utilised on flag and canopies where a notice or a lion motif is cutout in red cloth and then stitched on the white cloth. In the other type coloured cloth is cut into parochial stripes and sewn round the outlines of the design. This is generally done on pillow-cases.

The common ritual designs of Kanthas are lotus, the bull with the lingo on his back, the tiger representing Goddess Durga, the swastik and the mouse reminiscent of Ganesh. The symbols, faiths, rituals and myths are often kept alive in folk arts. These are particularly and only prepared by women and depicted as folk embroideries. Kanthas still continue to be made in Bengal by women in rural areas. They make them for their personal use only.

7. Kashmir Embroidery : Kashmir embroidery and shawls are well-known for the beauty of colours, design and technique allover the world.

The best embroidery is revealed in the shawls. It is a cottage industry run by many members of a family in their homes mainly around Shrinagar. Kashmir embroidery is practised by men and it is inevitably a commercial craft. According to Kamala S. Dongerkery, "the shawl industry in Kashmir was introduced by Zain-ul-Abidin, the ruler in the 15th century {1423-1474 A.D.). It seem that when he was yet a Prince, in Samarkand diverse crafts men worked for manufacturing different things. Zain-ul-Abidin got interested in the work of the craftsmen and when he returned to his own country he sent people in search of talented craftsmen. These shawl weavers from persia were brought to India to encourage this art.

Kind of woven Kashmir shawls :

(i) ***Pashmina shawls*** : The most of the woollen fabrics of Kashmir particularly the superior quality shawls are the Pashmina. Pashmina shawls were made from the wool of the upraharcus a species of the Asian mountain goat. Thus the shawls were known as Pashmina.

(ii) ***Dushala*** : Dushala or the double shawl are two resemble shawls stitched together so that when draped over the shoulder the wrong side was not visible.

(iii) ***Doroapha*** : This is double sided work in which there is no wrong side. Occasionally the same design is reproduced in two separate colours on the two sides creating double sided patterns. Thus it has simpler patterns with outlines and details woven in bright colours and being later on worked by hand.

(iv) ***Kasala shawl*** : These are square in shape and perhaps produced on European demand. They are commonly of twill weave or damask patterns woven them in a plain colour.

(v) ***Jamewar shawls*** : Woven completely of wool or with some cotton mixed but the floral design and brocaded parts are generally in silk or pashmina wool.

The colours most commonly used for Kashmiri shawls are white, green, purple, blue, yellow and black. They also use crimson colours (Gulnar). The motifs are mainly taken from nature. Animal and human figures are not seen in Kashmir embroidery probably due to of muslim influence in the area. The bird motifs used are parrots. magpie, wood-pecker and king fisher. The floral motifs are iris, lotus, lily, tulip and saffron flowers. The other designs are grapes, plums, cherries, almonds. The chenar, leaves is considered important motif.

The fabric utilised for embroidery is of several kind silk, cotton, wool. The threads utilised are cotton, wool and silk. The stitches utilised are simple the chief being the satin-stitch, stem-stitch and chain-stitch. Sometimes the darning stitch and the herringbone is also utilised. Kashida is the common term for Kashmir embroidery which comprises other stitches called as Zalakdozi (Chain-stitch.)

8. Doria (open work) and Talaibar (Gold work) : All the embroiders in Kashmir are men. They are trained from a very young age. Old man can do the finest work. Boys at the age of 6-7 do the outline on coarse material.

Kashmir also produces what is known as Gabhas. Gabha is a unique kind of floor covering. It is very cheap. It is devised from old or torn woollen blankets or torn shawls after being washed, milled and dyed in diverse colours. Here applique work in gay colours and bold floral or ornamental design is done. There are three types of Gabhas namely: 1. embroidered, 2. applique, and 3. both embroidered and applique combined. In the applique kind of Gabhas piece of dyed blanket clothes are joined together and interlaced with embroidery.

Hook or chain stitch rugs are also very fancied of the rich designs. It done in bright as well as light colours. The material utilised for hook rugs is hessian cloth. The embroidery is done completely with thick woollen threads.

9. Namda : This is an potent and popular part of Kashmir embroidery .It is a special work on a carpet called crewel for which chain stitch is the base foundation supplemented by other stitches like satin, cross, filling etc. Today Kashmir embroidery is of fine quality. Many workers are seen embroidering on shawls as well as silk sarees, dress materials, table linen, cushion cover, bed cover, purses and articles of personal uses.

10. Chicken Kari-work : Chicken Kar;-Chicken Kari work of U .P .was originated in Jammu and Kashmir.

This embroidery was first come into practice in Bengal and Dacca and later on brought to Jammu and Kashmir and Delhi. It is now seen in Bhopal, Gaya, Calcutta, Allahabad and Varanasi. But Jammu and Kashmir is a great modern centre where work of rather remarkable beauty and distinction is carried on.

1. ***Chicken Kari work*** is known as white embroidery .The fabric utilised for this work is plane white fabric. It is mostly done on white fine muslin cloth but today it is done on cambric and corresponding to fabrics. The patterns are printed from wood blocks in a washable colour. The designs are first prepared on paper and wooden stamping blocks are prepared from them. The designs are then stamped on the cloth and passed on to the embroiders. There are two kind of chicken kari work: the flat style and the knitted embossed, e.g. like jals or netting in types of design. The stitches are named as khatawa, bukhia. murri, taipchi, phanda and jali. Taipchi is a simple darning stitch used in a cheaper work. It comprise of strokes and straight lines drawn on the cloth in the direction needed to form the design. Taipchi is a flat style of chicken work.

2. ***Khatawa*** : This is an applique work prepared on white calico. This embroidery belongs to the flat style of chicken kari.

3. ***Bukhia*** : This is constituted of an invested satin stitch with designs outlined on the right side of the fabric. The thread is mainly below the cloth. Compact masson of thread are then worked on the wrong side so that the design appears opaque. It is also known as shadow work. The stitches that cover the wrong side of the cloth are in herringbone producing a shadow effect.

4. ***Murri*** : It implies rice shaped. It generally done on muslin cloth.

Murri is done on the centre of the flowers. Stitch is the french knot.

5. ***Phanda*** : This corresponding to grains like millet. This is a smaller and shorter form of Murri stitch. These are utilised to fill petals and leaves in a pattern.

6. ***Jali*** : This is done by breaking up the fabric into holes and not by drawing out the threads. The warp and weft threads are pushed apart with the needles into holes and tightened to give the cloth the appearance of a net. This is done by a kind of very fine button holing and then pulling the thread aside.

Moreover this work of Jammu and Kashmir is also famous for the Gold and Silver embroidery .This embroidery is done on velvette, satin and chiffon. Sari borders, kurtas, collars, hanky and white cape are all embroidered in chicken kari of grains and now as far as 30 designs exist in chiken kari work utilising ratine, stem and back stitch, herring bone and button hole stitches.

11. Phulkari of Punjab : Phulkari of Punjab belongs to Punjab. Phulkari literally implies flower- craft. The term phulkari is commonly utilised in East Punjab and the term Bag, for similar shawl in west Punjab, Peshawar and Rawalpindi.

Fabric used: The beauty of the Phulkari is relied on the great deal on colour of the ground material. Khaddar cloth was incessantly utilised for embroidering bagh and phulkaries. It was hand-spun and hand-woven cotton : material. The colour of the khaddar fabric was mainly red, white and blue or black. Khaddar was previously woven in narrow width. Hence two or more joints had to be made on the wrong side with running stitches different from the other. The work is very neat and is done without tracing and drawing and is divided as a work of art.

The motifs utilised are human and animal figures, floral and symbols which cover the surfaces from the four comers and reach out towards the main piece. The central design is generally a lotus with a variable number of petals and the field is interspersed with yielding patterns. The most recurrent being the tree of life, traditional animal figures, beads, chariots, kalkas and mythological stories. The borders comprise creepers, floral serials, spirals and several linear.

Thread used : It is pure silk. It is untwisted silken floss known as 'pot'. green, Golden yellow, white, crimson red and orange are the five colour prepared in selecting silk floss for phulkari work.

Motifs used : Motifs are made of horizontal, vertical and diagonal stitches yielding geometrical pattern in phulkari design while the bagh has an over all geometrically floral pattern as the name itself implies.

Stitches used : Although the darning stitch and geometrical pattern go hand and hand in phulkari still a number of designs can be yielded. The stitch of long and short darning stitches. It is a ubiquitous method of embroidery in the sense that it is worked on every side of the cloth.

The centre of this interesting art is Rohtak and the surrounding region. The best phulkari were produced in the district of Jhelum, Peshawar, Rawalpindi, Nazara and they are all now in Pakistan. In India in Punjab the phulkari embroidery was done in Amritsar, Ambala, Jallander, Patiala, Ludhiana, Rohtak and Kapurthala.

Particular authority has drawn a distinction in phulkari and bagh. In phulkari the ornamentation is dispersed mostly with large area of flower art. In Bagh the whole field is covered with pot and silk floss and not even a thread of base fabric is with beautifully mixed colours. The designs on phulkari are more or less floral in character with some geometrical pattern. Thus bagh or phulkari is the common name of these shawls with the distinction that in bagh or garden the whole surface is decorated with a connected pattern whereas in phulkari the pattern is dispersed at intervals over the earth.

Types of Phulkari : There are various types of phulkari. The motifs and designs are district from place to place. They may be grouped into 4 or.5 in classes. The chope and suber were wedding phulkari and were presented to the bride by the maternal relation during marriage ceremony. The plain red or dark red khaddar cloth known as saloo, were utilised in daily household ware. Til-patra shawl have very little embroidery and are of inferior quality khaddar. It was conventional custom to give servants this as presents during marriage and on auspicious occasion. Till-patra literally implies dotted with .till-seed design.

Nilak is worked on black or navy blue khaddar with yellow and crimson red pot. The nilak is pretty phulkari shawl and looks very attractive.

Kinds of Bagh : Bagh shawls are usually embroidered in one chief colour with other contrasting shape in little proportions. But two colour combinations like orange and yellow, green and crimson or white and gold look the best. One of the most splendid is the ghungat bagh or the veil shawl. It has a triangular patch of embroidery on that portion of which covers the head when worn. In this shawl there are usually two large motifs, triangular in shape and also very decorative.

Varida Bagh : The bridegroom's mother presents it to the bride. Reshmi sheesha meaning silken mirror of fine allover embroidery in white so perfect that it looks like a mirror. Bagh has several other varieties known by different names such as kakribagh, shalimar bagh, mircha bagh, dhania bagh each name derived from the motif suggested by objects with which the embroiders are familiar. The phulkari shawl would occasionally take even 10 years to be completed. Originally the phulkari embroidery covered almost the whole base and looked like the fabric itself. But the modern trend is to use the pulkari 's stitch just to embroider any cloth. Pulkari is done with great care which is a time and energy-consuming product and so each piece becomes a real heirloom handled down from generation to generation.

12. Kasuti : It is famous in the Kanataka areas. Kanataka is now in Karnataka state, which was earlier in the State of Bombay. The art of Kasuti embroidery is mainly done by women and men in house. The five garments on which kasuti was performed were kunchi (Bonnet) and cape combined; Lehenga (skirt), sharagu (Pallow of a saree), cusupa (Bodice) and Kulai (Bonnet). These were the garments the women and their children utilised and so after their children used.

A saree is generally worn with an embroidered Pallu by the Kannada women. Kulai, which is baby cap has a cape attached to the neck of the cap and also women's cholies have Kasuti design of the finest Texture.

The material on which the Kasuti embroidery was done previous was mostly khalls used as blouse pieces and Irkal sarees. Irkal is near Bejapur and the sarees produced there were generally yards in length with 3/4 of a yard as Pallow and borders about 6-8" with a varied colour in warp and weft. The pulak is in stripes of red and white and is called Teop and Tenni. Kasuti was done above the red and white stripes.

Kasuti Embroidery : It is done on any kind of fabric. It is made on cushion covers and several other household articles or hand-woven cloth.

The motifs used in Kasuti are from temple architecture. The Gopurams of South India and also lotus flowers, Palanquins, Raths, bird motifs such as parrot and peacock, snake and the squirrel are common. Animal motifs used for kasuti embroidery are the sacred bull, elephant and deer. One will rarely see mouse, lion or tiger but cats and dogs are never seen. The stitches utilised are the simplest and so minute that the effect of the work is intricate and pretty. Four kinds of stitches are used in kasuti, named such:

1. Gavanti, 2. Murgi, 3. Negi, 4. Menphi.

Kasuti is done by counting the threads. The four stitches are explained separately, as follows—

1. **Bandhani :** Bhandhari or Choonaries are the odhnis dyed by tie and dye method utilised by Sindhi ladies and Rajasthanis. The fabric is folded many times and tied in varied ways and dyed to produce the pattern. The patterns rely on the method of tieing. The commonly used patterns are' Ek bundi' (one dot), char bundi (four dots), sat bundi (seven dots) and Lahariya method. The motifs used are-flowers, birds, animals, dolls. When gold work in squares is made, it is known as Gharchola.

2. ***Murgi*** : Murgi appears like the steps of ladder. As the stitches are zig-zag running stitches. It is similar to Gavanti since both are neat with the design on the wrong and right side looking alike. The stitches are regular and uniform in length and so the distance between the two stitches remains the same.

3. ***Negi*** : Negi is ordinary running of darning stitch. It has the over all effect of a woven design. This stitch is used for larger designs by weaving the stitch in conformity with the surface to be covered with thread.

4. ***Menphi*** : It has a heavy appearance and a large amount of threads needed. Hence this stitch is not of much use. Nowadays several of the kasuti workers are taking to the use of simple stitch. It is most commonly utilised to cover up the background areas of design.

13. Kalmedar : These are the land painted cotton fabrics. The designs are made with fine stem brush (kalam). The process is like balik. In pali pink and fabric the material is dyed is designed with wax. Ultimately the cloth is dyed in darker shaes (syah red).

14. *Gavanti* : Gavanti is a line and back stitch or double running stitch. The patterns here are mainly geometrical. Since these are worked in vertical, horizontal and diagonal directions, this is the most common stitch. Here the design seems the same on both sides of the fabric.

15. Patola : In weave it is in plain. Before weaving the yarns are finished and dyed. The process of patola is very labourious and complex. Thus solely few designs are utilised in Patola. The designs of devnagari alphabets and mantras are woven on dhoties of men. Other designs utilised are Nari-Iunyar-bhat-danany girl, elephant and parrot, Pan bhat (Leaf design), Ratan Chowk bhat (Cross of diamonds), Okhas bhat (water crest), Phulvadi bhat (flowers), Chhabri bhat (basket), wagh-kunjar bhat (tiger-elephant), chawkadi bhat (Three flowers in a square).

3

Variation of Textile

A textile is a cloth, which is either woven by hand or machine. "Textile" has traditionally meant, "a woven fabric". The term comes from the Latin word texere, meaning to weave.

Fibres are the raw materials for all fabrics. Some fibres occur in nature as fine strands that can be twisted into yarns. These natural fibres come from plants, animals, and minerals. For most of history, people had only natural fibres to use in making cloth. But modern science has learned how to produce fibres by chemical and technical means. Today, these manufactured fibres account for more than two-thirds of the fibres processed by U.S. textile mills.

Plants provide more textile fibres than do animals or minerals. Cotton fibres produce soft, absorbent fabrics that are widely used for clothing, sheets, and towels. Fibres of the flax plant are made into linen. The strength and beauty of linen have made it a popular fabric for fine tablecloths, napkins, and handkerchiefs.

The main animal fibre used for textiles is wool. Another animal fibre, silk, produces one of the most luxurious fabrics. Sheep supply most of the wool, but members of the camel family and some goats also furnish wool. Wool provides warm, comfortable fabrics for dresses, suits, and sweaters. Silk comes from cocoons spun by silkworms. Workers unwind the cocoons to obtain long, natural filaments. Fabrics made from silk fibres have great luster and softness and can be dyed brilliant colours. Silk is especially popular for scarves and neckties.

Most manufactured fibres are made from wood pulp, cotton linters, or petrochemicals. Petrochemicals are chemicals made from crude oil and natural gas. The chief fibres manufactured from petrochemicals include nylon, polyester, acrylic, and olefin. Nylon has exceptional strength, wears well, and is easy to launder. It is popular for hosiery and other clothing and for carpeting and upholstery. Such products as conveyor belts and fire hoses are also made of nylon.

Most textiles are produced by twisting fibres into yarns and then knitting or weaving the yarns into a fabric. This method of making cloth has been used for thousands of years. But throughout most of that time, workers did the twisting, knitting, or weaving largely by hand. With today's modern machinery, textile mills can manufacture as much fabric in a few seconds as it once took workers weeks to produce by hand.

Woven fabrics are made of two sets of yarns - a lengthwise set called the Warp and a crosswise set called the Filling or Weft. The warp yarns are threaded into a loom through a series of frames called Harnesses. During the cloth-making process, the harnesses raise some warp yarns and lower others. This action creates a space, or shed, between the yarns. A device called a Shuttle carries the filling through the shed and so forms the crosswise yarns of the fabric. The pattern in which the harnesses are raised and lowered for each pass of the shuttle determines the kind of weave.

Knitted fabrics are made from a single yarn or a set of yarns. In making cloth, a knitting machine forms loops in the yarn and links them to one another by means of needles. The finished fabric consists of crosswise rows of loops, called courses, and lengthwise rows of loops, called Wales. This looped structure makes knitted fabrics more elastic than woven cloth. Garment manufacturers use knitted fabrics in producing comfortable, lightweight clothing that resists wrinkling. Other fabrics include tufted fabrics, nets and laces, braids, and felt. None of these fabrics is woven or knitted. However, the textile industry produces another class of fabrics specifically called Non-Woven Fabrics.

Cotton

Cotton is a soft white fibrous substance covering seeds of certain plants.

History of the use of cotton : Asiatic cottons first grew wild in East Africa. About 5000 years ago, the people in what is now Pakistan cultivated cotton. The army of Alexander the Great first brought cotton goods into Europe in the 300s B.C. but the cloth was too expensive and only the rich could afford it.

The English began to weave cotton in the 1600s. They imported raw cotton from other countries bordering the Mediterranean Sea. Later, they imported cotton from southern colonies in America. In the 1700s, English textile manufacturers developed machines that made it possible to spin thread and weave cloth into large quantities. Today, the United States, Russia, China and India are major producers of cotton.

Production of cotton : When cotton arrives at a textile mill, several blenders feed cotton into cleaning machines, which mix the cotton, break it into smaller pieces and remove trash. The cotton is sucked through a pipe into picking machines. Beaters in these machines strike the cotton repeatedly to knock out dirt and separate lumps of cotton into smaller pieces.

Cotton then goes to the carding machine, where the fibres are separated. Trash and short fibres are removed. Some cotton goes through a comber that removes more short fibres and makes a stronger, more lustrous yarn.

This is followed by spinning processes which do three jobs: draft the cotton, or reduce it to smaller structures, straighten and parallel the fibres and lastly, put twist into the yarn. The yarns are then made into cloth by weaving, knitting or other processes.

After inspectors check the cloth, it is passed through a gas flame that singes the fuzz off its surface. Boiling the cloth in an alkaline solution removes natural waxes, coloured substances or discolourations. Then the cloth is bleached in hypochlorite or peroxide. The cloth may then pass through a machine that prints designs on it. Cloth intended to be solid-coloured goes through a dye bath.

For fabrics made of 100% cotton:

- Set your washing machine to the low setting.
- Wash the cloth in cold water.
- Set your iron to Medium to iron it.
- Do not bleach the cloth.
- Hang to dry but do not tumble dry.

50% Cotton and 50% Polyester:

- Turn it inside out and machine wash with warm water.
- Wash with fabrics that are of light colours.
- Use only non-chlorine bleach to bleach the cloth.
- Tumble dry with a medium setting.
- Set your iron to medium for ironing.

Properties of the cotton:

- It is soft and comfortable.
- It wrinkles easily.
- It absorbs perspiration quickly.
- It has good colour retention and is good to print on.
- Cotton is also strong and durable.

Uses : Cotton is used to make blouses, shirts, singlets, bermudas, jackets and pants. It can also be made into bedspreads, pillowcases, carpets and curtains.

Wool

Woolen fabric is made from the fleece of sheep.

History of the use of wool : Wool was probably the first animal fibre to be made into cloth. The art of spinning wool into yarn developed about 4000 B.C. and encouraged trade among the nations in the region of the Mediterranean Sea.

The first wool factory in England was established in 50 A.D. in Winchester by the Romans. In 1797, the British brought 13 Merino sheep to Australia and started the country's Merino sheep industry.

There are 40 different breeds of sheep in the world producing a rough estimate of 200 types of wool with varying standards. The major wool producers in the world are Australia, Argentina, China and South Africa.

Production of Wool : The processing of wool involves four major steps. First comes shearing, followed by sorting and grading, making yarn and lastly, making fabric.

In most parts of the world, sheep are sheared once a year, in early spring or early summer. The best wool comes from the shoulders and sides of the sheep.

This is followed by grading and sorting, where workers remove any stained, damaged or inferior wool from each fleece and sort the rest of the wool according to the quality of the fibres. Wool fibres are judged not only on the basis of their strength but also by their fineness (diameter), length, crimp (waviness) and colour.

The wool is then scoured with detergents to remove the yolk and such impurities as sand and dust. After the wool dries, it is carded. The carding process involves passing the wool through rollers that have thin wire teeth. The teeth untangle the fibres and arrange them into a flat sheet called a web. The web is then formed into narrow ropes known as silvers.

After carding, the processes used in making yarn vary slightly, depending on the length of the fibres. Carding length fibres are used to make woolen yarn. Combing length fibres and French combing length fibres are made into worsted yarn.

Woolen yarn, which feels soft, has a fuzzy surface and is heavier than worsted. While worsted wool is lighter and highly twisted, it is also smoother, and is not as bulky, thus making it easier to carry or transport about.

Making worsted wool requires a greater number of processes, during which the fibres are arranged parallel to each other. The smoother the hard-surface worsted yarns, the smoother the wool it produces, meaning, less fuzziness. Fine worsted wool can be used in the making of athletics attire, because it is not as hot as polyester, and the weave of the fabric allows wool to absorb perspiration, allowing the body to "breathe".

Wool manufacturers knit or weave yarn into a variety of fabrics. Wool may also be dyed at various stages of the manufacturing process and undergo finishing processes to give them the desired look and feel.

The finishing of fabrics made of woolen yarn begins with fulling. This process involves wetting the fabric thoroughly with water and then passing it through the rollers. Fulling makes the fibres interlock and mat together. It shrinks the material and gives it additional strength and thickness. Worsteds go through a process called crabbing in which the fabric passes through boiling water and then cold water. This procedure strengthens the fabric.

Care of your woolen garment : It is better to hand wash your woolen products. Shampoos can be used to wash such garments. Use a good shampoo not one containing "crème rinse". If shampoo can clean your hair without leaving residues, it can clean your woolen products too. Be careful of what softener you use because softeners may add products to your wool. Some types of softeners may leave a coating on the fibre making it feel softer and smoother, but at the same time causing your wool to lose its absorbency.

Properties of the wool :

- It is hard wearing and absorbs moisture.
- It does not burn over a flame but smoulders instead.
- It is lightweight and versatile.
- Wool does not wrinkle easily.
- It is resistant to dirt and wear and tear.

Uses : Wool is used to make sweaters, dresses, coats, suits, jackets, pants and the lining of boots. It can also be made into blankets and carpets.

Silk

Silk is the fine strong soft lustrous fibre produced by silkworms.

History of the use of silk : The Chinese has used silk since the 27th century B.C.. Silk is mentioned by Aristotle and became a valuable commodity both in Greece and Rome. During the Roman Empire, silk was sold for its weight in gold. The Chinese domesticated silk worms and fed them with mulberry leaves. They unwound the silkworms' cocoons to produce long strands of silk fibre.

Farm women in China at that period were supposed to raise such silkworms as one of their chores. Silk was used in China and exported along the Silk Road (the ancient trade route linking China and the Roman Empire). This trade brought China great wealth, but the Chinese did not give away the secret on how silk was formed. Christian monks finally broke China's monopoly of the silk production by smuggling silkworm eggs out of the country, and soon other countries started to produce their own silk.

Production of silk : Silkworms are cultivated and fed with mulberry leaves. Some of these eggs are hatched by artificial means such as an incubator, and in the olden times, the people carried it close to their bodies so that it would remain warm.

Silkworms that feed on smaller, domestic tree leaves produce the finer silk, while the coarser silk is produced by silkworms that have fed on oak leaves. From the time they hatch to the time they start to spin cocoons, they are very carefully tended to. Noise is believed to affect the process, thus the cultivators try not to startle the silkworms.

Their cocoons are spun from the tops of loose straw. It will be completed in two to three days' a time. The cultivators then gather the cocoons and the chrysales are killed by heating and drying the cocoons.

In the olden days, they were packed with leaves and salt in a jar, and then burried in the ground, or else other insects might bite holes in it. Modern machines and modern methods can be used to produce silk but the old-fashioned hand-reels and looms can also produce equally beautiful silk.

Care of your silk garment : It is best to dry clean your silk garment either by individual or bulk method, in order to maintain the characteristic of the silk.

Dry clean: Sending it to the dry cleaners may be done but make sure that you inform the dry cleaner that your garment is made of silk.

Hand wash :

- Make sure you wash in cool water.
- Use a small amount of soap or mild detergent to wash the silk.
- After washing it, rinse in cold water.
- Hang it or lay it flat in a shaded area to dry.
- If pressing is needed, use an all cotton iron board cover, a low or moderate steam setting, and press on the wrong side of the fabric while ironing.

Other Tips :

- To keep white silk white, add peroxide and ammonia to the wash.
- Do not use bleach or any washing detergent with bleach.
- To remove yellow from white silk, add a few teaspoons of white vinegar to the wash.

Properties of the silk :

- It is versatile and very comfortable.
- It absorbs moisture.
- It is cool to wear in the summer yet warm to wear in winter.
- It can be easily dyed.
- It retains its shape and is relatively smooth.
- It has a poor resistance to sunlight exposure.
- It is the strongest natural fibre and is lustrous.

Uses : Silk is used to make blouses, dresses, scarves, pants and ties. It can also be made into curtains, draperies, cushion covers and sofa covers.

Nylon

Nylon is a strong, light synthetic fibre. It is a man-made.

History of the use of nylon : This synthetic fibre was introduced in the 1930s. It was another early substitute for silk and soon quickly became the fibre of choice for women's stockings. The first commercial production of nylon in the United States was in 1939 by the E.I. du Pont de Nemours and Company. Wallace H.

Carothers, a chemist of the Dupont Company played the leader in this development of nylon. This man-made fibre is the second most used fibre in the United States.

Production of nylon : Nylon is made by forcing molten nylon through very small holes in a device called a spinneret. The streams of nylon harden into filament once they come in contact with air. They are then wound onto bobbins. These fibres are drawn (stretched) after they cool.

Drawing involves unwinding the yarn or filaments and then winding it around another spool. Drawing makes the molecules in each filament fall into parallel lines. This gives the nylon fibre strength and elasticity.

After the whole drawing process, the yarn may be twisted a few turns per yard or metres as it is wound onto spools. Further treatment to it can give it a different texture or bulk.

Other Tips :

- Extensive washing and drying in an automatic dryer can lead to piling.
- White nylon should be washed separately to avoid it turning grey.
- To avoid yellowing of your white nylon, you should bleach it frequently with Sodium Perborate bleach.

Properties of the nylon :

- It is strong and elastic.
- It is easy to launder.
- It dries quickly.
- It retains its shape.
- It is resilient and responsive to heat setting.

Uses : Nylon is popular for hosiery and is used to make track pants, shorts, swimwear, active wear, windbreakers, bedspread and draperies. It can also be made into parachutes, flak vests, combat uniforms, tires and life vests, or used as the netting of bridal veils, umbrellas and luggage.

Polyester

Polyester is the general name for any group of widely used

synthetic products. Polyesters are strong, tough materials that are manufactured in a variety of colours, shapes and sizes.

History of the use of polyester : The first commercial production of polyester was by the du Pont de Nemours Company. It is the most used fibre in the United States.

Production of polyester : Polyesters are made from chemical substances found mainly in petroleum. Polyesters are manufactured in three basic forms - fibres, films and plastics.

Polyester fibres are used to make fabrics. Poly (Ethylene Terephthalate or simply PET) is the most common polyester used for fibre purposes. This is the polymer used for making soft drink bottles. Recycling PET by re-melting it and extruding it as fibre saves much raw materials as well as energy.

PET is made by ethylene glycol with either terephthalic acid or its methyl ester in the presence of an antimony catalyst. In order to achieve high molecular weights needed to form useful fibres, the reaction has to be carried out at high temperature and in a vacuum.

Care of your polyester garment :

- Machine-wash your fabric in cold water.
- Wash with light colours.
- Use a gentle cycle while washing.
- Tumble dry with the setting low.
- Do not bleach.
- If needed, iron with a cool iron.

Properties of the polyester :

- It is resists wrinkling.
- It is easy to launder.
- It dries quickly.
- It is resistant to stretching and shrinking.

Uses : Polyester is used to make most forms of clothing like shirts, running shorts, track pants, windbreakers, and lingerie. It can also be made into curtains and draperies.

Textile of Different Countries

India Textile : Heritage of textile in India. In India textile enjoys a rich heritage and the origin of **Textiles in India** traces back to the Indus Valley Civilization where people used homespun cotton for weaving their clothes. Rigveda, the earliest of the Veda contains the literary information about textiles and it refers to weaving. Ramayana and Mahabharata, the eminent Indian epics depict the existence of wide variety of fabrics in ancient India. These epics refer both to rich and stylized garment worn by the aristocrats and ordinary simple clothes worn by the common people. The contemporary Indian textile not only reflects the splendid past but also cater to the requirements of the modern times. The rich tradition of textile in India has been favored by a number of factors. The favorable factors leading to the extensive growth of **Textile tradition in India** follows:

- Easy availability of abundant raw materials like cotton, wool, silk, jute and many more.
- Widely prevalent social customs.
- Variety of distinct local culture.
- Constructive geographic and climatic conditions.

Each and every region of India contributes in creating a myriad of textile tradition. The hilly region of the country produces a rich variety of woolen textiles. The pashmina and shahtoosh shawls of Kashmir, shawls and woolen garments of Himachal Pradesh and other north eastern states provides excellent examples of world famous woolen **Indian textiles**. The barren and semi barren regions like Rajasthan and Gujarat usually prefers embroidered.

The coastal areas of the south eastern regions prefer light coloured fabrics and particularly cotton and silk textiles are very popular over here. The home furnishing utilitarian textile products like bedspreads and sheets, pillows and cushions, linens and mats, curtains and napkins, carpets and rugs and many such other items are produced by all parts of the country.

Distinct style and tradition of Indian textiles :

- Silk and cotton weaving predominates the rich tradition of weaving in India. Silk weaving is most popular in various parts of the country. Assam, Banaras, Mysore, Surat, Kanchipuram and Surat are all important centers of silk weaving. All these centers specialize mostly in cotton and silk saree weaving and some of the popular traditional Indian sarees are Banarasi, Patola, Baluchari, Pochampalli, Paithani and many others.

- The ornate Style of appliqué Most commonly done bright coloured fabrics from the Kutchh region of Gujarat is very popular in the country as well as in abroad.
- The state of Punjab is famous for its phulkari work.
- Lucknow, a city in Uttar Pradesh is famous for its chicken work

Apart from those mentioned, each and every region and state of India has its own distinct individual style in textile.

Chinese Textile

China enjoys an excellent heritage in textile sector and occupies a prominent position in the global textile market. Chinese textiles are world famous and extraordinary for their fine quality and profound symbolic meanings. Textiles in china often form an integral aspect of its heritage and symbolically reflect its tradition and culture.

In China, textile is often closely associated with prosperity and involved in the process of elaborate rituals. Parents' spontaneous love for their children is most visibly reflected through the excellent clothes they provide on festive occasions to their children. These clothes are made up of expensive materials and excellent craftsmanship.

Different types of Chinese textile products

- Compound Fabric
- Bedding
- Chemical Fabric
- Feather & Down
- Fur Fabric
- Grey Cloth
- Other Textiles
- Sack & Bag for Packing
- Silk
- Adhesive bonded fabric
- Carpet
- Color Card & Color Comparator
- Functional Textile
- Glistening Fabric
- Industrial Textile
- Printed & Color-woven Cloth
- Sewing Thread & Tape
- Cotton

- Table Cloth
- Curtain
- Edging & Tassel
- Label & Tag
- Leather & Leatheroid
- Materials for Cap & shoes
- Textile Stocks
- Towel & Handkerchief
- Wool & Animal Hair
- Adhesive bonded fabric
- Decorative Cloth
- Embroidery & Drawn work
- Lace & Purfle
- Linen
- Military Material
- Textile Waste
- Twine, Rope & Netting

Carpets and other flooring traditions have been an essential part of Indian housing management from ages. Indian households have used carpets and various kinds of floorings crafted in wool, silk, jute, coir, bamboo and wool. Till today, Indian carpets and floorings are enjoying patronage of large international clientele. Carpets and floorings are an integral part of Indian homes. Carpets are generally made from wool and silk. However, floorings like mats and durries are made up of a variety of material, ranging from wool, cotton, jute, coir, bamboo and grass. One can trace the origins of carpet weaving tradition in India to the Mughal dynasty.

Mughals not only used the Persian technique of carpet weaving, but were also influenced by traditional designs and motifs from Persia. Mughal carpets were as intricate as their miniatures and often depicted court life, animals and floral decorations. From the Mughals, the craft of weaving carpets spread to different regions of India, and the trend of using them became an international craze.

States like Kashmir, Uttar Pradesh, and others have their distinctive tradition of carpet weavings. Gabbe woolen carpets, chain stitch rugs and carpets, and namdas are also made in India. Durries are traditional Indian flooring and a cheap alternate to carpets. Durries come in a variety of designs and styles. Durrie weaving is common to many states. Mats are made out of a variety of natural material like, bamboo, grass, jute, coir etc. India has a varied mat making tradition. Bihar, Orissa, TamilNadu, Kerala, West Bengal and Northeastern states all have distinct mat weaving traditions of their own.

Indians have known weaving of material from Cotton since 5000 years. The traditional Indian cotton weaving revolves around 'Khadi'. Khadi is a cloth woven by hand using handspun yarn only. Fine cotton fabrics are also referred as Muslin. India has been famous for its ultra fine Muslins in the past. As handspun yarn is used in making Khadi, this activity is mainly carried out in the rural areas of the country.

Cotton weaving is the heart and soul of Indian textiles. There are 23 different varieties of cotton found in India and there are about 4 million handlooms producing cotton fabric. Cotton is used in producing a wide range of items like: saree, bed sheets, covers, napkins, shirts, summer wear, tablemats etc.

Cotton fabric is very popular in a tropical country like India, because of the soft twist imparted by the hand, maintains the hairiness of the yarn to an extent, which gives maximum comfort. Handloom producing Khadi weave cotton in such a way that the interlacing of threads provides maximum passage of air to the body, thus creating a cooling effect, making Khadi an ideal summer wear.

Every state has its own traditional cotton weaving tradition:

Fine embroidery and appliqué work done on garments, from various parts of Gujarat and mainly from Kutchh is done on cotton fabric.

Cotton is used to create beautiful saris and is an integral part of the saree weaving tradition of India. The tasteful varieties of sarees from Chander in Madhya Pradesh are not only produced in silk but also have silk- cotton types. The tribal regions of Madhya Pradesh are also known for their cotton sarees or Gamchhas.

The jamdani cotton sarees from Tanda and Banaras in Uttar Pradesh are popular. So are the tangail cottons Of West Bengal and Sambalpuri and Vichitrapuri sarees of Orissa. These saris come in a variety of colours and traditional motifs inspired by nature.

The city of Hyderabad is known for its ancient cotton weaving tradition. The Venkatgiri fine cotton sarees are produced here, which are ideal for summers. These sarees are mainly in off-white colour and decorated with dull golden motifs.

Andhra Pradesh is also known for Ponduru Khadi, which is obtained from wild variety of cotton. It is used in shirting and furnishings.

Cotton fabrics from the handlooms from West Bengal, Gujarat, Assam, Rajasthan, Karnataka, Madhya Pradesh, Maharashtra etc. are used in creating a variety of items ranging from dress material, shirting, furnishing, hosiery, bedspreads etc.

The craft of weaving cotton fabric in India has achieved the status of small and medium scale industry. It not only caters to the local demands but is also exported to other countries on a large scale. Being eco-friendly and 100% natural, the demand for products made out of cotton is on the rise.

African Textile

The weavers, dyers and other textile artists of Africa together makes an active contribution in creating exquisite and amazing range of textiles. African textiles usually embody a great variety of styles. Adinkara, kente and bogolan are some of the some of the African textiles which are becoming increasingly popular while some others like Yoruba, ase-oke and adire are equally beautiful but less well known.

In the ancient times the most important aspect of textiles or more precisely cloth in Africa was that cloth was used as form of money. The width of cloth strip was usually standardized in each region of Africa and therefore there used to be a regular number of such standard length cloth strips required to make a woman's wrapper cloth.

This would then be used to serve as the unit of value. Cloth was a convenient form of money primarily because it was used by everybody, fairly durable and easily sub dividable.

Though textile has great social relevance in Africa, but to the majority of textile workers, more than any other aspect of textile it is primarily an occupation.

African textiles usually use the following raw materials:

- Bast fibres
- Wool
- Cotton
- Silk
- Raffia

- Bark of certain trees

Various types of African textiles : An extensive range of hand made African textile follows :

- Adinkra
- Adire
- Akwete
- Aso-oke
- Bagolan
- Ewe
- Kente
- kuba
- Nupe clothes

African textiles are usually decorated either by dyeing the thread or the finished product.

African textile sector is busy getting influenced by the various developments in the global scenario and accordingly updating itself. Nowadays African designers are increasingly attempting to add a local appeal and flavour to their creations by using the tradition of weaving and textile design in contemporary dress styles.

Japanese Textile

Textiles offer a fascinating and revealing reflection of any society and this is particularly applicable in case of Japanese textiles. Starting with the modern age when Japan augmented its urbanization; textiles have served the purpose of acting as an emblem of social status and position. The style, colour motif and shape of the garment effectively depict the tradition and culture of Japan and at the same time also provides personalized information about an individual.

History of Japanese Textile In 1869 the capital of Japan was shifted from Kyoto to Tokyo and from this time onwards the Nishijin weaving tradition seemed threatened with extinction. Though it had a negative impact on the weaving industry and consequently on the entire economy of Kyoto but the Nishijin weavers exhibited a remarkable spirit and flexibility in preserving their own craft and soon enough highly developed weaving technology and equipment was introduced.

The industry again started to grow along with Japan's new capitalist economy by 1890 when the Nishijin weavers embraced and applied modern technology to their own ancient and original textile art. The textile art of Japan particularly reached an epitome of excellence by exhibiting a cultural distinction and remarkable artistic skill in the Edo and succeeding Meiji periods (1868 - 1912).

Exclusive Japanese Textile Japanese textiles present an extraordinary and extensive collection of textiles. The rich heritage of Japanese textiles gets reflected through its traditional textiles like the kimono which is the traditional Japanese garment for men, women and children haori which is typical formal Japanese overcoat or obi which is a hand woven Japanese belt or sash tied around the waist or the fukusa which is an elaborately decorated and beautiful piece of cloth used for wrapping a gift while presenting it formally.

Exclusive Japanese Textile Art Tsujigahana textiles which belong to the period of fourteenth and early seventh century often reflect the epitome of excellence in Japanese Textile Art.

Tsujigahana textiles which were extremely creative and beautiful depicts the diverse changes in the history of Japan and these textiles were mainly utilized for making clothes, banners and such other items. The ornamental lavishness of the later Edo period often gets reflected through the best pieces of tsujigahana.

Southern Textile

Southern Textile is an organization that is involved in apparel/ general merchandise wholesale, liquidation and exporting business. Southern Textile was established in 1973 and it comprise of a team of experienced professionals who are operating all over the world and serve the buyers and customers of all the continents.

Southern Textile caters to the diversified needs of retail stores, wholesale distribution center or an e commerce market place as it offers a variety of branded products which are widely available for purchasing. The selected category comprise of computers, computer components, home office products, consumer electronics, digital cameras and video equipment, house wares, sports, hobbies, jewelry, gifts, accessories, apparel, shoes, furniture, domestics, home improvement, collectibles, and many more at reasonable low wholesale prices.

Southern Textile enjoys 30 years of experience and expertise in wholesaling and is devoted completely in finding the most excellent deals for its clients from all over the world. In this context it is necessary to clearly define and describe the term, Wholesale is a term that is closely associated with commercial aspect of textile product and textile industry. The practice of selling of textile goods or merchandise to retailers, commercial, institutional, or other professional business users or to other textile wholesalers is known as textile wholesaling. Wholesalers often physically assemble, sort and grade products in huge quantities, then break the bulk repack and redistribute them in smaller quantities. Southern Textile is one of the leading remarked of reverse supply chain merchandise to professional as well as wholesale buyers. This company enjoys 30 years of experience in liquidation industry. With over 30 years experience in the liquidation industry and it has long-term business relationships with major retailers, manufacturers and distributors. Southern Textile has expertise product range in major categories of consumer merchandise such as electronics, apparel, footwear, toys, furniture, entertainment and general merchandise.

The warehouse locations and national presence of Southern Textile offer professional purchasers fast and reliable access to bulk lots of wholesale and discount goods to fulfill their requirements.

Southern Textile also has the credit of successfully using the internet to generate an interactive market place which helps the professional buyers to access conveniently the brand name merchandise at concession in a short span of time. Apart from providing access to live inventory the website of this organization also offers the convenient and time saving option of placing online orders and arrangements for shipping requirements.

To take full advantage of online facilities, a business associate of need to have an account with Southern Textile and this account in turn offers the following access :

- Real time product availability.
- Real time order placement.

- Real time order status.
- Downloadable manifests.
- Quicker responses from sales representatives.
- Overview of recent online transactions.

Textile Converting

Textile Converting refers to the process of converting the textile fabrics to varying size and shape according to the requirement of the product. The product can be anything from a stylized garment to any home furnishing product. Textile Converting generally comprise of the following processes :

- Fabric designing based on the requirement of the product.
- Purchasing both dyed and undyed yarns and commissioning the knitting mills to knit the yarns into fabric according to the requirements of the specific product.
- Commissioning the finishers to finish the fabrics by using the process of washing, dyeing, bleaching and applying certain chemical finishes to the fabrics.

Chemical Conversion :

- Purified cellulose is chemically converted into a soluble compound in rayon production. A solution of this compound is passed through the spinneret to form soft filaments which are then converted or regenerated into almost pure cellulose. Rayon is termed as regenerated cellulose fibre due to the re-conversion of soluble compound to cellulose.
- Various types of rayon fibres are now a days used in commercial purposes and they are termed according to the process of conversion of cellulose into soluble form and consecutive regeneration. Rayon fibres are wet spun and it means that filaments developing from the spinneret pass directly into chemical bathing for solidification or regeneration.

Textile Printing

Textile printing is one of the procedure of textile decoration. **Textile printing** requires the correct coordination between the printing machinery support and the human skill for producing the best of the results. **Textile printing** uses various printing techniques of which screen printing is most predominant.

Screen printing was previously known as silk screening which refers to the printing technique that utilizes a stencil or a porous fabric to create a sharp edged image. Now a days it is very popular in both the fields of commercial printing and fine arts. Because of its advantage of low cost and ability to print on many mediums it is preferred over other processes like dye sublimation or inkjet printing. It started off during the First World War as an industrial process used primarily for printing flags and banners. Guy Mc Roy was the pioneer of screen printing technique. The greatest advantage of screen printing is that it possesses more versatility than any other traditional printing techniques.

- **Block Printing**–It was first developed in china. In this technique , first an original needs to be created ,then block with ink is used to create duplicates which involves a wide variety of skilled crafts men
- **Ink jet printing**–In this technique, the intended pattern along with the individual colour is formed by projecting small drops of ink which are special dye liquors in predetermined micro arrays onto the surface of the substrate.
- **Hand printing**–This is earliest form of printing used for the purpose of increasing the decorative value of textiles. This is the traditional technique of tie and dye.
- **Spray Printing**–In this technique, a spray gun is used to force the colour through a screen and electro-coating is used to apply a patterned pile.
- **Tie and dye**–This is particularly done on bright colours. This technique involves tying up of both wrap and weft threads where original colour needs to be retained and then dyed.
- **Kalamkari**–It is an exclusive and ancient craft done on textile fabrics. Kalamkari derives its name from the word Kalam which means Pen and Kari means Work and thus it means Pen Work. This art undergoes the laborious process of resist dyeing and hand printing.

- **Batik**–It is the procedure of dyeing the fabric by using the resist technique which covers the areas of the cloth to prevent it from colour absorption by using a dye resistant substance.
- Printing with the use of mordant is another technique of textile printing. Mordants are chemicals that absorb dye.

Phulkari Art

Sitting on the charpoys (beds woven with jute strings) pulled into the protective shade of a tree, or ensconced against a wall, women in villages and small towns all over Punjab are often busy creating spectacular **flower-embroidery** on dupattas, shawls or other garments. Called phulkari in local parlance, the origin of this beautiful art can be traced back to the 15th century AD.

The word phulkari literally means flowering. It is a form of craft in which embroidery is done in a simple and sparse design over shawls and dupattas. In some cases where the design is worked over very closely, covering the material entirely, it is called bagh (a garden of flowers).

The Making

The **embroidery of phulkari** and bagh is done in long and short darn stitch, which is created into innumerable designs and patterns. It is the skillful manipulation of this single stitch that lends an interesting and characteristic dimension to this needlework. While the stitch itself is uncomplicated, the quality of the phulkari depends upon the size of the stitch. The smaller the stitch, the finer the embroidery.

The threads used were of a silk yarn called pat. In the past, the silk threads were brought in from different parts of India, like Kashmir and Bengal and also from Afghanistan and China.

Using Colours : Bright colours were always preferred and among these, golden yellow, red, crimson, orange, green, blue, pink etc., were the popular ones.

For the embroidery, only a single strand was used at a time, each part worked in one colour. Shading and variation were not done by using various colours of thread. Instead, the effect was obtained by the dexterous use of horizontal, vertical or diagonal stitches. This resulted in giving an illusion of more than one shade when light fell on it and when it was viewed from different angles.

To keep the embroidered part clean while working on the cloth, the finished portion was rolled and covered with a muslin cloth. Specially created designs varied from village to village or region to region in Punjab and were given suitable names descriptive of their form. While phulkari was used to ornament cloth, the bagh ensured that not even a square inch of the base cloth was visible.

Base Cloth : The cloth primarily used and preferred by the women, was the home-spun, locally woven and dyed khadi. It was strong, long-lasting, and cheap and served the purpose of keeping the wearer warm during winters. Another reason was that the embroidery involved the counting of threads while doing the straight darn stitch. The coarse weave made this task easier. In addition, the thick cloth did not pucker and pull and could be worked upon without a frame. Usually, pieces of small width, about 45 to 60 centimeters, were worked on separately and the two or three strips were joined together to form the required size.

Repertoire of Motifs : Beginning with geometrical patterns, flowers and leaves, the repertoire of motifs was constantly enlarged. Birds, animals and human figures and objects of everyday use were inducted, along with vegetables, pots, buildings, rivers, the sun and the moon, scenes of village life, and other imagery. Phulkaris and baghs came to be embroidered in a stunning range of exquisite designs. In dhoop chaon, which literally means "sun and shade", an amazing interactive display of light and shade was created. The designs remained earthy and true to life. There was dhaniya bagh (coriander garden), motia bagh (jasmine garden), satranga bagh (garden of rainbow), leheria bagh (garden of waves) and many other depictions.

Today the most intricate and sought after phulkaris are the sainchi phulkaris, which bring scenes from rural Punjab to life. An incredible wealth of detail is embroidered onto cloth.

Reflecting Emotions : With time, the **phulkaris** became closely interwoven with the lives of the women of Punjab.

The joys, sorrows, hopes, dreams and yearnings of the young girls and women who **embroidered the phulkaris** were often transferred onto cloth. Many folk songs grew out of this expressive combination of skills and intense feelings. So, it is that one hears a young woman, whose betrothed has not sent a promised message to her, murmuring sadly, softly, as she *embroiders peacocks on a phulkari*. It was not long before phulkari folk songs became a part of the famous, pulsating folk dances of Punjab - the gidda and the bhangra.

Phulkari for Different Occasions : Phulkaris were also made for religious ceremonies or to be used at other festive times.

A phulkari is sanctified to be used as the canopy over the holy book of the Sikhs, the 'Guru Granth Sahib'.

For each different occasion, for each different setting, the versatile fingers and fertile imagination of the women of Punjab designed an impressive selection of phulkaris.

A New Form of Phulkari : A new form of phulkari is being embroidered these days.

It is not as detailed or time consuming as the older variety. Using a range of different fast coloured synthetic threads, it is embroidered from the top of the cloth rather than on its reverse.

The Punjab Government's Emporium, Phulkari, boasts of the best collection of this form of embroidery in the country. Their sizeable assemblage of a variety of these original pieces has been garnered from the villages in the state. Many of these are being exported, especially to the Middle-East.

Different Varieties : There are different varieties of phulkaris and baghs made in Punjab.

The Chope, usually presented to the bride by her grandmother during a ceremony before the wedding, is embroidered with straight, two-sided line stitch and appears the same on the reverse. Only the border is embroidered and the center is left plain. It is usually red in colour and worn as a veil.

Vari-da-bagh (bagh of the trousseau) is also on a red cloth with golden yellow embroidery symbolizing happiness and fertility.

The entire cloth is covered in a lozenge design with smaller ones within the border and is again intricately worked in different colours.

Ghunghat bagh or sari-pallu (covering for the head) has a small border on all four sides. In the center of each side, which covers the head, a large triangular motif is worked.

Bawan bagh (fifty-two in Punjabi) has as many geometrical patterns.

Darshan dwar (the gate offering a view of the deity) is usually for presentation in temples or to adorn the walls of the home when the Granth Sahib (holy book of the Sikhs) is brought to a house. The gate motif has been inspired by the arched verandahas of the temples. It is again, always on a red cloth. The architectural design depicts two outer panels of all gates with arched tops. The bases face each other with motifs of humans, animals, birds, flowers etc., giving the impression of passing through a crowded street.

Suber is a phulkari worn by a bride during marriage rites. It comprises five motifs, one in the center and one each in the four corners.

Chamba is a hybrid phulkari having a series of wavy creepers, stylized leaves and flowers. It came into vogue earlier this century.

Besides this, designs inspired by various day to day items, fauna and flora around us also found their way into this craft.

Surajmukhi (sunflower) is a cross between a chope and ordinary bagh in brilliant yellow, which creates a stunning effect.

Mor or tota is one that has a peacock or parrot motif.

Mirchi, as the name suggests, has chilies in red, orange or green usually on brown.

Belan and parantha symbolize the rolling pin and leavened bread.

Ikka or ace of diamonds has been inspired by playing cards.

Satrang is a seven-coloured phulkari.

Jewellery items like bangles, earrings, etc., are also embroidered At times, a snake was embroidered, guarding a woman's treasure. Another variety popular in Haryana was the Sheeshedar where small, round, matt-dull mirror pieces were included in the embroidered motifs.

Traditionally, the phulkaris and baghs were never sold in the markets as they were only woven by the women of the house for their personal use.

A Symbol of Familial Ties : The women of Punjab created **phulkari** mostly for personal use. The cycle began with the young girl who followed her mother's chores and learned household work including this embroidery. When the girl got married, phulkari formed a part of her bridal trousseau. If a son was born to her, her mother would start preparing a vari da bagh, a gift she would present to her grand daughter-in- law.

The bagh was considered a symbol of marriage and among the wealthy families; sometimes up to fifty-one pieces of various designs were given to the bride. She, in turn, wore them for auspicious and ceremonial occasions. In some parts of Punjab, it was customary to drape the new mother with a bagh on the eleventh day after the birth of the child, when she left the maternity room for the first time.

4

Natural Fibre

Until the advent of the manufactured fibers near the beginning of the twentieth century, the chief fibers for apparel and home furnishings were linen and wool in the temperate climates and cotton in the tropical climates. However, with the invention of the cotton gin in 1798, cheap cotton products began to replace the more expensive linen and wool until by 1950 cotton accounted for about 70% of the world's fiber production. Despite the development of new fibers based on fossil fuels, cotton has managed to maintain its position as the fiber with the largest production volume, although its use has fallen. A fiber obtained from a plant, animal, or mineral. The commercially important natural fibers are those cellulosic fibers obtained from the seed hairs, stems, and leaves of plants; protein fibers obtained from the hair, fur, or cocoons of animals; and the crystalline mineral asbestos.

Sources of natural fibers : Natural fibers are made from plant, animal and mineral sources. Natural fibers can be classified according to their origin.

Vegetable Fiber

Vegetable fibers are generally comprised mainly of cellulose:

examples include cotton, jute, flax, ramie, sisal, and hemp. Cellulose fibers serve in the manufacture of paper and cloth. This fiber can be further categorized into the following:

- Seed fiber: Fibers collected from seeds or seed cases. e.g. cotton and kapok

Agave is a succulent plant of a large botanical genus of the same name, belonging to the family Agavaceae. Chiefly Mexican, agaves occur also in the southern and western United States and in central and tropical South America. The plants have a large rosette of thick fleshy leaves, each ending generally in a sharp point and with a spiny margin; the stout stem is usually short, the leaves apparently springing from the root. Along with plants from the related genus *Yucca*, various *Agave* species are popular ornamental plants.

Cotton is used to make a number of textile products. These include terrycloth, used to make highly absorbent bath towels and robes; denim, used to make blue jeans; chambray, popularly used in the manufacture of blue work shirts (from which we get the term "blue-collar"); and corduroy, seersucker, and cotton twill. Socks, underwear, and most T-shirts are made from cotton. Bed sheets often are made from cotton. Cotton also is used to make yarn used in crochet and knitting.

Kapok (***Ceiba pentandra***) is a tropical tree of the order *Malvales* and the family *Malvaceae* (previously separated in the family *Bombacaceae*), native to Mexico, Central America and the Caribbean, northern South America, and (as the variety *C. pentandra* var. *guineensis*) to tropical west Africa. The word is also used for the fiber obtained from its seed pods. The tree is also known as the Java cotton, Java kapok, or ceiba. It is a sacred symbol in Maya mythology.

The tree of life grows to 60-70 m (200-230 ft) tall and has a very substantial trunk up to 3 m (10 ft) in diameter with buttresses. The trunk and many of the larger branches are densely crowded with very large, robust simple thorns. The leaves are compound of 5 to 9 leaflets, each up to 20 cm (8 in) and palm like. Adult trees produce several hundred 15 cm (6 in) seed pods. The pods contain seeds surrounded by a fluffy, yellowish fiber that is a mix of lignin and cellulose.

- Leaf fiber: Fibers collected from leaves. e.g. sisal and agave.

Sisal is an agave *Agave sisalana* that yields a stiff fiber traditionally used in making twine and rope. (The term may refer either to the plant or the fiber, depending on context.) It is has sometimes been incorrectly referred to as *sisal hemp* because hemp was for centuries a major source for fiber, so other fibers were sometimes named after it.

The plant's origin is uncertain; while traditionally it was deemed to be a native of Yucatan, there are no records of botanical collections from there. Gentry hypothesized a Chiapas origin, on the strength of traditional local usage. In the 19th century, sisal cultivation spread to Florida, the Caribbean islands and Brazil, as well as to countries in Africa, notably Tanzania and Kenya, and Asia. The first commercial plantings in Brazil were made in the late 1930's and the first sisal fiber exports from there were made in 1948.

- Bast fiber or skin fiber: Fibers are collected from the skin or bast surrounding the stem of their respective plant. These fibers have higher tensile strength than other fibers. Therefore, these fibers are used for durable yarn, fabric, packaging, and paper. Some examples are flax, jute, kenaf, industrial hemp, ramie, rattan, soybean fiber, and even vine fibers and banana fibers.
- Fruit fiber: Fibers are collected from the fruit of the plant, e.g. coconut (coir) fiber.
- Stalk fiber: Fibers are actually the stalks of the plant. E.g. straws of wheat, rice, barley, and other crops including bamboo and grass. Tree wood is also such a fiber.

The most used natural fibers are cotton, flax and hemp, although sisal, jute, kenaf, and coconut are also widely used.

Jute is a long, soft, shiny vegetable fiber that can be spun into coarse, strong threads. It is produced from plants in the genus *Corchorus*, family Tiliaceae.

Jute is one of the cheapest natural fibers and is second only to cotton in amount produced and variety of uses. Jute fibers are composed primarily of the plant materials cellulose (major component of plant fiber) and lignin (major components, wood fiber). It is thus a ligno-cellulosic fiber that is partially a textile fiber and partially wood. It falls into the bast fiber category (fiber collected from bast or skin of the plant) along with kenaf, industrial hemp, flax (linen), ramie, etc. The industrial term for jute fiber is *raw jute*. The fibers are off-white to brown, and 1–4 meters (3–12 feet) long.

Jute fiber is often called hessian; jute fabrics are also called hessian cloth and jute sacks are called gunny bags in some European countries. The fabric made from jute is popularly known as burlap in North America.

Flax (also known as **common flax** or **linseed**) (binomial name: ***Linum usitatissimum***) is a member of the genus *Linum* in the family Linaceae. It is native to the region extending from the eastern Mediterranean to India and was probably first domesticated in the Fertile Crescent. This is called as Jawas/Javas or Alashi in Marathi. Flax was extensively cultivated in ancient Egypt. (New Zealand flax is not related to flax, but was named after it as both plants are used to produce fibers.)

Ramie (*Boehmeria nivea*) is a flowering plant in the nettle family Urticaceae, native to eastern Asia. It is a herbaceous perennial growing to 1 - 2.5 m tall; the leaves are heart-shaped, 7-15 cm long and 6-12 cm broad, and white on the underside with dense small hairs - this gives it a silvery appearance; unlike nettles, the hairs do not sting. The true ramie or China Grass also called Chinese plant or white ramie is the Chinese cultivated plant. A second type, is known as green ramie or rhea and is believed to have originated in the Malay Peninsula.

Cotton is a soft, staple fiber that grows in a form known as a **boll** around the seeds of the cotton plant (*Gossypium* sp.), a shrub native to tropical and subtropical regions around the world, including the Americas, India and Africa. The fiber most often is spun into yarn or thread and used to make a soft, breathable textile, which is the most widely used natural-fiber cloth in clothing today.

Sisal is an agave *Agave sisalana* that yields a stiff fiber traditionally used in making twine and rope. (The term may refer either to the plant or the fiber, depending on context.) It is has sometimes been incorrectly referred to as *sisal hemp* because hemp was for centuries a major source for fiber, so other fibers were sometimes named after it.

The plant's origin is uncertain; while traditionally it was deemed to be a native of Yucatan, there are no records of botanical collections from there. Gentry hypothesized a Chiapas origin, on the strength of traditional local usage. In the 19th century, sisal cultivation spread to Florida, the Caribbean islands and Brazil, as well as to countries in Africa, notably Tanzania and Kenya, and Asia. The first commercial plantings in Brazil were made in the late 1930's and the first sisal fiber exports from there were made in 1948. It was not until the 1960's that Brazilian production really accelerated and the first of many spinning mills were established. Today Brazil is the major world producer of sisal. There are both positive and negative environmental impacts from sisal growing.

Traditionally used for rope and twine, sisal has many uses, including paper, cloth, wall coverings and carpets.

Hemp fibers are mainly used for ropes and aerofoils because of their high suppleness and resistance within an aggressive environment. Hemp fibers are, for example, currently used as a seal within the heating and sanitary industries.

Hemp is used for a wide variety of purposes, including the manufacture of cordage of varying tensile strength, clothing, and nutritional products. The *bast fibers* can be used in 100% hemp products, but are commonly blended with fibers such as flax, cotton or silk, for apparel and furnishings, most commonly at a 55%/45% hemp/cotton blend. The inner two fibers of hemp are more woody, and are more often used in non-woven items and other industrial applications, such as mulch, animal bedding and litter.

Cellulose Fiber- Cellulose is an organic compound with the formula $(C_6H_{10}O_5)_n$, a polysaccharide consisting of a linear chain of several hundred to over ten thousand β(1'!4) linked D-glucose units.

Cellulose is the structural component of the primary cell wall of green plants, many forms of algae and the oomycetes. Some species of bacteria secrete it to form biofilms. Cellulose is the most common organic compound on Earth. About 33 percent of all plant matter is cellulose (the cellulose content of cotton is 90 percent and that of wood is 50 percent). Cellulose fibers serve in the manufacture of paper and cloth.

Paper is thin material mainly used for writing upon, printing upon or packaging. It is produced by pressing together moist fibers, typically cellulose pulp derived from wood, rags or grasses, and drying them into flexible sheets. Paper is a versatile material with many uses. Whilst the most common is for writing and printing upon, it is also widely used as a packaging material, in many cleaning products, and in a number of industrial and construction processes, and occasionally as a food ingredient, particularly in Asian cultures.

Textile is a flexible material consisting of a network of natural or artificial fibers often referred to as thread or yarn. Yarn is produced by spinning raw wool fibers, linen, cotton, or other material on a spinning wheel to produce long strands known as yarn. Textiles are formed by weaving, knitting, crocheting, knotting, or pressing fibers together (felt).

The words *fabric* and *cloth* are used in textile assembly trades (such as tailoring and dressmaking) as synonyms for *textile*. However, there are subtle differences in these terms. *Textile* refers to any material made of interlacing fibers. *Fabric* refers to any material made through weaving, knitting, crocheting, or bonding. *Cloth* refers to a finished piece of fabric that can be used for a purpose such as covering a bed.

Bast fiber (fiber) or **skin fiber** is plant fiber collected from the phloem (the "inner bark" or the skin) or **bast** surrounding the stem of certain, mainly dicotyledonic, plants. They support the conductive cells of the phloem and provide strength to the stem. Most of the technically important bast fibers are obtained from herbs cultivated in agriculture, as for instance flax, hemp, or ramie, but also bast fibers from wild plants, as stinging nettle, and trees as the lime tree, have been used to some extent. Since the valuable fibers are located in the phloem, they must often be separated from the xylem material ("woody core"), and sometimes also from epidermis. The process for this is called retting, and can be performed by microoganisms either on land (nowadays the most important) or in water, or by chemicals (for instance high pH and chelating agents) or by pectinolytic enzymes. In the phloem bast fibers occur in bundles that are glued together by pectin and calcium ions. More intense retting separates the fiber bundles into elementary fibers, that can be several cm long. The bast fibers have often higher tensile strength than other kinds, and are therefore used for textiles (not seldom very exclusive textiles, sometimes in blends with cotton or synthetic fibers) ropes, yarn, paper, composite materials and burlap. A special property of bast fibers are that the fiber contain a special structure, *the fiber node*, that represents a weak point. Fibre nodes seems not to be present in seed hairs as cotton.

Examples are:

- Jute
- Hemp
- Flax (Linen)
- Ramie
- Kenaf
- Roselle hemp
- Rattan
- Soybean fiber
- Okra fiber
- Banana fiber
- Abaca
- Nettles

Use of bast fiber

Bast fibers are processed for use in carpet yarn, rope, geotextile (netting or matting), traditional carpets, hessian or burlap, paper, sacks, etc. Bast fibers are also used in the non-woven, moulding, and composite technology industries for the manufacturing of non-woven mats and carpets, composite boards as furniture materials, automobile door pannels and headliners, etc. From prehistoric times through at least the early 20th century, bast shoes were woven from bast strips in the forest areas of Eastern Europe.

Animal Fibers

Animal fibers generally comprise proteins; examples include silk, wool, angora, mohair and alpaca. **Animal fibers** are natural fibers that consist largely of particular proteins. Instances are silk, hair/fur (including wool) and feathers. The most commonly used type of animal fiber is hair.

Not all animal fibers have the same properties. Alpaca fiber is known for its softness, and silk for its sheen and strength. Even within a species the fiber is not consistent. Merino is a very soft, fine wool, while Cotswold is coarser, and yet both merino and Cotswold are types of sheep. This comparison can be continued on the microscopic level, comparing the diameter and structure of the fiber.

With animal fibers, and natural fibers in general, the individual fibers look different, whereas all synthetic fibers look the same. This provides an easy way to differentiate between natural and synthetic fibers under a microscope. The animal fibers used most commonly both in the manufacturing world as well as by the hand spinners are wool and silk.

- Animal hair (wool or hairs): Fibre or wool taken from animals or hairy mammals. e.g. sheep's wool, goat hair (cashmere, mohair), alpaca hair, horse hair, etc.
- Silk fiber: Fibre collected from dried saliva of bugs or insects during the preparation of cocoons. Examples include silk
- Avian fiber: Fibers from birds, e.g. feathers and feather fiber.

Silk

Silk is a natural protein fiber, some forms of which can be woven into textiles. The best-known type of silk is obtained from cocoons made by the larvae of the mulberry silkworm *Bombyx mori* reared in captivity (sericulture). The shimmering appearance for which silk is prized comes from the fibers' triangular prism-like structure which allows silk cloth to refract incoming light at different angles.

Wild silks are produced by caterpillars other than the mulberry silkworm and can be artificially cultivated. A variety of wild silks have been known and used in China, South Asia, and Europe since early times, but the scale of production was always far smaller than that of cultivated silks. They differ from the domesticated varieties in color and texture, and cocoons gathered in the wild usually have been damaged by the emerging moth before the cocoons are gathered, so the silk thread that makes up the cocoon has been torn into shorter lengths. Commercially reared silkworm pupae are killed by dipping them in boiling water before the adult moths emerge, or by piercing them with a needle, allowing the whole cocoon to be unraveled as one continuous thread. This permits a much stronger cloth to be woven from the silk. Wild silks also tend to be more difficult to dye than silk from the cultivated silkworm.

Silks are produced by several other insects, but only the silk of moth caterpillars has been used for textile manufacture. There has been some research into other silks, which differ at the molecular level. Silks are mainly produced by the larvae of insects that complete metamorphosis, but also by some adult insects such as webspinners. Silk production is especially common in the Hymenoptera (bees, wasps, and ants), and is sometimes used in nest construction. Other types of arthropod produce silk, most notably various arachnids such as spiders.

History of Silk

According to Chinese tradition, the **history of silk** begins in the 27th century BCE. Its use was confined to China until the Silk Road opened at some point during the latter half of the first millennium BC. China maintained its virtual monopoly over silk for another thousand years. Not confined to clothing, silk was also used for a number of other applications, including writing, and the colour of silk worn was an important indicator of social class during the Tang Dynasty.

Silk cultivation spread to Japan in around 300 CE, and by 522 the Byzantines managed to obtain silkworm eggs and were able to begin silkworm cultivation. The Arabs also began to manufacture silk during this same time. As a result of the spread of sericulture,

Chinese silk exports became less important, although they still maintained dominance over the luxury silk market. The Crusades brought silk production to Western Europe, in particular to many Italian states, which saw an economic boom exporting silk to the rest of Europe. Changes in manufacturing techniques also began to take place during the Middle Ages, with devices such as the spinning wheel first appearing. During the 16th century France joined Italy in developing a successful silk trade, though the efforts of most other nations to develop a silk industry of their own were unsuccessful.

The Industrial Revolution changed much of Europe's silk industry. Due to innovations in spinning cotton, it became much cheaper to manufacture and therefore caused more expensive silk production to become less mainstream. New weaving technologies, however, increased the efficiency of production. Among these was the Jacquard loom, a precursor to modern computers, developed for silk embroidery. An epidemic of several silkworm diseases caused production to fall, especially in France, where the industry never recovered. In the 20th century Japan and China regained their earlier role in silk production, and China is now once again the world's largest producer of silk. The rise of new fabrics such as nylon reduced the prevalence of silk throughout the world, and silk is now once again a somewhat rare luxury good.

Properties

Physical Properties

Silk fibers have a triangular cross section with rounded corners. This reflects light at many different angles, giving silk a natural shine. It has a smooth, soft texture that is not slippery, unlike many synthetic fibers. Its denier is 4.5 g/d when dry and 2.8-4.0 g/d when moist.

Silk is one of the strongest natural fibers but loses up to 20% of its strength when wet. It has a good moisture regain of 11%. Its elasticity is moderate to poor: if elongated even a small amount it remains stretched. It can be weakened if exposed to too much sunlight. It may also be attacked by insects, especially if left dirty.

Silk is a poor conductor of electricity and thus susceptible to static cling.

Unwashed silk chiffon may shrink up to 8% due to a relaxation of the fiber macrostructure. So silk should either be pre-washed prior to garment construction, or dry cleaned. Dry cleaning may still shrink the chiffon up to 4%. Occasionally, this shrinkage can be reversed by a gentle steaming with a press cloth. There is almost no gradual shrinkage or shrinkage due to molecular-level deformation.

Chemical Properties

Silk is made up of the amino acids GLY-SER-GLY-ALA-GLY and forms Beta pleated sheets. Interchain H-bonds are formed while side chains are above and below the plane of the H-bond network.

The high proportion (50%) of glycine, which is small, allows tight packing and the fibers are strong and resistant to stretching. The tensile strength is due to covalent peptide bonds. Since the protein forms a Beta sheet, when stretched the force is applied to these strong bonds and they do not break.

Silk is resistant to most mineral acids but will dissolve in sulfuric acid. It is yellowed by perspiration.

Uses

Silk's good absorbency makes it comfortable to wear in warm weather and while active. Its low conductivity keeps warm air close to the skin during cold weather. It is often used for clothing such as shirts, blouses, formal dresses, high fashion clothes, negligees, pyjamas, robes, skirtsuits, sun dresses and underwear.

Silk's elegant, soft luster and beautiful drape makes it perfect for many furnishing applications. It is used for upholstery, wall coverings, window treatments (if blended with another fiber), rugs, bedding and wall hangings.

While on the decline now, due to artificial fibers, silk has had many uses; parachutes, bicycle tires, comforter filling and artillery gunpowder bags. From the blackpowder era, until roughly World War I, early bulletproof vests were made from silk. A special manufacturing process makes it suitable as non-absorbable surgical sutures. Chinese doctors have used it to make prosthetic arteries. Silk cloth is also used as a material on which to write.

Cultivation

Silk moths lay eggs on specially prepared paper. The eggs hatch and the caterpillars (silkworms) are fed fresh mulberry leaves. After about 35 days and 4 moltings, the caterpillars are 10,000 times heavier than when hatched, and are ready to begin spinning a cocoon. A straw frame is placed over the tray of caterpillars, and each caterpillar begins spinning a cocoon by moving its head in a "figure 8" pattern. Two glands produce liquid silk and force it through openings in the head called spinnerets. Liquid silk is coated in sericin, a water-soluble protective gum, and solidifies on contact with the air. Within 2-3 days, the caterpillar spins about 1 mile of filament and is completely encased in a cocoon. The silk farmers then kill most caterpillars by heat, leaving some to metamorphose into moths to breed the next generation of caterpillars.

Animal Rights

As the process of harvesting the silk from the cocoon kills the larvae, sericulture has been criticized in the early 21st century by animal rights activists, especially since artificial silks are available. Mahatma Gandhi was also critical of silk production based on the Ahinsa philosophy. Ahinsa is part of the three millennial Jain and Buddhist philosophy of India, "not to hurt any living thing". This led to development of a cotton spinning machine which Gandhi distributed and can be seen at the Gandhi Institute. *Ahinsa Silk*, made from the cocoons of wild and semi-wild silk moths, is promoted in parts of Southern India for those who prefer not to wear silk produced by killing silkworms.

Silk Waste

Silk waste includes all kinds of raw silk which may be unwindable, and therefore unsuited to the throwing process. Before the introduction of machinery applicable to the spinning of silk waste, the refuse from cocoon reeling, and also from silk winding, which is now used in producing spun silk fabrics, was nearly all destroyed as being useless, with the exception of that which could be hand-combed and spun by means of the distaff and spinning wheel, a method which is still practised by some of the peasantry in India and other countries in Asia.

Sources

The supply of waste silk is drawn from the following sources:

- The silkworm, when commencing to spin, emits a dull, lustreless and uneven thread with which it suspends itself to the twigs and leaves of the tree upon which it has been feeding, or to the straws provided for it by attendants in the worm-rearing establishments: this first thread is unreliable, and, moreover, is often mixed with straw, leaves and twigs.
- The outside layers of the true cocoon are too coarse and uneven for reeling; and as the worm completes its task of spinning, the thread becomes finer and weaker, so both the extreme outside and inside layers are put aside as waste.
- Pierced cocoons, that is, those from which the moth of the silkworm has emerged-and damaged cocoons.
- During the process of reeling from the cocoon the silk often breaks; and both in finding a true and reelable thread, and in joining the ends, there is unavoidable waste.
- Raw silk skeins are often re-reeled; and in this process part has to be discarded: this being known to the trade as gum-waste. The same term — gum-waste — is applied to " waste "made in the various processes of silk throwing; but manufacturers using threads known technically as organizes and trams call the surplus "manufacturer's waste."

Processing

A silk "throwster" receives his silk in skein form, the thread of which consists of a number of silk fibers wound together to make a certain diameter or size, the separate fiber having actually been spun by the worm. The silk-waste spinner receives his silk in quite a different form: merely the raw material, packed in bales of various sizes and weights, the contents being a much-tangled mass of all lengths of fiber mixed with much foreign matter, such as ends of straws, twigs, leaves, worms and chrysalis. It is the spinner's business to straighten out these fibers, with the aid of machinery, and then to so join them that they become a thread, which is known as spun silk.

There are two distinct kinds of spun silk: one called *schappe* and the other *spun silk* or *discharged spun silk.* All silk produced by the worm is composed of two substances: fibroin, the true thread, and sericin, which is a hard, gummy coating of the fibroin. Before the silk can be manipulated by machinery to any advantage, the gum coating must be removed, really dissolved and washed away - and according to the method used in achieving this operation the result is either a schappe or a discharged yarn. The former, schapping, is the French, Italian and Swiss method, from which the silk when finished is neither so bright nor so good in colour as the discharged silk; but it is very clean and level, and for some purposes absolutely essential, as, for instance, in velvet manufacture.

Wool

Wool is the fiber derived from the fur of animals of the Caprinae family, principally sheep, but the hair of certain species of other mammals such as goats, alpacas, and rabbits may also be called wool. **Wool** is the fiber derived from the specialized skin cells, called follicles, of animals in the Caprinae family, principally sheep, but the hair of certain species of other mammals such as goats, llamas, rabbits and keeshond may also be called wool. Wool has several qualities that distinguish it from hair or fur: it is crimped; it has a different texture or handle; it is elastic; and it grows in staples (clusters).

Characteristics

Wool's scaling and crimp make it easier to spin the fleece. They help the individual fibers attach to each other so that they stay together. Because of the crimp, wool fabrics have a greater bulk than other textiles and retain air, which causes the product to retain heat. Insulation also works both ways; Bedouins and Tuaregs use wool clothes to keep the heat out.

The amount of crimp corresponds to the thickness of the wool fibers. A fine wool like Merino may have up to a hundred crimps per inch, while the coarser wools like karakul may have as few as one to two crimps per inch. Hair, by contrast, has little if any scale and no crimp, and little ability to bind into yarn. On sheep, the hair part of the fleece is called kemp. The relative amounts of kemp to wool vary from breed to breed, and make some fleeces more desirable for spinning, felting, or carding into batts for quilts or other insulating products.

Wool fibers are hygroscopic. This means wool has the power to readily absorb and give off moisture. It can absorb moisture almost one-third of its own weight. Wool absorbs sound like many other fabrics. Wool is generally a creamy white color, although some breeds of sheep produce natural colors such as black, brown, silver, and random mixes.

Wool ignites at a higher temperature than cotton fibers and some synthetics. It has lower rate of flame spread, low heat release, and low heat of combustion; doesn't melt or drip; forms a char which is insulating and self-extinguishes; and contributes less to toxic gases and smoke than other flooring products when used in carpets. Wool carpets are specified for high safety environments such as trains and aircraft. Wool is usually specified for garments for fire-fighters, soldiers, and others in occupations where they are exposed to the likelihood of fire.

Wool is static resistant as the retention of moisture within the fabric prevents a build up of static electricity. Wool garments are much less likely to spark or cling to the body. The use of wool car seat covers or carpets reduces the risk of a shock when a person touches a grounded object. Wool is considered by the medical profession to be hypoallergenic.

Processing : Wool straight off a sheep contains a high level of grease which contains valuable lanolin, as well as dirt, dead skin, sweat residue, and vegetable matter. This state is known as "grease wool" or "wool in the grease". Before the wool can be used for commercial purposes it must be scoured, or cleaned. Scouring may be as simple as a bath in warm water, or a complicated industrial process using detergent and alkali. In commercial wool, vegetable matter is often removed by chemical carbonization. In less processed wools, vegetable matter may be removed by hand, and some of the lanolin left intact through use of gentler detergents. This semi-grease wool can be worked into yarn and knitted into particularly water-resistant mittens or sweaters, such as those of the Aran Island fishermen. Lanolin removed from wool is widely used in cosmetics products such as hand creams.

After shearing, the wool is separated into five main categories: fleece (which makes up the vast bulk), broken, pieces, bellies, and locks. The latter four are pressed into wool packs and sold separately. The quality of fleece is determined by a technique known as wool classing, whereby a qualified wool class groups wools of similar gradings together to maximise the return for the farmer or sheep owner. Prior to Australian auctions, all Merino fleece wool is objectively measured for micron, yield (including the amount of vegetable matter), staple length, staple strength, and sometimes color and comfort factor.

Quality

The quality of wool is determined by the following factors, fiber diameter, crimp, yield, color, and staple strength. Fibre diameter is the single most important wool characteristic determining quality and price.

Merino wool is typically 3-5 inches in length and is very fine (between 12-24 microns). The finest and most valuable wool comes from Merino hoggets. Wool taken from sheep produced for meat is typically more coarse, and has fibers that are 1.5 to 6 inches in length. Damage or breaks in the wool can occur if the sheep is stressed while it is growing its fleece, resulting in a thin spot where the fleece is likely to break.

Wool is also separated into grades based on the measurement of the wool's diameter in microns. These grades may vary depending on the breed or purpose of the wool.

Alpaca Fiber

Alpaca fiber is that of an alpaca. It is warmer than sheep's wool and lighter in weight. It is soft, fine, glossy, and luxurious. The thickness of quality fiber is between 12-29 micrometres. Most alpaca fiber is white, but it also comes in various shades of brown and black.

Alpaca fleece is a lustrous and silky natural fiber. While similar to sheep's wool, it is warmer, not prickly, and bears no lanolin, which makes it hypoallergenic. Without lanolin, it does not repel water. It is also soft and luxurious. In physical structure, alpaca fiber is somewhat akin to hair, being very glossy. The preparing, carding, spinning, weaving and finishing process of alpaca is very similar to the process used for wool.

Alpaca fleece is the natural fiber harvested from an Alpaca. It is light weight or heavy weight, depending on how it is spun, soft, durable, luxurious and silky natural fiber. While similar to sheep's wool, it is warmer, not prickly, and has no lanolin which makes it hypoallergenic. However, this lack of lanolin also prevents Alpaca fiber from being naturally water-repellent. It also has less crimp, thus making it much less elastic. Alpaca fleece is made into various exports, from very simple and inexpensive garments made by the aboriginal communities to sophisticated, industrially made and expensive products such as suits. In the United States, groups of smaller alpaca breeders have banded together to create "fiber co-ops," in order to make the manufacture of alpaca fiber products less expensive.

In physical structure, alpaca fiber is somewhat akin to hair, being very glossy. Alpaca fiber is generally coarser than wool fiber, and alpaca yarns are weaker than most wool yarns. In processing, slivers lack fiber cohesion and single alpaca rovings lack strength. More twisting is necessary to improve strength, but this reduces yarn softness.

Alpaca has generally higher medullated fiber than wool. These are fibers with a central core, which may be continuous, interrupted, or fragmented. The cells of the central core may contract or disappear, forming air pockets which assist insulation. However the higher incidence of medullated fibers in alpaca, compared to wool and mohair, can be an objectionable trait. They can take less dye, standing out in the finished garment, and are weaker. The proportion of medullated fibers is higher in the coarser, unwanted guard hairs: there is less or no medullation in the finer, lower micrometre fibers.

Good quality alpaca fiber is approximately 18 to 25 micrometres in diameter. Whilst breeders report fiber can sell for 2 to 4 dollars per ounce, the world wholesale price for processed pre-spun alpaca "tops" is only between about $10 to $24 US/kg (according to quality), i.e. about $0.28 to $0.68 per oz. Finer fleeces, ones with a smaller diameter, are preferred, and thus are more expensive. As an alpaca gets older the width of the fibers gets thicker, at between 1 μm and 5 μm per year. This is often caused by over nutrition; if fed too much nutritious food the animal doesn't get fat, instead the fiber gets thicker. Any alpaca fiber exceeding 34μ is classified as llama.

As with all fleece-producing animals, quality varies from animal to animal, and some alpacas produce fiber which is less than ideal. Fibre and conformation are the two most important factors in determining an alpaca's value.

Alpacas come in many shades from a true-blue black through browns-black, browns, fawns, white, silver-greys, and rose-greys. However, white is predominant, because of selective breeding: the white fiber can be dyed in the largest ranges of colors. In South America, the preference is for white as they generally have better fleece than the darker-colored animals. This is because the dark colors had been all but bred out of the animals. The demand for darker fiber sprung up in the United States and elsewhere, however in order to reintroduce the colors, the quality of the darker fiber has decreased slightly. Breeders have been diligently working on breeding dark animals with exceptional fiber, and much progress has been made in these areas over the last 5-7 years.

Types of alpacas

There are two types of alpaca: Huacaya (which produce a dense, soft, crimpy sheep-like fiber), and the mop-like Suri (with silky pencil-like locks, resembling dread-locks but not actually matted fibers). Suris are prized for their longer and silkier fibers, and estimated to make up between 19-20% of the Alpaca population. Since its import into the United States, the number of Suri alpacas has grown substantially and become more color diverse. The Suri is thought to be rarer, possibly because it is less hardy in the harsh South American mountain climates, as its fleece offers less insulation against the cold.

Angora

Angora wool or Angora fiber refers to the downy coat produced by the Angora rabbit. Angora is prized for its softness, thin fibers of around 12-16 micrometres for quality fiber, and what knitters refer to as a halo (fluffiness). The fiber felts very easily. Angora fiber comes in white, black, and various shades of brown.

Angora wool or **Angora fiber** refers to the downy coat produced by the Angora rabbit. While their names are similar, Angora fiber is distinct from mohair, which comes from the Angora goat. Angora is known for its softness, low micron count (i.e. thin fibers), and what knitters refer to as a halo (fluffiness). It is also known for its silky texture. Angora rabbits produce coats in a variety of colours, from white to black. Good quality angora fiber is around 12-16 microns in diameter, and can cost around 10 - 16 dollars per ounce. It felts very easily, even on the animal itself if the animal is not groomed frequently.

The fiber is normally blended with wool to give the yarn elasticity, as angora fiber is not naturally elastic. The blend decreases the softness and halo as well as the price of the finished object.

The fibers are hollow which gives them their characteristic floating feel.

Fur Production

Angora fur is produced in Europe, Chile, China and the United

States. Harvesting occurs up to four times a year (about every 4 months) and is collected by plucking, shearing, or collection of the molting fur.

Most breeds of Angora rabbits molt with their natural growth cycle about every four months. Many producers of the fiber pluck the fur of these breeds. Plucking is, in effect, pulling out the molted fur. Plucking ensures a minimum of guard hair, and the fur is not as matted when plucked as when it is collected from the rabbit's cage. However, plucking a rabbit is time consuming, so some producers shear the rabbit instead. While this results in slightly lower quality fleece as the guard hairs are included, it does take less time and results in more fleece. Also, not all breeds of angora molt, and if the rabbit does not naturally molt, it cannot be plucked. German angoras do not molt.

The rabbits must be groomed at least once or twice a week to prevent the fur from matting and felting. There is also a danger that a rabbit will ingest its own molted fur; unlike a cat, a rabbit cannot easily be rid of the build up.

Quality of Wool

The premium 1st quality wool is taken from the back and upper sides of the rabbit. This is usually the longest and cleanest fiber on the rabbit. There should not be hay or vegetable matter in the fiber. Second quality is from the neck and lower sides and may have some vegetable matter. Third quality is the buttocks and legs and any other areas that easily felt and are of shorter length. Fourth quality is totally unsalvageable and consists of the larger felted bits or stained fiber. Third and fourth quality are perfect for cutting up for the birds to use in lining their nests. With daily brushing, felting of the fiber can be avoided, increasing the usable portion of fiber.

Uses

Angora wool can be used in all sorts of ways. It is commonly used in apparel such as sweaters and suitings, knitting yarn, and felting.

Cashmere

Cashmere wool is wool obtained from the Cashmere goat. Cashmere is characterized by its luxuriously soft fibers, with high capability and loft. In order for a natural goat fiber to be considered Cashmere, it must be under 18.5 micrometers in diameter and be at least 3.175 centimeters long. It is noted as providing a natural light-weight insulation without bulk. Fibers are highly adaptable and are easily constructed into fine or thick yarns, and light to heavy-weight fabrics.

Cashmere wool, usually simply known as **cashmere**, is a fiber obtained from the Cashmere goat. The word cashmere derives from an archaic spelling of *Kashmir. Cashmere* wool is fine in texture, and it is also strong, light, and soft; when it is made into garments, they are extremely warm to wear.

Characteristics

Cashmere is characterized by its soft fibers. It is noted as providing a natural light-weight insulation without bulk. Fibers are highly adaptable and are easily constructed into fine or thick yarns, and light to heavy-weight fabrics. The original undyed or natural colors of cashmere wool are various shades of grey, brown and white.

The Cashmere and Camel Hair Manufacturers Institute defines cashmere as:

- The fine (dehaired) undercoat fibers produced by a Cashmere goat (Capra hircus laniger).
- The fiber is generally non-medullated and has a mean maximum diameter of 19 microns. The co-efficient of variation around the mean shall not exceed 24%. There can be no more than 3% (by weight) of cashmere fibers over 30 microns

Source of the fiber

Cashmere wool fiber for clothing and other textile articles is obtained from the Cashmere domestic goat. The goat (*Capra hircus laniger*) is a mammal belonging to the subfamily Caprinae of the family Bovidae. The goats produce a double fleece consisting of the fine, soft undercoat or underdown of hair mingled with a straighter and much coarser outer coating of hair called guard hair. In order for the fine under down to be sold and processed further, it must first be de-haired. De-hairing is a mechanical process that separates the coarse hairs from the fine hair and after de-hairing the resulting "cashmere" is ready to be dyed and converted into yarn, fabrics and garments.

Gathering

Cashmere is collected during the spring moulting season when the goats naturally shed their winter coat. In the Northern Hemisphere the goats moult over a period beginning as early as March and as late as May.

In some regions, the mixed mass of down and coarse hair is removed by hand with a coarse comb that pulls tufts of fiber from the animal as the comb is raked through the fleece. The collected fiber then has a higher yield of pure cashmere after the fiber has been washed and dehaired. The long, coarse guard hair is then typically clipped from the animal and is often used for brushes, interlinings and other non-apparel uses. Animals in Iran, Afghanistan, New Zealand and Australia are typically shorn of their fleece, resulting in a higher coarse hair content and lower pure cashmere yield. In America, the most popular method is combing. The process takes up to two weeks but, with a trained eye for when the fiber is releasing, sometimes it is possible to comb the fibers out in about a week.

Types of fiber

- Raw — fiber that has not been processed and is essentially straight from the animal
- Processed — fiber that has been through the processes of de-hairing, washing, carding, and is ready either to spin or to knit/crochet/weave
- Virgin — new fiber which has been made into yarns, fabrics or garments for the first time
- Recycled — fibers reclaimed from scraps or fabrics that were

previously woven or felted, and which may or may not have been previously used by the consumer.

Mohair

Mohair is a silk-like fabric or yarn made from the hair of the Angora goat. It is both durable and resilient. It is notable for its high luster and sheen, and is often used in fiber blends to add these qualities to a textile. Mohair also takes dye exceptionally well. Mohair fiber is approximately 25-45 microns in diameter. It is one of the oldest textile fibers in use. It is both durable and resilient. It is notable for its high luster and sheen, and is often used in fiber blends to add these qualities to a textile. Mohair also takes dye exceptionally well. Mohair is also warm as it has great insulating properties. It is durable, moisture-wicking, stretch and flame resistant, and crease resistant.

Mohair is composed mostly of keratin, a protein found in the hair, wool, horns and skin of all mammals. While it has scales like wool, the scales are not fully developed, merely indicated. Thus, mohair does not felt like wool does.

Mohair increases its diameter with the age of the goat, growing along with the animal. This means fine hair from younger animals is used for finer applications such as clothing, and the thicker hair from older animals is more often used for carpets and heavy fabrics intended for outerwear.

The term mohair is sometimes used to describe a type of material used for the folding roof on convertible cars. In this instance, mohair refers to a form of denim-like canvas. Also, in Poland, mohair berets, which are particularly popular with elderly women, have become a symbol of bigotry and are usually associated with the ultra-Catholic Radio Maryja. Mohair should not be confused with the fur from the angora rabbit, which is called *angora wool*.

Production

Mohair is shorn from the goat without harming the animal. Shearing is done twice a year, in the spring and in the fall. One goat will produce 11 to 17 pounds of mohair a year. Shearing is done on a clean swept floor with extra care taken to keep the hair clean and free of debris. The hair is then processed to remove natural grease, dirt and vegetable matter. Mohair grows in uniform locks. Angora is a single-coat breed, and unlike Pygora or Cashmere, there is no need to dehair a mohair fleece to separate the coarse hair from the down hair.

Uses

Mohair is used in scarves, suits, sweaters, coats, socks and home furnishing. Mohair fiber is also found in carpets, wall fabrics, craft yarns, and many other fabrics, and may be used as a substitute for fur. Because its texture resembles fine human hair, mohair is often used in making high grade doll wigs or in rooting customized dolls.

Mohair is also used in 'climbing skins' for randonnee skiing. The mohair is used in a carpet allowing the skier an appropriate ascension method without sliding downhill.

Sheep's wool

Wool has two qualities that distinguish it from hair or fur: it has scales which overlap like shingles on a roof and it is crimped; in some fleeces the wool fibers have more than 20 bends per inch. Wool varies in diameter from below 17 micrometres to over 35 micrometres. The finer the wool, the softer it will be, while coarser grades are more durable and less prone to pilling.

Qiviut

Qiviut is the fine underwool of the muskox. Qiviut fibers are long (about 5 to 8 cm), fine (between 15 and 20 micrometers in diameter), and relatively smooth. It is approximately eight times warmer than sheep's wool and does not felt or shrink.

Qiviut (qiviuq ; sometimes spelled **qiveut**, and pronounced *kiv-ee-yut*) is an Inuit word commonly used to indicate the wool of the muskox. The word was originally used to refer to the down feathers of birds as well as the inner wool of the muskox. It is valued for its use as a fiber as, unlike sheep's wool, it does not shrink in water at any temperature. (However, this means that it also is not useful for felting.) It is most commonly used for hats and scarves, and is among the softest wools, though this softness comes with a price. A high quality "smoke ring" — essentially a knitted scarf — will cost about $175, but will last over 20 years with good care.

The muskox has a two-layered coat, and *qiviut* refers specifically to the soft underwool beneath the longer outer wool. The muskox sheds this layer of wool each spring. Qiviut is plucked from the coat of the muskox during the molt or gathered from objects the animals have brushed against; unlike sheep, the animals are not sheared. Much of the commercially available qiviut comes from Canada, and is obtained from the pelts of muskoxen after hunts. In Alaska, qiviut is obtained from farmed animals or gathered from the wild during the molt.

Qiviut is stronger and eight times warmer than sheep's wool, and softer than cashmere wool. Wild muskoxen have qiviut fibers approximately 18 micrometres in diameter. Females and young animals have slightly finer wool.

Fibre from other animals

Hand spinners also use fiber from animals such as llamas, camels, yak, and possums. These fibers are generally used in clothing. Hair from animals such as horses is also an animal fiber. Horsehair is used for brushes, the bows of musical instruments and many other things.

Chiengora

Chiengora is a yarn or wool spun from dog hair. The word is a portmanteau of "chien", the French word for dog, and "angora." It is up to 80% warmer than wool and is not elastic. Often chiengora is blended with wool during the carding process. This blend has some give to it, which is preferable when knitting. It is also often blended with wool in order to create a yarn with less heat insulation.

Benefits of chiengora

Chiengora is similar in appearance to Angora and is furry and very soft. Chiengora tends to "fluff" with use, creating a halo effect. It is warm, even in frigid temperatures, and it sheds water well.

Wood Fiber

Wood fibers are usually cellulosic elements that are extracted from trees, straw, bamboo, cotton seed, hemp, sugar cane and other sources. The end paper product (paper, paperboard, tissue, etc.) dictates the species, or species blend, that is best suited to provide the desirable sheet characteristics, and also dictates the required fiber processing (chemical treatment, heat treatment, mechanical 'brushing' or refining etc.).

In North America, virgin (non-recycled) wood fiber is primarily extracted from **hardwood** (deciduous) trees and **softwood** (coniferous) trees. Wood fibers can also be recycled from used paper materials. Wood fibers are treated by combining them with other additives. They are then processed into a network of wood fibers, which constitutes the sheet of paper.

The term **hardwood** is used to describe wood from non-monocot angiosperm trees and for those trees themselves. These are usually broad-leaved; in temperate and boreal latitudes they are mostly deciduous, but in tropics and subtropics mostly evergreen.

Hardwood contrasts with softwood, which comes from conifer trees. On average, hardwood is of higher density and hardness than softwood, although there is an enormous variation in actual wood hardness in both groups, with the range in density in hardwoods completely including that of softwoods; some hardwoods (e.g. balsa) are softer than most softwoods, while yew is an example of a hard softwood.

Hardwoods are more varied than softwood. There are about a hundred times as many hardwoods as softwoods. The dominant feature separating hardwoods from softwoods is the presence of pores, or vessels. The vessels may show considerable variation in size, shape of perforation plates (simple, scalariform, reticulate, foraminate), and structure of cell wall (e.g. spiral thickenings).

Hardwoods are employed in a large range of applications including: construction, furniture, flooring, utensils, etc. Solid hardwood joinery tends to be expensive compared to softwood. In the past, tropical hardwoods were easily available but the supply of some species such as Burma teak and mahogany is now becoming restricted due to overexploitation. Cheaper "hardwood" doors, for instance, now consist of a thin veneer bonded to a core of softwood, plywood or medium-density fibreboard (MDF). Hardwoods can also be used in a variety of objects but mainly for furniture or musical instruments because of their density.

Softwood is timber obtained from coniferous trees (mainly of the pine and fir families). With the exception of bald cypress, tamarack, and larch, softwood trees are evergreens. Softwood is mostly obtained from the Baltic, Scandinavia, and North America and is the source of about 80% of the world's production of timber. Softwoods of longleaf pine, douglas fir, and yew are much harder in the mechanical sense than several hardwoods.

Properties

Perhaps the most noticeable difference between softwood and hardwood is found in the microscopic structure of the wood. Softwood contains only two types of cells, tracheids and parenchyma. Thus, softwoods lack the vessel elements for water transport that hardwoods have; these vessels elements manifest in hardwoods as pores. In softwood water transport within the tree is via the tracheids only. Some softwoods, such as pine, spruce, larch, and Douglas fir, have resin canals, which provide transport of resin as a defense against injury.

Applications

In general softwood is easy to work: it forms the bulk of wood used by humans.

- Prime material for structural building components
- Furniture
- Millwork (mouldings, doors, windows)
- Raw material as pulp in the production of paper and board
- The finer softwoods find many specialty uses.

Straw

Straw is an agricultural by-product, the dry stalk of a cereal plant, after the grain or seed has been removed. Straw makes up about half of the yield of cereal crops such as barley, oats, rice, rye and wheat. In times gone by, it was regarded as a useful by-product of the harvest, but with the advent of the combine harvester, straw has become more burdensome to agriculture.

However, straw can be put to many uses, old and new.

Uses

- Biofuels
  - The use of straw as a carbon-neutral energy source is increasing rapidly, especially for biobutanol. **Biofuel** is defined as solid, liquid or gaseous fuel derived from relatively recently dead biological material and is distinguished from fossil fuels, which are derived from long dead biological material. Theoretically, biofuels can be produced from any (biological) carbon source; although, the most common sources are photosynthetic plants. Various plants and plant-derived materials are used for biofuel manufacturing. Globally, biofuels are most commonly used to power vehicles, heating homes, and cooking stoves. Biofuel industries are expanding in Europe, Asia and the Americas. Recent technology developed at Los Alamos National Lab even allows for the conversion of pollution into renewable bio fuel. Agrofuels are biofuels which are produced from specific crops, rather than from waste processes such as landfill off-gassing or recycled vegetable oil.
- Biomass
  - The use of straw in large-scale biomass power plants is becoming mainstream in the EU, with several facilities already online. The straw is either used directly in the form of bales, or densified into pellets which allows for the feedstock to be transported over longer distances. Finally, torrefaction of straw with pelletization is gaining attention, because it increases the energy density of the resource, making it possible to transport it still further. This processing step also makes storage much

easier, because torrefied straw pellets are hydrophobic. Torrefied straw in the form of pellets can be directly co-fired with coal or natural gas at very high rates and make use of the processing infrastructures at existing coal and gas plants. Because the torrefied straw pellets have superior structural, chemical and combustion properties to coal, they can replace all coal and turn a coal plant into an entirely biomass-fed power station. First generation pellets are limited to a co-firing rate of 15% in modern IGCC plants.

- Bedding humans or livestock
  - The straw-filled mattress, also known as palliasse, is still used in many parts of the world.
  - It is commonly used as bedding for ruminants and horses. It may be used as bedding and food for small animals, but this often leads to injuries to mouth, nose and eyes as straw is quite sharp.
- Animal feed
  - Straw may be fed as part of the roughage component of the diet to cattle that are on a near maintenance level of energy requirement. It has a low digestible energy and nutrient content. The heat generated when microorganisms in a herbivore's gut digest straw can be useful in maintaining body temperature in cold climates. Due to the risk of impaction and its poor nutrient profile, it should always be restricted to part of the diet.
- Hats
  - There are several styles of straw hats that are made of woven straw.
  - Until about 100 years ago, thousands of women and children in England were employed in plaiting straw for making hats. These days the straw plait is imported.
- Thatching
  - Thatched roofs are becoming increasingly popular, and the skills of a master thatcher are once again in demand.
- Packaging
  - Straw is resistant to being crushed and therefore makes a good packing material. A company in France makes a straw mat sealed in thin plastic sheets.

- o Straw envelopes for wine bottles have become rarer, but are still to be found at some wine merchants.
- Paper
- o Straw can be pulped to make paper.
- Archery targets
- o Heavy gauge straw rope is coiled and sewn tightly together. This is no longer done entirely by hand, but is partially mechanized.
- Horse collars
- o Working horses are making a comeback, and there is a need for horse collars stuffed with good quality rye straw. Being a "long straw filler" is a highly skilled job.
- Construction material: bricks / cob
- o In many parts of the world, straw is used to bind clay and concrete. This mixture of clay and straw, known as cob, can be used as a building material. There are many recipes for making cob.
- o When baled, straw has excellent insulation characteristics. It can be used, alone or in a post-and-beam construction, to build straw bale houses.
- o Enviroboard can be made from straw.
- Rope
- o Rope made from straw was used by thatchers, in the packaging industry and even in iron foundries.
- Basketry
- o Bee skeps and linen baskets are made from coiled and bound together continuous lengths of straw. The technique is known as lip work.
- Sandals
- o Koreans wear Jipsin, sandals made of straws.
- Horticulture
- o Straw is used in cucumber houses and for mushroom growing.
- o In Japan, certain trees are wrapped with straw to protect them from the effects of a hard winter as well as to use them as a trap for parasite insects.
- o It is also used in ponds to reduce algae by changing the nutrient ratios in the water.

- The soil under strawberries is covered with straw to protect the ripe berries from dirt, and straw is also used to cover the plants during winter to prevent the cold from killing them.
- Straw also makes an excellent mulch.

Bamboo

The **bamboos** are a group of woody perennial evergreen (except for certain temperate species) plants in the true grass family **Poaceae**, subfamily Bambusoideae, tribe **Bambuseae**. Some are **giant bamboos**, the largest members of the grass family. Bamboos are the fastest growing woody plants in the world. Their growth rate (up to 60 centimeters (24 in.)/day) is due to a unique rhizome-dependent system, but is highly dependent on local soil and climate conditions.

They are of economic and high cultural significance in East Asia and South East Asia where they are used extensively in gardens, as a building material, and as a food source.

There are more than 70 genera divided into about 1,000 species. They are found in diverse climates, from cold mountains to hot tropical regions. Major areas with no native bamboos include Europe, North Africa, Western Asia, Canada, and Antarctica.

Growth

Bamboo is the fastest-growing plant on Earth; it has been clocked surging skyward as fast as 121 cm (47.6 inches) in a 24-hour period, and can also reach maximal growth rate exceeding one meter (39 inches) per hour for short periods of time. Many prehistoric bamboos exceeded heights of 250 feet. Primarily growing in regions of warmer climates during the Cretaceous, vast fields existed in what is now Asia. Modern bamboos can only sustain their maximal growth rate for short periods of time. Bamboo can grow six or more inches a day though there are exceptions (below).

Mass flowering

Although some bamboos flower every year, most species flower infrequently. In fact, many bamboos only flower at intervals as long as 60 or 120 years. These taxa exhibit mass flowering (or gregarious flowering), with all plants in the population flowering simultaneously. The longest mass flowering interval known is 130 years, and is found for all the species *Phyllostachys bambusoides* (Sieb. & Zucc.). In this species, all plants of the same stock flower at the same time, regardless of differences in geographic locations or climatic conditions, then the bamboo dies. The lack of environmental impact on the time of flowering indicates the presence of some sort of "alarm clock" in each cell of the plant which signals the diversion of all energy to flower production and the cessation of vegetative growth. This mechanism, as well as the evolutionary cause behind it, is still largely a mystery.

One theory to explain the evolution of this semelparous mass flowering is the predator satiation hypothesis. This theory argues that by fruiting at the same time, a population increases the survival rate of their seeds by flooding the area with fruit so that even if predators eat their fill, there will still be seeds left over. Thus, according to this hypothesis, the death of the adult clone is due to resource exhaustion, as it would be more effective for parent plants to devote all resources to creating a large seed crop than to hold back energy for their own regeneration.

A second theory, the fire cycle hypothesis, argues that the death of the adult plants has evolved as a mechanism to create disturbance in the habitat, thus providing the seedlings with a gap to grow in. This hypothesis argues that the dead culms create a large fuel load, and also a large target for lightning strikes, increasing the likelihood of wildfire. Because bamboos are very aggressive as early successional plants, the seedlings would be able to outstrip other plants and take over the space left by their parents. However, both of these theories contain flaws, and the cause of this mass flowering and fruiting remains uncertain.

The mass fruiting also has direct economic consequences, however. The huge increase in available fruit in the forests often causes a boom in rodent populations, leading to increases in disease and famine in nearby human populations. For example, there are devastating consequences when the *Melocanna bambusoides* population flowers and fruits once every 30-35 years around the Bay of Bengal. The death of the bamboo plants following their fruiting means the local people lose their building material, and the large increase in bamboo fruit leads to a rapid increase in rodent populations. As the number of rodents increase, they consume all available food, including grain fields and stored food, sometimes leading to famine. These rats can also carry dangerous diseases such as typhus, typhoid, and bubonic plague, which can reach epidemic proportions as the rodents increase in number.

Cultivation

Commercial timber : Timber is harvested from cultivated and wild stands and some of the larger bamboos, particularly species in the genus *Phyllostachys*, are known as "timber bamboos".

Ornamental bamboos : Many bamboos are popular in cultivation as garden trees. There are two general patterns for the growth of bamboo: "clumping" (sympodial) and "running" (monopodial). Clumping bamboo species tend to spread slowly, as the growth pattern of the rhizomes is to simply expand the root mass gradually, similar to ornamental grasses. "Running" bamboos, on the other hand, need to be taken care of in cultivation because of their potential for aggressive behavior. They spread mainly through their roots and/or rhizomes, which can spread widely underground and send up new culms to break through the surface. Running bamboo species are highly variable in their tendency to spread; this is related to both the species and the soil and climate conditions. Some can send out runners of several meters a year, while others can stay in the same general area for long periods. If neglected, over time they can cause problems by moving into adjacent areas.

Bamboos seldom and unpredictably flower, and the frequency of flowering varies greatly from species to species. Once flowering takes place, a plant will decline and often die entirely. Seeds collected from a flowering may be used to rebuild a species, but flowering can also introduce unexpected alterations in the characteristics of the bamboo, so that new variants ("sports") are created instead. There are a number of interesting types of bamboo which did not exist several decades ago that have been introduced as a result of flowering. Seeds generally have a relatively short period of viability (3-12 months). Germination rates can often be improved by use of cold stratification, which involves refrigerating the seeds for a period of 4-8 weeks before planting. Although there are always a few species of bamboo in flower at any given time, collectors desiring to grow specific bamboo typically obtain their plants as divisions of already-growing plants, rather than waiting for seeds to be produced.

Once established as a grove, it is difficult to completely remove bamboo without digging up the entire network of underground rhizomes. If bamboo must be removed, an alternative to digging it up is to cut down the culms, and then repeatedly mow down new shoots as they arise, until the root system exhausts its energy supply and dies. If any leaves are allowed to photosynthesize, the bamboo survives and may continue spreading. Chemical methods involving herbicides are also used to control bamboo.

There are two main ways to prevent the spread of running bamboo into adjacent areas. The first method is rhizome pruning or "edging", which involves removing any rhizomes escaping the desired bamboo area. Pruning shears, shovels, and pickaxes are useful tools for this task. Under typical soil conditions the rhizomes are generally very close to the surface (usually within 0-3 inches, sometimes as deep as a foot). Rhizome pruning maintenance should be done at least once per year, but better is to check in the spring, summer, and fall. Some species may be deep running (beyond typical spade depth). These are much harder to control and deeper cuts will need to be made. Regular maintenance will indicate major growth directions and locations. Once the rhizomes are cut, they are typically removed; however, rhizomes take a number of months to mature and an immature, severed rhizome will usually cease growing if left in-ground. If any bamboo shoots come up outside of the bamboo area afterwards, their presence indicates the precise location of the missed rhizome. The fibrous roots that radiate from the rhizomes do not grow up to be more bamboo so if they stay in the ground, that's not a problem.

The second way to control growth is by surrounding the plant or grove with a physical barrier. This method is very detrimental to ornamental bamboo as the bamboo within quickly becomes rootbound—showing all the signs of any unhealthy containerized plant. Symptoms include rhizomes escaping over the top, down underneath, and bursting the barrier. The bamboo within generally deteriorates in quality as fewer and fewer culms grow each year, culms live shorter periods, new culm diameter decreases, fewer leaves grow on the culms, and leaves turn yellow as the unnaturally contained rootmass quickly depletes the soil of nutrients, and curling leaves as the condensed roots cannot collect the water they need to sustain the foliage. Concrete and specially-rolled HDPE plastic are the usual materials used. This is placed in a 60-90 cm (2-3 feet) deep ditch around the planting, and angled out at the top to direct the rhizomes to the surface. (This is _only_ possible if the barrier is installed in a straight line.) Strong rhizomes and tools can penetrate plastic barriers with relative ease, so great care must be taken. Barriers usually fail sooner or later, or the bamboo within suffers greatly. Casual observation of many failed barriers has shown bursting of 60 mil HDPE in 5-6 years, and rhizomes diving underneath in as few as 3 years post install. In small areas regular maintenance is the only perfect method of controlling the spreading bamboos. Bamboo in barriers is much more difficult to remove than free-spreading bamboo. Barriers and edging are unnecessary for clump-forming bamboos. Clump-forming bamboos may eventually need to have portions removed if they get too large.

Uses

Culinary

The shoots (new bamboo culms that come out of the ground) of bamboo are edible. They are used in numerous Asian dishes and broths, and are available in supermarkets in various sliced forms, both fresh and canned version. A health warning is appropriate in the case of the shoots of the *giant bamboo*, as they contain cyanide. Despite this, the Golden Bamboo Lemur ingests many times the quantity of toxin that would kill a human.

The bamboo shoot in its fermented state (called *khorisa*) forms an important ingredient in the cuisine of Assam.

In Indonesia, they are sliced thin and then boiled with *santan* (thick coconut milk) and spices to make a dish named *gulai rebung*. Other recipes using bamboo shoots are *sayur lodeh* (mixed vegetables in coconut milk) and *lun pia* (sometimes written *lumpia*: fried wrapped bamboo shoots with vegetables). Note that the shoots of some species contain toxins that need to be leached or boiled out before they can be eaten safely.

Medicine

Bamboo is used in Chinese medicine for treating infections. It is also a low calorie source of potassium. It has also been known for its sweet taste and good source of nutrients. In Ayurveda, the Indian system of traditional medicine, the silicious concretion found in the culms of the bamboo stem is called *banslochan*. It is known as *tabashir* or *tawashir* in *Unani-Tibb* the Indo-Persian system of Medicine. In English this concretion is called "bamboo manna". This concretion is said to be a tonic for the respiratory diseases. This concretion, which was earlier obtained from *Melocanna bambusoides* is very hard to get now and has been largely replaced by synthetic silicic acid.

Construction

When treated, bamboo forms a very hard wood which is both lightweight and exceptionally durable. In tropical climates it is used in elements of house construction, construction scaffolding, as a substitute for steel reinforcing rods in concrete construction, and so on. Modern companies are also attempting to popularize bamboo flooring made of bamboo pieces steamed, flattened, glued together, finished, and cut. However, bamboo wood is easily infested by wood-boring insects unless treated with wood preservatives or kept very dry (see picture). A lot of institutes and universities are working on the bamboo as an ecological construction material. It is possible to get in the United States and France houses 100% made with bamboo, earthquake and cyclone-resistant, with international certification. Three ISO standards are for bamboo as construction material.

Other

Besides its use as a construction material, it is also used for fencemaking, bridges, toilets, walking sticks, canoes, tableware, decorative artwork carving, furniture, chopsticks, food steamers, toys, bicycles, hats, and martial arts weaponry, including fire arrows, flame throwers and rockets. Also, abaci and various musical instruments such as the dizi, xiao, shakuhachi, palendag, jinghu, angklung, it can also be used in building tree forts that can hold a normal child's body weight. The Bamboo Organ of Las Piñas, Philippines has pipes made of bamboo culms. Bamboo is the traditional material used for fly fishing rods. When bamboo is harvested for wood, care is needed to select mature stems that are several years old, as first-year stems, although full sized, are not fully developed and are not as strong as more mature stems.

Bamboo canes are normally round in cross-section, but square canes can be produced by forcing the young culms to grow through a tube of square cross-section slightly smaller than the culm's natural diameter, thereby constricting the growth to the shape of the tube. Every few days the tube is removed and replaced higher up the fast-growing culm.

The fiber of bamboo has been used to make paper in China since early times. A high quality hand-made paper is still produced in small quantities. Coarse bamboo paper is still used to make spirit money in many Chinese communities.

Fabric/Clothing: The wood is used for knitting needles and a rayon type fabric made of bamboo fiber can be used for yarn and fabrics. A technique of making bamboo fiber from bamboo pulp has been developed in East Asian countries. The textile industry benefits from the many properties of this kind of fabric: soft, absorbent, antibacterial, UV resistant, hypoallergenic, thermo-regulating. It is also called the eco-fiber of the 21st century:

-Naturally organic: Bamboo is grown without pesticides and fertilizers.

-Sustainable: Bamboo is arguably the most renewable resource on our planet. It has an extensive rooting system and needs little water, growing 4–6 new shoots per year. It is, in fact, considered to be the fastest growing plant in the world.

-Eco-friendly: Bamboo absorbs nearly 5 times the amount of greenhouse gases and produces 35% more oxygen than the same amount of trees. It is critical in the fight to end global warming. Bamboo is rain-fed only and helps to reduce soil erosion. It is a grass, so it regenerates without the need for replanting.

-100% biodegradable: Bamboo fiber comes from nature and it returns entirely to nature in the end. Clothing made from bamboo fiber started as a popular alternative for activities such as yoga but is now very well appreciated by women, men and also babies. Thanks to its hypoallergenic properties, bamboo fiber is perfect for baby's sensitive skin. Bed sheets and towels made from bamboo have become luxury items (Woolworths, South Africa sells towels made of a cotton/bamboo mix) and are becoming more popular as an environmentally-friendly option compared to other fabrics, particularly since bamboo can be grown quickly without pesticides or fertilizers.

Sharpened bamboo is also traditionally used to tattoo in Japan, Hawaii and elsewhere.

Bamboo is used for the stems of traditional Vietnamese, Chinese and Japanese smoking pipes, and was also utilized for crafting the stems of opium pipes.

A variety of species of bamboo was one of about two dozen plants carried by Polynesian voyagers to provide all their needs settling new islands; in the Hawaiian Islands, among many uses, »Ohe (bamboo) carried water, made irrigation troughs for taro terraces, was used as a traditional knife for cutting the umbilical cord of a newborn, as a stamp for dyeing bark tapa cloth, and for four hula instruments — nose flute, rattle, stamping pipes and Jew's harp.

Some skateboard and snowboard deck manufacturers as well as surfboard builders are beginning to use bamboo construction. It is both lighter and stronger than traditional materials and its cultivation is environmentally friendly. At least one snow ski manufacturing company, Liberty Skis, now uses bamboo construction for these reasons.

Bamboo has been used in the construction of fishing rods since the mid 1800s. However, following the invention of fiberglass and graphite, bamboo use in fishing rods has declined dramatically. There is something of a resurgence of the use of bamboo, particularly for bamboo fly rods as demonstrated by some companies because of their aesthetics and impact on the environment.

Bamboo is also used to make enclosures in fish farming, where cages can be made from a wooden frame and bamboo lattices.

A single shoot of Bamboo can also be made into a didgeridoo, a wind instrument that is indigenous to Australia. Bamboo has gained increasing popularity in the culinary world as a material for cutting boards, as they are hard enough to withstand years of knife abuse, yet more forgiving to the knife blade, causing less damage to the edged utensils over time

Sugarcane

Sugarcane (*Saccharum*) is a genus of 6 to 37 species (depending on taxonomic interpretation) of tall perennial grasses (family Poaceae, tribe Andropogoneae), native to warm temperate to tropical regions of the Old World. They have stout, jointed, fibrous stalks that are rich in sugar and measure 2 to 6 meters tall. All of the sugar cane species interbreed, and the major commercial cultivars are complex hybrids.

Pests

The most important sugarcane pests are the larvae of some butterfly/moth species, including the turnip moth, the sugarcane borer (*Diatraea saccharalis*), the Mexican rice borer (*Eoreuma loftini*), leaf-cutting ants, termites; spittlebugs (especially *Mahanarva fimbriolata* and *Deois flavopicta*), and the beetle *Migdolus fryanus*. The planthopper *Eumetopina flavipes* is an insect which acts as a vector for the phytoplasma which causes the sugarcane disease ramu stunt.

Diseases

Bacterial diseases	
Gumming disease	Xanthomonas campestris pv. vasculorum
Leaf scald	Xanthomonas albilineans
Mottled stripe	Herbaspirillum rubrisubalbicans
Ratoon stunting disease	Leifsonia xyli subsp. xyli
Red stripe (top rot)	Acidovorax avenae

Fungal diseases	
Banded sclerotial (leaf) disease	Thanatephorus cucumeris= Pellicularia sasakii Rhizoctonia solani [anamorph]
Black rot	Ceratocystis adiposa Chalara sp. [anamorph]
Black stripe	Cercospora atrofiliformis
Brown spot	Cercospora longipes
Brown stripe	Cochliobolus stenospilus Bipolaris stenospila [anamorph]
Downy mildew	Peronosclerospora sacchari= Sclerospora sacchari
Downy mildew, leaf splitting form	Peronosclerospora miscanthi= Sclerospora mischanthi- Mycosphaerella striatiformans
Eye spot	Bipolaris sacchari= Helminthosporium sacchari
Fusarium sett and	Gibberella fujikuroi Fusarium moniliforme [anamorph] Gibberella subglutinans
stem rot Iliau	Clypeoporthe iliau= Gnomonia iliau Phaeocytostroma iliau [anamorph]
Leaf blast	Didymosphaeria taiwanensis
Leaf blight	Leptosphaeria taiwanensis Stagonospora tainanensis [anamorph]
Leaf scorch	Stagonospora sacchari

Disease	Pathogen
Marasmius sheath and shoot blight	Marasmiellus stenophyllus= Marasmius stenophyllus
Myriogenospora leaf binding (tangle top)	Myriogenospora aciculispora
Phyllosticta leaf spot	Phyllosticta hawaiiensis
Phytophthora rot of cuttings	Phytophthora spp.Phytophthora megasperma
Pineapple disease	Ceratocystis paradoxa Chalara paradoxa= Thielaviopsis paradoxa [anamorph]
Pokkah boeng (that may have knife cut symptoms)	Myriogenospora aciculispora xmoniliforme [anamorph] Gibberella subglutinans
Red leaf spot (purple spot)	Dimeriella sacchari
Red rot	Glomerella tucumanensis= Physalospora tucumanensis Colletotrichum falcatum [anamorph]
Red rot of leaf sheath and sprout rot	Athelia rolfsii= Pellicularia rolfsii Sclerotium rolfsii [anamorph]
Red spot of leaf sheath	Mycovellosiella vaginae= Cercospora vaginae
Rhizoctonia sheath and shoot rot	Rhizoctonia solani
Rind disease (sour rot)	Phaeocytostroma sacchari= Pleocyta sacchari= Melanconium sacchari
Ring spot	Leptosphaeria sacchari Phyllosticta sp. [anamorph]
Root rots	Marasmius sacchari Pythium arrhenomanes Pythium graminicola Rhizoctonia sp. Unidentified Oomycete
Rust, common	Puccinia melanocephala= Puccinia erianthi
Rust, orange	Puccinia kuehnii
Schizophyllum rot	Schizophyllum commune
Sclerophthora disease	Sclerophthora macrospora

Seedling blight	Alternaria alternata Bipolaris sacchari Cochliobolus hawaiiensis Bipolaris hawaiiensis [anamorph] Cochliobolus lunatus Curvularia lunata [anamorph] Curvularia senegalensis Setosphaeria rostrata Exserohilum rostratum [anamorph]= Drechslera halodes
Sheath rot	Cytospora sacchari
Smut, culmicolous	Ustilago scitaminea
Target blotch	Helminthosporium sp.
Veneer blotch	Deightoniella papuana
White rash	Elsinoë sacchari Sphaceloma sacchari [anamorph]
Wilt	Fusarium sacchari= Cephalosporium sacchari
Yellow spot	Mycovellosiella koepkei= Cercospora koepkei
Zonate leaf spot	Gloeocercospora sorghi
Miscellaneous diseases and disorders	
Bud proliferation	Undetermined
Bunch top	Undetermined
Cluster stool	Undetermined
Internal stalk necrosis	Undetermined
Leaf freckle	Undetermined
Leaf stipple	Undetermined
Multiple buds	Undetermined
Stem galls	Undetermined
Nematodes, parasitic	
Lesion	Pratylenchus spp.
Root-knot	Meloidogyne spp.
Spiral	Helicotylenchus Scutellonema spp.

Viral diseases	
Chlorotic streak	Virus (assumed)
Dwarf	Sugarcane dwarf virus
Fiji disease	Sugarcane Fiji disease virus
Grassy shoot	MLO
Mosaic	Sugarcane mosaic virus
Sereh	Virus (assumed)
Streak disease	Maize streak virus, sugarcane strain
White leaf	MLO

Processing

Traditionally, sugarcane has been processed in two stages. Sugarcane mills, located in sugarcane-producing regions, extract sugar from freshly harvested sugarcane, resulting in raw sugar for later refining, and in "mill white" sugar for local consumption. Sugar refineries, often located in heavy sugar-consuming regions, such as North America, Europe, and Japan, then purify raw sugar to produce refined white sugar, a product that is more than 99 percent pure sucrose. These two stages are slowly becoming blurred. Increasing affluence in the sugar-producing tropics has led to an increase in demand for refined sugar products in those areas, where a trend toward combined milling and refining has developed.

Milling

Sugarcane first has to be moved to a mill which is usually located close to the area of cultivation. Small rail networks are a common method of transporting the cane to a mill. Once the factories acquire the cane it will be subjected to the quality test. In Sri Lanka cane will be evaluated according to the brix and trash percentage.

In a sugar mill, sugarcane is washed, chopped, and shredded by revolving knives. The shredded cane is repeatedly mixed with water and crushed between rollers; the collected juices (called garapa in Brazil) contain 10–15 percent sucrose, and the remaining fibrous solids, called bagasse, are burned for fuel. Bagasse makes a sugar mill more than self-sufficient in energy; the surplus bagasse can be used for animal feed, in paper manufacture, or burned to generate electricity for the local power grid.

The cane juice is next mixed with lime to adjust its pH to 7. This mixing arrests sucrose's decay into glucose and fructose, and precipitates out some impurities. The mixture then sits, allowing the lime and other suspended solids to settle out, and the clarified juice is concentrated in a multiple-effect evaporator to make a syrup about 60 percent by weight in sucrose. This syrup is further concentrated under vacuum until it becomes supersaturated, and then seeded with crystalline sugar. Upon cooling, sugar crystallizes out of the syrup. A centrifuge is used to separate the sugar from the remaining liquid, or molasses. Additional crystallizations may be performed to extract more sugar from the molasses; the molasses remaining after no more sugar can be extracted from it in a cost-effective fashion is called blackstrap.

Raw sugar has a yellow to brown colour. If a white product is desired, sulfur dioxide may be bubbled through the cane juice before evaporation; this chemical bleaches many color-forming impurities into colourless ones. Sugar bleached white by this *sulfitation* process is called "mill white", "plantation white", and "crystal sugar". This form of sugar is the form most commonly consumed in sugarcane-producing countries. Traditionally, sugarcane has been processed in two stages. Sugarcane mills, located in sugarcane-producing regions, extract sugar from freshly harvested sugarcane, resulting in raw sugar for later refining, and in "mill white" sugar for local consumption. Sugar refineries, often located in heavy sugar-consuming regions, such as North America, Europe, and Japan, then purify raw sugar to produce refined white sugar, a product that is more than 99 percent pure sucrose. These two stages are slowly becoming blurred. Increasing affluence in the sugar-producing tropics has led to an increase in demand for refined sugar products in those areas, where a trend toward combined milling and refining has developed.

Refining

In sugar refining, raw sugar is further purified. It is first mixed with heavy syrup and then centrifuged clean. This process is called 'affination'; its purpose is to wash away the outer coating of the raw sugar crystals, which is less pure than the crystal interior. The remaining sugar is then dissolved to make a syrup, about 70 percent by weight solids.

The sugar solution is clarified by the addition of phosphoric acid and calcium hydroxide, which combine to precipitate calcium phosphate. The calcium phosphate particles entrap some impurities and absorb others, and then float to the top of the tank, where they can be skimmed off. An alternative to this "phosphatation" technique is 'carbonization,' which is similar, but uses carbon dioxide and calcium hydroxide to produce a calcium carbonate precipitate.

After any remaining solids are filtered out, the clarified syrup is decolorized by filtration through a bed of activated carbon; bone char was traditionally used in this role, but its use is no longer common. Some remaining colour-forming impurities adsorb to the carbon bed. The purified syrup is then concentrated to supersaturation and repeatedly crystallized under vacuum, to produce white refined sugar. As in a sugar mill, the sugar crystals are separated from the molasses by centrifuging. Additional sugar is recovered by blending the remaining syrup with the washing from affination and again crystallizing to produce brown sugar. When no more sugar can be economically recovered, the final molasses still contains 20–30 percent sucrose and 15–25 percent glucose and fructose.

To produce granulated sugar, in which the individual sugar grains do not clump together, sugar must be dried. Drying is accomplished first by drying the sugar in a hot rotary dryer, and then by conditioning the sugar by blowing cool air through it for several days.

Ribbon cane Syrup

Ribbon cane is a subtropical type that was once widely grown in southern United States, as far north as coastal North Carolina. The juice was extracted with horse or mule-powered crushers; the juice was boiled, like maple syrup, in a flat pan, and then used in the syrup form as a sweetener for other foods. It is not a commercial crop nowadays, but a few growers try to keep alive the old traditions and find ready sales for their product.

Cane ethanol

This is generally available as a by-product of sugar mills producing sugar. It can be used as a fuel, mainly as a biofuel alternative to gasoline, and is widely used in cars in Brazil. It is steadily becoming a promising alternative to gasoline throughout much of the world and thus instead of sugar may be produced as a primary product out of sugar canes processing.

Sugarcane as food

In most countries where sugarcane is cultivated, there are several foods and popular dishes derived from it, such as:

- Direct consumption of raw sugarcane cylinders or cubes, which are chewed to extract the juice, and the bagasse is spat out
- Freshly extracted juice (garapa, *guarab, guarapa, guarapo, papelón,* '*aseer asab*, Ganna sharbat, mosto or *caldo de cana*) by hand or electrically operated small mills, with a touch of lemon and ice, makes a popular drink.
- Molasses, used as a sweetener and as a syrup accompanying other foods, such as cheese or cookies
- Rapadura, a candy made of flavored solid brown sugar in Brazil, which can be consumed in small hard blocks, or in pulverized form (flour), as an add-on to other desserts.
- Sugarcane is also used in rum production, especially in the Caribbean.
- Cane sugar syrup was the traditional sweetener in soft drinks for many years, but has been largely supplanted (in the US at least) by high-fructose corn syrup, which is less expensive, but is considered by some to not taste quite like the sugar it replaces.
- Hard rock candy is a confection that is enjoyed by people around the world.
- Jaggery - solidified molasses of sugarcane, known as Gur or Gud in South Asia. Traditionally produced by heat evaporating sugarcane juice until it is a thick sludge and then letting it cool

in buckets used as molds. Modern production methods make use of partial freeze drying to give reduce caramelization and give it lighter color. It is used as sweetener in cooking traditional meal entrees as well as sweets and desserts.

Nitrogen fixation

Some sugarcane varieties are known to be capable of fixing atmospheric nitrogen in association with a bacterium, Acetobacter diazotrophicus. Unlike legumes and other nitrogen fixing plants which form root nodules in the soil in association with bacteria, Acetobacter diazotrophicus lives within the intercellular spaces of the sugarcane's stem.

5

Introduction of Wool

Wool, the essential fabric of the North and North Eastern states due to the geographical factors. Wool usually comes from sheep, but it can also come from rabbits, goats and llamas. There are many different types of wool, but they all share certain characteristics. The most important characteristic is that it easily absorbs moisture. It can absorb up to 30 percent of its weight without feeling wet, plus the moisture content in the wool helps to prevent a build-up of static electricity. Wool will keep you warmer than other fibres. Wool is also very elastic and can easily be stretched when wet; yet it is still able to return to its normal shape once it is dry. All of these factors make it very comfortable to wear.

Wool is generally a creamy white colour, although some breeds of sheep produce natural colors such as black, brown (also called moorit) and grey. The fabric is very resilient and resistant to wrinkling. It is renewed by moisture and is well known for it's warmth. In addition to clothing, wool is used for carpeting, felt, insulation and upholstery.

Wool is the fiber derived from the specialized skin cells, called follicles, of animals in the Caprinae family, principally sheep, but the hair of certain species of other mammals such as goats, llamas, rabbits and keeshonds may also be called wool. Wool has several qualities that distinguish it from hair or fur: it is crimped; it has a different texture or handle; it is elastic; and it grows in staples (clusters).

Characteristics

Wool's scaling and crimp make it easier to spin the fleece. They help the individual fibers attach to each other so that they stay together. Because of the crimp, wool fabrics have a greater bulk than other textiles and retain air, which causes the product to retain heat. Insulation also works both ways; Bedouins and Tuaregs use wool clothes to keep the heat out.

The amount of crimp corresponds to the thickness of the wool fibers. A fine wool like Merino may have up to a hundred crimps per inch, while the coarser wools like karakul may have as few as one to two crimps per inch. Hair, by contrast, has little if any scale and no crimp, and little ability to bind into yarn. On sheep, the hair part of the fleece is called kemp. The relative amounts of kemp to wool vary from breed to breed, and make some fleeces more desirable for spinning, felting, or carding into batts for quilts or other insulating products.

Wool fibers are hygroscopic. This means wool has the power to readily absorb and give off moisture. It can absorb moisture almost one-third of its own weight. Wool absorbs sound like many other fabrics. Wool is generally a creamy white color, although some breeds of sheep produce natural colors such as black, brown, silver, and random mixes.

Wool ignites at a higher temperature than cotton fibers and some synthetics. It has lower rate of flame spread, low heat release, and low heat of combustion; doesn't melt or drip; forms a char which is insulating and self-extinguishes; and contributes less to toxic gases and smoke than other flooring products when used in carpets. Wool carpets are specified for high safety environments such as trains and aircraft. Wool is usually specified for garments for fire-fighters, soldiers, and others in occupations where they are exposed to the likelihood of fire.

Wool is static resistant as the retention of moisture within the fabric prevents a build up of static electricity. Wool garments are much less likely to spark or cling to the body. The use of wool car seat covers or carpets reduces the risk of a shock when a person touches a grounded object. Wool is considered by the medical profession to be hypoallergenic.

Wool is a protein fibre chiefly composed of keratin. The fibre is made up of overlapping cuticle scales and an inner cortex. Both the cortex and the cuticle influence the fibre properties of the wool and the fibre is slightly elliptical, unlike other animal fibres. With the wide range of sheep breeds, the fibre properties of the wool produced are equally wide ranging. The particular fibre characteristic of specific breeds can be exploited by processing the fibre into appropriate end products. In a general sense, wool varies from the super fine Merino producing a fibre similar to cashmere, very high lustre English breeds producing mohair-like fibre, and coarse hairy wools similar to the guard coat of some goats.

The range of fleece weights produced annually by sheep in the IWS member countries is from 2-5 kg clean depending on the breed of sheep and the farming environment. In the countries where sheep owners income from wool is less important, the annual fleece weights are lower, ie. from 1-3 kg clean.

The first shearing of the sheep as a lamb occurs from 3-11 months of age and produces lambs wool which is the finest diameter wool the sheep produces. The diameter is from 2-6 microns finer than the second time the sheep is shorn usually at 9-18 months. The amount of change that occurs is influenced by the interval between shearing, feeding levels and animal health and possible breed effects. The third time shorn, the wool maybe from 1-3 microns coarser that the previous shearing . From then the change in diameter is small. The range of fibre diameters between the different breeds of the sheep varies from 15 microns grown by superfine Merinos through to 45 microns produced by the carpet wool sheep.

The length of wool produced is influenced by breed and fibre diameter. Merinos range from 60-110 mm if shorn annually through to the coarse carpet wools ranging from 100-200 mm annually.

Scientific breeding programmes in the major producing countries have almost eliminated melanin pigmentation and consequently the wool is of very white colour. However, this is not the case with wools grown in many of the other producing countries.

Wool constitutes 5% of the world textile fibre production. Wool's limited supply coupled with its excellent textile performance properties has resulted in wool products being positioned in the luxury end of most markets. The promotional activities of IWS have focused on the "woolmark" and have assisted greatly with enhancing this position in the market place. The "woolmark" is an internationally recognised registered trade mark denoting products made from pure new wool, which also meets strict performance criteria.

Owing to the range of sheep breeds and wool types produced wool is processed into an equally wide range of end products. End uses of wool is determined by the main fibre characteristics. These include fibre diameter, fibre length/strength, colour and handle, plus others such as lustre, bulk, presence of faults like vegetable matter and the level of felting.

The two major end uses for wool are apparel products and carpets (both machine made and hand-knotted).

The three systems for making wool yarns are:

- Woollen (condenser spun)
- Semi-worsted, or
- Worsted.

There are however, a vast number of other products made from wool and a few of the more interesting ones include:

- Mattress and furniture stuffings
- Tennis ball covers
- Piano hammers
- Insulation
- Felt hats and toys

Processing

Wool straight off a sheep contains a high level of grease which contains valuable lanolin, as well as dirt, dead skin, sweat residue, and vegetable matter. This state is known as "grease wool" or "wool in the grease". Before the wool can be used for commercial purposes it must be scoured, or cleaned. Scouring may be as simple as a bath in warm water, or a complicated industrial process using detergent and alkali. In commercial wool, vegetable matter is often removed by chemical carbonization. In less processed wools, vegetable matter may be removed by hand, and some of the lanolin left intact through use of gentler detergents. This semi-grease wool can be worked into yarn and knitted into particularly water-resistant mittens or sweaters, such as those of the Aran Island fishermen. Lanolin removed from wool is widely used in cosmetics products such as hand creams.

After shearing, the wool is separated into five main categories: fleece (which makes up the vast bulk), broken, pieces, bellies, and locks. The latter four are pressed into wool packs and sold separately. The quality of fleece is determined by a technique known as wool classing, whereby a qualified wool classer groups wools of similar gradings together to maximise the return for the farmer or sheep owner. Prior to Australian auctions, all Merino fleece wool is objectively measured for micron, yield (including the amount of vegetable matter), staple length, staple strength, and sometimes color and comfort factor.

Quality

The quality of wool is determined by the following factors, fiber diameter, crimp, yield, color, and staple strength. Fiber diameter is the single most important wool characteristic determining quality and price.

Merino wool is typically 3-5 inches in length and is very fine (between 12-24 microns). The finest and most valuable wool comes from Merino hoggets. Wool taken from sheep produced for meat is typically more coarse, and has fibers that are 1.5 to 6 inches in length. Damage or breaks in the wool can occur if the sheep is stressed while it is growing its fleece, resulting in a thin spot where the fleece is likely to break.

Wool is also separated into grades based on the measurement of the wool's diameter in microns. These grades may vary depending on the breed or purpose of the wool. For example:

- < 17.5 - Ultrafine Merino
- 17.6-18.5 - Superfine Merino
- < 19.5 - Fine Merino
- 19.6-20.5 - Fine medium Merino
- 20.6-22.5 - Medium Merino
- 22.6 < - Strong Merino

or

- < 24.5 - Fine
- 24.5–31.4 - Medium
- 31.5-35.4 - Fine crossbred
- 35.5 < - coarse crossbred

In general, anything finer than 25 microns can be used for garments, while coarser grades are used for outerwear or rugs. The finer the wool, the softer it will be, while coarser grades are more durable and less prone to pilling.

The finest Australian and New Zealand Merino wools are known as 1PP which is the industry benchmark of excellence for Merino wool that is 16.9 micron and finer. This style represents the top level of fineness, character, color, and style as determined on the basis of a series of parameters in accordance with the original dictates of British Wool as applied today by the Australian Wool Exchange (AWEX) Council. Only a few dozen of the millions of bales auctioned every year can be classified and marked 1PP

History of Wool

As the raw material has been readily available since the widespread domestication of sheep - and of goats, another major provider of wool - the use of felted or woven wool for clothing and other fabrics characterizes some of the earliest civilizations. Prior to invention of shears - probably in the Iron Age - the wool was plucked out by hand or by bronze combs. The oldest known European wool textile, ca. 1500 BCE, was preserved in a Danish bog.

In Roman times, wool, linen, and leather clothed the European population; the cotton of India was a curiosity that only naturalists had heard of; and silk, imported along the Silk Road from China, was an extravagant luxury. Pliny the Elder records in his Natural History that the reputation for producing the finest wool was enjoyed by Tarentum, where selective breeding had produced sheep with a superior fleece, but which required special care.

In medieval times, as trade connections expanded, the Champagne fairs revolved around the production of wool cloth in small centers such as Provins; the network that the sequence of annual fairs developed meant that the woollens of Provins might find their way to Naples, Sicily, Cyprus, Majorca, Spain, and even Constantinople (Braudel, 316). The wool trade developed into serious business, the generator of capital. In the thirteenth century, the wool trade was the economic engine of the Low Countries and of Central Italy; by the end of the following century Italy predominated, though in the 16th century Italian production turned to silk (Braudel p 312). Both pre-industries were based on English raw wool exports - rivaled only by the sheepwalks of Castile, developed from the fifteenth century - which were a significant source of income to the English crown, which from 1275 imposed an export tax on wool called the "Great Custom". The importance of wool to the English economy can be shown by the fact that since the 14th Century, the presiding officer of the House of Lords has sat on the "Woolsack", a chair stuffed with wool.

Economies of scale were instituted in the Cistercian houses, which had accumulated great tracts of land during the twelfth and early thirteenth centuries, when land prices were low and labor still scarce. Raw wool was baled and shipped from North Sea ports to the textile cities of Flanders, notably Ypres and Ghent, where it was dyed and worked up as cloth. At the time of the Black Death, English textile industries accounted for about 10% of English wool production (Cantor 2001, 64); the English textile trade grew during the fifteenth century, to the point where export of wool was discouraged. Over the centuries, various British laws controlled the wool trade or required the use of wool even in burials. The smuggling of wool out of the country, known as owling, was at one time punishable by the cutting off of a hand. After the Restoration, fine English woollens began to compete with silks in the international market, partly aided by the Navigation Acts; in 1699 English crown forbade its American colonies to trade wool with anyone but England herself.

A great deal of the value of woollen textiles was in the dyeing and finishing of the woven product. In each of the centers of the textile trade, the manufacturing process came to be subdivided into a collection of trades, overseen by an entrepreneur in a system called by the English the "putting-out" system, or "cottage industry", and the *Verlagssystem* by the Germans. In this system of producing wool cloth, until recently perpetuated in the production of Harris tweeds, the entrepreneur provides the raw materials and an advance, the remainder being paid upon delivery of the product. Written contracts bound the artisans to specified terms. Fernand Braudel traces the appearance of the system in the thirteenth-century economic boom, quoting a document of 1275 (Braudel, 317) The system effectively by-passed the guilds' restrictions.

Before the flowering of the Renaissance, the Medici and other great banking houses of Florence had built their wealth and banking system on their textile industry based on wool, overseen by the Arte della Lana, the wool guild: wool textile interests guided Florentine policies. Francesco Datini, the "merchant of Prato", established in 1383 an *Arte della Lana* for that small Tuscan city. The sheepwalks of Castile shaped the landscape and the fortunes of the *meseta* that lies in the heart of the Iberian peninsula; in the sixteenth century, a unified Spain allowed export of Merino lambs only with royal permission. The German wool market - based on sheep of Spanish origin - did not overtake British wool until comparatively late. Australia's colonial economy was based on sheep raising, and the Australian wool trade eventually overtook that of the Germans by 1845, furnishing wool for Bradford, which developed as the heart of industrialized woollens production.

- Fernand Braudel, 1982. *The Wheels of Commerce*, vol 2 of *Civilization and Capitalism* (New York:Harper & Row)

Due to decreasing demand with increased use of synthetic fibers, wool production is much less than what it was in the past.

The collapse in the price of wool began in late 1966 with a 40% drop; with occasional interruptions, the price has tended down. The result has been sharply reduced production and movement of resources into production of other commodities, in the case of sheep growers, to production of meat.

Superwash wool (or washable wool) technology first appeared in the early 1970s to produce wool that has been specially treated so that it is machine washable and may be tumble-dried. This wool is produced using an acid bath that removes the "scales" from the fiber, or by coating the fiber with a polymer that prevents the scales from attaching to each other and causing shrinkage. This process results in a fiber that holds longevity and durability over synthetic materials, while retaining its shape.

In December 2004, a bale of the world's finest wool, averaging 11.8 micron, sold for $3,000 per kilogram at auction in Melbourne, Victoria. This fleece wool tested with an average yield of 74.5%, 68 mm long, and had 40 newtons per kilotex strength. The result was $AUD279,000 for the bale. The finest bale of wool ever auctioned sold for a seasonal record of 269,000 cents per kilo during June 2008. This bale was produced by the Hillcreston Pinehill Partnership and measured 11.6 microns, 72.1% yield and had a 43 Newtons per kilotex strength measurement. The bale realized $247,480 and was exported to India.

During 2007 a new wool suit was developed and sold in Japan that can be washed in the shower, and dries off ready to wear within hours with no ironing required. The suit was developed using Australian Merino wool and it enables woven products made from wool, such as suits, trousers and skirts, to be cleaned using a domestic shower at home.

In December 2006 the General Assembly of the United Nations proclaimed 2009 to be the International Year of Natural Fibres, so as to raise the profile of wool and other natural fibers.

Production

Global wool production is approximately 1.3 million tonnes per annum of which 60% goes into apparel. Australia is the leading producer of wool which is mostly from Merino sheep. New Zealand is the second largest producer of wool, but is the largest producer of crossbred wool. China is the third largest producer of wool. Breeds such as Lincoln, Romney, Tukidale, Drysdale and Elliotdale produce coarser fibers, and wool off these sheep is usually used for making carpets.

In the United States, Texas, New Mexico and Colorado also have large commercial sheep flocks and their mainstay is the Rambouillet (or French Merino). There is also a thriving home-flock contingent of small-scale farmers who raise small hobby flocks of specialty sheep for the hand spinning market. These small-scale farmers may raise any type of sheep they wish, so the selection of fleeces is quite wide.

Global wool clip 2004/2005

1. Australia: 25% of global wool clip (475 million kg greasy, 2004/2005)
2. China: 18%
3. New Zealand: 11%
4. Argentina: 3%
5. Turkey: 2%
6. Iran: 2%
7. United Kingdom: 2%
8. India: 2%
9. Sudan: 2%
10. South Africa: 1%
11. United States: 0.77%

Keeping with the times, organic wool is becoming more and more popular. This wool is very limited in supply and much of it comes from New Zealand and Australia. Organic wool is becoming easier to find in clothing and other products, though these products often carry a higher price. Wool is environmentally preferable (as compared to petroleum-based Nylon or Polypropylene) as a material for carpets as well, in particular when combined with a natural binding and the use of formaldehyde-free glues.

Animal rights groups have noted issues with the production of wool, such as Mulesing.

Wool Marketing

Australia

The dominant form of marketing for about 85 per cent of Australian wool is sale by open cry auction. **Sale by Sample** is a method in which a mechanical claw takes a sample from each bale in a line or lot of wool. These grab samples are bulked, objectively measured, and a sample of not less than 4 kg is displayed in a box for the buyer to examine. The Australian Wool Exchange (AWEX) conducts sales primarily in Sydney, Melbourne, Newcastle, and Fremantle. There are about eighty brokers and agents throughout Australia.

About 15 percent of wool is sold by **private treaty** on-farm or to local wool-handling facilities. This option gives wool growers benefit from reduced transport, warehousing, and selling costs. This method is preferred for small lots or mixed butts in order to make savings on reclassing and testing.

Sale by tender can achieve considerable cost savings on wool clips large enough to make it worthwhile for potential buyers to submit tenders. Some marketing firms sell wool on a **consignment** basis, obtaining a fixed percentage as commission.

Forward selling: Some buyers will offer a secure price for forward delivery of wool based on estimated measurements or the results of previous clips. Prices are quoted at current market rates and are locked in for the season. Premiums and discounts are added to cover variations in micron, yield, tensile strength, etc., which are confirmed by actual test results when available.

Another method of selling wool includes sales direct to wool mills.

Other countries

The British Wool Marketing Board operates a central marketing system for UK fleece wool with the aim of achieving the best possible net returns for farmers.

Less than half of New Zealand's wool is now sold at auction, but many farmers (around 45%) now sell wool directly to private buyers and end-users. Some businesses in New Zealand like Blue House Yarns have turned to selling organic wool, a new trend on wool production.

United States sheep producers market wool with private or cooperative wool warehouses, but wool pools are common in many states. In some cases, wool is pooled in a local market area but sold through a wool warehouse. Wool offered with objective measurement test results is preferred. Imported apparel wool and carpet wool goes directly to central markets where it is handled by the large merchants and manufacturers.

Uses

In addition to clothing, wool has been used for blankets, horse rugs, saddle cloths, carpeting, felt, wool insulation (also see links) and upholstery. Wool felt covers piano hammers, and it is used to absorb odors and noise in heavy machinery and stereo speakers. Ancient Greeks lined their helmets with felt, and Roman legionnaires used breastplates made of wool felt.

Wool has also been traditionally used to cover cloth diapers. Wool fiber exteriors are hydrophobic (repel water) and the interior of the wool fiber is hygroscopic (attracts water; this makes a wool garment able to cover a wet diaper while inhibiting wicking so outer garments remain dry. Wool felted and treated with lanolin is water resistant, air permeable, and slightly antibacterial, so it resists the buildup of odor. Some modern cloth diapers use felted wool fabric for covers, and there are several modern commercial knitting patterns for wool diaper covers.

Yarns

Virgin wool is wool spun for the first time, as contrasted with shoddy.

Shoddy

Shoddy or **recycled wool** is made by cutting or tearing apart existing wool fabric and respinning the resulting fibers. As this process makes the wool fibers shorter, the remanufactured fabric is inferior to the original. The recycled wool may be mixed with raw wool, wool noil, or another fiber such as cotton to increase the average fiber length. Such yarns are typically used as weft yarns with a cotton warp. This process was invented in the Heavy Woollen District of West Yorkshire and created a micro-economy in this area for many years.

Recycled or remanufactured wool which is of inferior quality compared to the original wool. Historically generated from loosely woven materials. Benjamin Law invented shoddy and mungo, as such, in 1813. He was the first to organise, on a larger scale, the activity of taking old clothes and grinding them down into a fibrous state that could be re-spun into yarn. The shoddy industry was centred on the towns of Batley, Morley, Dewsbury and Ossett in West Yorkshire, and concentrated on the recovery of wool from rags. The importance of the industry can be gauged by the fact that even in 1860 the town of [Batley] was producing over 7000 tonnes of shoddy. At the time there were 80 firms employing a total of 550 people sorting the rags. These were then sold to shoddy manufacturers of which there were about 130 in the West Riding.

Ragg

Ragg is a sturdy wool fiber made into yarn and used in many rugged applications like gloves.

Worsted

Worsted is the name of a yarn, the cloth made from this yarn, and a yarn weight category. The name derives from the village of Worsted in the English county of Norfolk. This village became, along with North Walsham and Aylsham, a centre for the manufacture of yarn and cloth after weavers from Flanders arrived in Norfolk in the 12th century. **Worsted** is a strong, long-staple, combed wool yarn with a hard surface.

Technique & Preparation

The essential feature of a worsted yarn is straightness of fibre, in that the fibres lie parallel to each other. Traditionally, long, fine staple wool was spun to create worsted yarn, but other long fibres are also used today.

Many spinners differentiate between worsted preparation and worsted spinning. Worsted preparation refers to the way the fibre is prepared before spinning, using gilling machines which force the fibre staples to lie parallel to each other. Once these fibres have been made into a top, they are then combed to remove the short fibres. The long fibres are combined in subsequent gilling machines to again make the fibres parallel. This produces overlapping untwisted strands called slivers. Worsted spinning refers to using a worsted technique, which produces a smooth yarn where the fibres lie parallel .

Roving and wool top are often used to spin worsted yarn. Many hand spinners buy their fibre in roving or top form. Top and roving are ropelike in appearance, in that they can be thick and long. While some mills put a slight twist in the rovings they make, it is not enough twist to be a yarn. The fibers in top and rovings all lie parallel to one another along the length, which makes top ideal for spinning worsted yarns.

Worsted-spun yarns, used to create **worsted** fabric, are spun from wool fibers that have been combed, to ensure that the woollen fibers all run the same direction, butt-end (end that was cut in shearing the sheep) to tip, and remain parallel. A short-draw is used in spinning worsted fibers (as opposed to a long -draw).

In short draw spinning, spun from combed roving, sliver or wool top, the spinners keep their hands very close to each other. The fibers are held fanned out in one hand while the other hand pulls a small number from the mass. The twist is kept between the second hand and the wheel - there is never any twist between the two hands.

The cloth

Worsted cloth, archaically also known as stuff, is lightweight and has a coarse texture. The weave is usually twill or plain. Twilled fabrics such as whipcord, gabardine and serge are often made from worsted yarn. Worsted fabric made from wool has a natural recovery, meaning that it is resilient and quickly returns to its natural shape, but non-glossy worsted will shine with use or abrasion.

Worsteds differ from woolens, in that the natural crimp of the wool fibre is removed in the process of spinning the yarn. In Tropical Worsteds this use of tightly-spun straightened wool combined with a looser weave permits the free flow of air through the fabric.

Worsted is also used for carpets, garments, hosiery, gloves and baize.

Weight

The term "worsted" is often applied to any yarn spun from fibres three inches in length or longer that have been carded or combed, and spun, not just wool. Acrylic and other yarns can be called "worsted," as much a reference to the weight of the yarn as the production process.

A worsted yarn has a thickness of 12 wraps per inch. Depending on a knitter's personal technique, a worsted yarn generally has a gauge of about 16-20 stitches per 10 centimeters using 5.5mm (US size 9) needles.

History

Prior to the introduction of automatic machinery there was little difficulty in attaining a straight fibre, as long wool was always used, and the sliver was made up by hand, using combs. However, with the introduction of Richard Arkwright's water frame in 1771, and the later introduction of cap and mule spinning machines, the need for perfectly prepared slivers became apparent, and many manufactories used one or more preparatory "gill-boxes" (combing machines) before the worsting process, to ensure straightness of fibre and distribute the lubricant evenly.

Woollen

Woollen (American English: ***woolen***) is the name of a yarn and cloth usually made from wool. Woollen yarn is known for being light, stretchy, and full of air. It is thus a good insulator, and makes a good knitting yarn. Woollen yarn is in contrast to worsted yarn, which doesn't contain air and doesn't stretch as much. **Woollen** is a soft, short-staple, carded wool yarn typically used for knitting. In traditional weaving, woollen weft yarn (for softness and warmth) is frequently combined with a worsted warp yarn for strength on the loom.

Commercial manufacture

The woollen and worsted process both require that the wool (and other similar amimal fibres, cashmere, camel etc.) are cleaned before mechanical processing. Woollen and worsted nomenclatures apply only to the textile processing of animal fibres, but it has become common to include fibre blends under these terms.

The resultant fabrics will be classified as being either woollen or worsted, but this designation is assigned during fibre processing and yarn formation, not in the cloth or finished garment.

A woven woollen fabric is one which is subjected to fabric finishing techniques designed to add a directional pile - in that the end consumer can 'stroke' the garment in a single direction (shoulder to cuff etc.), such as a casual jacket. This feels like the fibres are directionally arranged.

Woollen yarn formation is also very common for knitwear, where the resultant garment has some bulk and the requirement for visual aesthetics (of fibre alignment) is minimal.

The worsted processing route is more complex and requires the removal of short fibers and the use of a focussed mechanical process to make the individual fibres parallel with respect to each other. The yarn formation process is significantly more comprehensive and results in a very sleek yarn which will offer a clean looking woven fabric, such as for suitings. The worsted process is significantly more expensive and is seldom used for knitwear.

We can get into a lot of specific details here, including when and how to impart colour, if desired.

Handspinning woollen yarn

Woollen yarn is handspun using the long draw technique, and

the yarn is spun from a rolag. Most handspinners make a blend of a woollen and worsted yarn, using techniques from both categories, and thus ending up with a mix. The first step to spin a true woollen yarn, however, is to card the fiber into a rolag using handcarders.

The rolag is spun without much stretching of the fibers from the cylindrical configuration. This is done by allowing twist into a short section of the rolag, and then pulling back, without letting the rolag change position in your hands, until the yarn is the desired thickness. The twist will concentrate in the thinnest part of the roving, thus when the yarn is pulled, the thicker sections with less twist will tend to thin out. Once the yarn is the desired thickness, enough twist is added to make the yarn strong. Then the yarn is wound onto the bobbin, and the process starts again.

Other meanings

"Woollen", as an adjective, also refers to a thing which is composed of wool, in the same vein as wheaten, golden, and the somewhat rarer silvern and leathern.

Events

Being one of the biggest buyers of Merino wool, Ermenegildo Zegna has encouraged, supported, and rewarded the efforts of the Australian wool producers since 1963 in the production of finer and softer wools. In 1963, the first Ermenegildo Zegna Perpetual Trophy was presented in Tasmania for growers of "Superfine skirted Merino fleece." In 1980, a national award, the Ermenegildo Zegna Trophy for Extrafine Wool Production, was launched. In 2004, this award became known as the Ermenegildo Zegna Unprotected Wool Trophy. In 1998, an Ermenegildo Zegna Protected Wool Trophy was launched for fleece from sheep coated for around nine months of the year.

In 2002, the Ermenegildo Zegna Vellus Aureum Trophy was launched for wool that is 13.9 micron and finer. Wool from Australia, New Zealand, Argentina, and South Africa may enter, and a winner is named from each country. In April 2008, New Zealand won the coveted Ermenegildo Zegna Vellus Aureum Trophy for the first time with a fleece which measured 10.8 microns. This contest awards the winning fleece weight with the same weight in gold as a prize, hence the name.

Since 2000, Loro Piana has awarded a cup for the world's finest bale of wool which produces just enough fabric for 50 tailor-made suits. The prize is awarded to an Australian or New Zealand wool grower who produces the year's finest bale.

The New England Merino Field days which display local studs, wool, and sheep are held during January, every two years (in even numbered years) around the Walcha, New South Wales district. The Annual Wool Fashion Awards, which showcase the use of Merino wool by fashion designers, are hosted by the city of Armidale, New South Wales in March each year. This event encourages young and established fashion designers to display their talents. During each May, Armidale hosts the annual New England Wool Expo to display wool fashions, handicrafts, demonstrations, shearing competitions, yard dog trials, and more.

In July, the annual Australian Sheep and Wool Show is held in Bendigo, Victoria. This is the largest sheep and wool show in the world, with goats and alpacas as well as woolcraft competitions and displays, fleece competitions, sheepdog trials, shearing, and wool handling. The largest competition in the world for objectively-measured fleeces is the Australian Fleece Competition, which is held annually at Bendigo. In 2008, there were 475 entries from all states of Australia with first and second prizes going to the Northern Tablelands, New South Wales fleeces.

Wool insulation

Wool insulation is made from sheep wool that is mechanically bonded together to form insulating batts and ropes. Batts are commonly used in timber-frame buildings and ropes are primarily used between the logs in log homes. Wool insulation is used for both thermal and acoustic insulating applications. Sheep wool is a natural, sustainable, renewable, recyclable material that does not endanger the health of people or the environment. Wool is a highly effective insulating material that has been used for years insulating people in the form of clothing. Mongolian nomads also used felted and woven sheep wool pads as an insulating layer on the walls and floors of their dwellings called, ger or yurts. Presently the use of wool for insulation is starting to rise in popularity. It is used more in Europe, Australia and Canada than it is the United States; manufacturers are, however, trying to expand their distribution to the US.

Insulating qualities

Sheep wool is a natural insulator because it has a crimped nature which traps air in millions of tiny pockets. Sheep wool insulation has an R-value (resistance to heat flow) of approximately 3.5 to 3.8 per inch of material thickness which is 0.3 to 0.6 points higher than fiberglass, cellulose, or mineral wool. The crimp also allows the wool to retain its structure and overall thickness instead of breaking down and settling like many other insulating materials. Wool is a hygroscopic material which means that it will absorb up to 30% to 40% of its own weight in moisture without becoming wet to the touch. This moisture absorption is unique to sheep wool and does not compromise the wool's insulating abilities unlike cellulose or fiberglass insulation. When used as acoustic insulation wool provides rates starting at 44dB for a 60mm (2.4in) thick partition, and goes up to 53dB for a 100mm (4in) thickness. Wool has a long life span and can be used over and over again. Wool also has a low embodied energy at approximately 15 kilowatt hours per cube meter of material produced. The low embodied energy of wool is just over half of that of cellulose insulation and practically one sixth of the embodied energy required to produce mineral wool. However, the issues of transportation energy costs need to be factored in, as the embodied energy figures usually do not consider this. Consumers must think about both transportation stages, pre-production, as a raw material, and post-production as insulation, to be careful to choose a manufacturer that is as close as possible to the building site.

Health considerations

Wool is not irritating to the respiratory system or the skin like fiberglass and other alternative insulating materials because its fibers are more than 30 micrometres thick which is too big to be a health risk; potentially carcinogenic fibers are 1 to 4 micrometres thick. Wool insulation also helps prevent the sick building syndrome because it permanently traps substances like formaldehyde, nitrogen dioxide and sulfur dioxide emitted by other common building materials and combustion processes. Sheep wool is naturally flame retardant, self extinguishing and won't melt. In the case that the wool does ignite, its inflammation point is 560 degrees Celsius, it will not emit any toxic gases. Because wool insulation is mechanically bonded there are no chemicals or glues needed. Sheep wool is biodegradable so used wool insulation, if it not going to be recycled, can be composed without causing harm to the environment.

Building considerations

Wool insulation commonly comes in rolls of batts or ropes with varied widths and thicknesses depending on the manufacturer. Generally, wool batts have thicknesses of 50 mm (2 in) to 100mm (4 in), with widths of 400 mm (16in) and 600 mm (24 in), and lengths of 4000 mm (13 ft 4 in), 5000 mm (16 ft 8 in), 6000 mm (20ft) and 7200 mm (24 ft). The widths of 16 in and 24 in are the standard measurements between studs in a stud frame wall. Most manufacturers provide custom sizes as well and batts and ropes are easy to cut once on site. Wool insulation can be used in the roof, walls and floors of any building type as long as there are spaces to put the insulation in. The construction costs when installing wool insulation are lower due to having no need for protective clothing or respiratory equipment, this also makes installation slightly faster. Installing wool insulation is very similar to installing conventional insulation batts, it can be held into place with staples or it can be friction-fit which involves cutting the insulation slightly bigger than the space it occupies, using friction to hold it in place.

Environmental factors

There are some primary environmental factors that need to be considered when looking for a source of wool, such as the way the flock is treated for pesticides, the chemicals used in the treatment of the wool after shearing, and the distance from the source to its final destination. Sheep are often treated with insecticide and fungicide in a process called dipping. This leaves a residue on the fleece and can result in groundwater contamination if used improperly. These residues are often washed off once the fleece is sheared, but this results in three by-products, grease, liquor, and sludge. The first two can be safely disposed of, but the latter contains remnants of the pesticides which cause a concern for disposal. When used in insulation wool is often treated with Borax to enhance its fire retardant and pest repellent qualities. Borax mining employs one of the cleanest mining techniques available and the Borax product has a low toxicity with no need for special safety precautions when handling it and requiring nothing more than washing hands and changing clothes daily after contact.

Micron (Wool)

A **micron** (micrometre) is the measurement used to express the diameter of a wool fibre. The lower microns are the finer fibres. Fibre diameter is the most important characteristic of wool in determining its greasy value.

Every fleece comprises a very wide range of fibre diameters - for example a typical Merino fleece will contain fibres of as low as 10 microns in diameter, and there could be fibres with diameters exceeding 25 microns, depending on the age and health (or nutrition) of the sheep. What is usually referred to as wool's "micron" is the mean of the fibre diameters or average diameter. This may be measured in a number of different ways.

Small samples can be taken from the side or fleece of a sheep and measured using a portable instrument such as an OFDA2000 (Optical Fibre Diameter Analyser); or a mobile instrument system called a Fleecescan. Both these systems have been studied extensively and used correctly should give reasonably reliable results. Pre wool classing micron test results are a useful guide for classes in determining lines of wool to be made. Samples of fleece can also be shorn from the animal and sent to a laboratory for measurement ("midside sampling"). Most fleece-testing laboratories nowadays use related instruments to those mentioned - either the OFDA models or the Laserscan. Merino stud rams are mid-side sampled and the test results are displayed in the sale catalogues.

Once the fleeces are baled and prepared for sale as lots, they are commonly sampled by coring in the broker store and the samples sent to certification laboratories. Here the core samples are cleaned, dried and prepared for measurement under strict test methods. Merino wools are normally measured on Laserscan instruments in Australia, New Zealand and South Africa, although OFDA instruments may also be used in some cases (the results from these two types of instrument are quite similar). The "coefficient of variation of fibre diameter" (CVD) is a measure of the variation in fibre fineness within the sample fleece, relative to the average fibre diameter. Crossbred and coarse wools are often measured for mean fibre diameter by older instruments - "Airflow" in many parts of the world, and even a projection microscope in some cases.

Weaner and hogget wool is finer and generally more valuable than the wool from older sheep. Most wool between 11.5 and 24 microns in fibre diameter is made into clothing. The remainder is used for other textiles such as blankets, insulation and furnishings.

The finest bale of wool ever auctioned sold for a seasonal record of 269,000 cents per kilo during June, 2008. This bale was produced by the Hillcreston Pinehill Partnership and measured 11.6 microns, 72.1% yield and had a 43 Newtons per kilotex strength measurement. The bale realised $247,480 and was exported to India.

Staple (wool)

Staple is a term referring to naturally formed clusters or locks of wool fibres throughout a fleece that are held together by cross fibres. The staple strength of wool is one of the major determining factors when spinning yarn as well as the sale price of greasy wool.

Virtually all fleece and better grade wool skirtings sold at auction in Australia are objectively measured prior to the sale with the average results printed in a catalogue.

Staple strength is calculated as the force required to break per unit staple thickness, expressed as newtons per kilotex or N/tex. Position of Break (POB) is measured in conjunction with staple strength and is a measure of the position in the staple (base, mid or tip) where it will break given enough force. Forty or more staples must be measured to in order to conform to the Australian Standard. Wools under 30 newtons per kilotex are considered tender. Currently wools over 40 newtons per kilotex are preferred and attract a premium. Seasonal conditions or the health of the sheep may influence the soundness (strength) of the wool.

The Australian Standard requires that sale lot has a minimum of 55 staples measured with the average calculated and produced. The variability of this measure is reported as the coefficient of variation (CV%). Staple length generally determines the end use of wool, that is, whether it will be used in weaving or knitting. The longer wools are processed in the worsted system (weaving), which are called combing types, and are generally around 51 millimeters (mm) and longer. Short stapled wools are more profitably used in the woolen section where high grade material may be produced from superfine wool. Staple length (mm) is highly correlated with mean fibre length in the top (hauteur). Although traditionally, staple length only referred to animal fibres, it is now used when referring to animal and manufactured fibres as well.

The opposite term is **filament** fibre, which is fibre that comes in continuous to near continuous lengths for use. Silk, taken from the cocoon of a silkworm, is called a silk filament.

Types of Wool

Angora wool

Angora wool or **Angora fiber** refers to the downy coat produced by the Angora rabbit. While their names are similar, Angora fiber is distinct from mohair, which comes from the Angora goat. Angora is known for its softness, low micron count (i.e. thin fibers), and what knitters refer to as a halo (fluffiness). It is also known for its silky texture.

Angora rabbits produce coats in a variety of colours, from white to black. Good quality angora fibre is around 12-16 microns in diameter, and can cost around 10 - 16 dollars per ounce. It felts very easily, even on the animal itself if the animal is not groomed frequently.

The fiber is normally blended with wool to give the yarn elasticity, as angora fiber is not naturally elastic. The blend decreases the softness and halo as well as the price of the finished object. The fibers are hollow which gives them their characteristic floating feel.

The Angora rabbit

The **Angora rabbit** is a variety of domestic rabbit bred for its long, soft hair. The Angora is one of the oldest types of domestic rabbit, originating in Ankara, Turkey, along with the Angora cat and Angora goat. The rabbits were popular pets with French royalty in the mid 1700s, and spread to other parts of Europe by the end of the century. They first appeared in the United States in the early 1900s. They are bred largely for their long angora wool, which may be removed by shearing, combing, or plucking (gently pulling loose wool).

There are many individual breeds of Angora rabbits, four of which are ARBA recognized. Such breeds include French, German, Giant, English, Satin, Chinese, Swiss and Finnish, to name a few.

Cost, appearance, and personality

Angoras are bred mainly for their wool because it is silky and soft. They have a humorous appearance, as they oddly resemble a fur ball. Most are calm and docile but should be handled carefully. Grooming is necessary to prevent the fiber from matting and felting on the rabbit. Because they are prone to hairballs, they should be groomed everyday or every other day. A condition "wool block" is common in angora rabbits and should be treated quickly. Sometimes they are shorn in the summer as the long fur can cause the rabbits to overheat.

Breeds

There are four different ARBA-recognized Angora rabbit

breeds: English, French, Giant and Satin. The German Angora is also common, but is not ARBA recognized. It has its own association; the IAGARB.

English

- **Weight:** 2.0-3.5 kg (5-7½ lb).
- **ARBA-accepted varieties:** Ruby Eye White, Pointed White, Self, Shaded, Agouti

Prior to the 1939, there was one breed of "Angora Wooler". In 1939, ARBA reclassified "Angora Wooler" into "English Type" and "French Type". In 1944, ARBA officially separate Angora rabbit into two breeds: English Angora and French Angora.

Rabbits of the angora breed are adorned with "fur," growths of wool on the ears and the entire face except above the nose, and front feet, along with their thick body, and wool. They are gentle in nature, but they are not recommended for those who do not groom their animals. Their fur is very thick and needs to be groomed a lot.

This is the smallest Angora rabbit of the four breeds recognized by ARBA. This breed is more common as a pet because of the facial features that give it a puppy dog or teddy bear look. If the texture of the wool is correct, the maintenance is relatively easy; if the texture of the rabbit is cottony, it requires a great deal of maintenance.

The English angora can be bred to have broken colors, (ex: the rabbit is white with black spots.) This is not accepted by ARBA standards and would lead to a disqualification when showing the rabbit. When showing an English angora rabbit the toe nails should also be only one color, the ears could be folded over at the tips, and the furnishings on the face may cover their eyes.

French

- **Weight:** 3.5-4.5 kg (7½-10 lb).
- **ARBA-accepted varieties:** Agouti, Pointed White, Self, Shaded, Ticked, Wide Band, and Broken.

This breed has a preponderance of guard hair on the surface, with wool as an undercoat. If the texture is correct, it requires less maintenance than other Angora breeds. Ear tufts are allowed but not preferred by breeders. The ARBA recognizes the same colors as with English Angora, plus broken. The French Angora is one of the largest Angora breeds at 7 1/2 to 10 lbs, with a commercial body type. It differs from the English and German Angora in that it possesses a clean face and front feet with only minor tufting on the rear legs.

German

- **Weight:** 2.0-5.5 kg (5-12 lb).
- **IAGARB-accepted varieties:** all (not subject to ARBA standards)

This breed, while not ARBA recognized, is common in the United States and Canada. It looks much like the Giant Angora, except it almost always comes in ruby-eyed white or albino. Many spinners breed the German Angora with another Angora breed for the bountiful German Angora wool in many beautiful colors. These Angora crosses are called hybrids.

Giant angoras were created in the United States using imported German angoras and also other large breed short haired rabbits. In a certain sense, a Giant is a cross-bred German. Many people confuse the Germans with Giants, which are only ruby eyed white.

A separate club for German angoras exists in the United States, caled the International Association of German Angora Rabbit Breeders, or IAGARB. Instead of conformation showing, the emphasis is on the wool bearing properties of the rabbit for commercial purposes. The rabbit must meet objective standards and perform well on 90 day shearing tests in order to be officially recognized as a registered German angora rabbit.

IAGARB, unlike ARBA, recognizes colored rabbits and a colored rabbit may achieve merit-based registration if it conforms to the standard and proves its wool bearing ability via the witnessed 90 day shearing tests. IAGARB also recognizes the worth of the rabbit based strictly upon its tests and judging, welcoming all breeds to test for registration status. It does not require breed purity.

Since IAGARB registration is independent of parentage, any colored angora rabbit that meets the registration standards of the club can be registered as a German Angora. The notion that they come only in white is a common misconception, as the rules have only recently been changed to include colored angoras as well as ruby eyed white.

Giant

- **Weight:** 4.5 kg (9½ lb) or larger
- **ARBA-accepted varieties:** Ruby-Eyed White

The Giant Angora is larger than other varieties of Angora, having been created to be an efficient wool rabbit on economical feed and housing. It has three hair types in its wool: underwool, awn fluff, and awn hair.

This is the largest of the four ARBA recognized Angora breeds. It produces more wool than the others in general. This breed may or may not have furnishings on the face and ears. In addition to the underwool and guard hairs, it has an "Awn Fluff" that does not exist in the other three breeds of Angora.

Satin

- **Weight:** 3.0-4.5 (6½-9½ lb).
- **ARBA-accepted varieties:** Agouti, Pointed White, Self, Shaded, Ticked, Wide Band

The Satin Angora is derived from a cross between a Satin and a French Angora. This breed is named for the extremely soft texture of its wool. It has no furnishings on face, ears, or feet, and it is also easy to groom compared to the English variety. Satin Angora's wool is said to be stronger for spinning than other varieties of Angora.

Spinners love the wool and sheen of this breed. However, this breed does not produce as much wool as other breeds of Angora rabbits. This trait is being improved upon by selective breeding. The wool should have a silky texture with good guard hair for ease of maintenance.

Fur production

Angora fur is produced in Europe, Chile, China and the United

States. Harvesting occurs up to four times a year (about every 4 months) and is collected by plucking, shearing, or collection of the molting fur.

Most breeds of Angora rabbits molt with their natural growth cycle about every four months. Many producers of the fiber pluck the fur of these breeds. Plucking is, in effect, pulling out the molted fur. Plucking ensures a minimum of guard hair, and the fur is not as matted when plucked as when it is collected from the rabbit's cage. However, plucking a rabbit is time consuming, so some producers shear the rabbit instead. While this results in slightly lower quality fleece as the guard hairs are included, it does take less time and results in more fleece. Also, not all breeds of angora molt, and if the rabbit does not naturally molt, it cannot be plucked. German angoras do not molt.

The rabbits must be groomed at least once or twice a week to prevent the fur from matting and felting. There is also a danger that a rabbit will ingest its own molted fur; unlike a cat, a rabbit cannot easily be rid of the build up.

Quality of Wool

The premium 1st quality wool is taken from the back and upper sides of the rabbit. This is usually the longest and cleanest fiber on the rabbit. There should not be hay or vegetable matter in the fiber. Second quality is from the neck and lower sides and may have some vegetable matter. Third quality is the buttocks and legs and any other areas that easily felt and are of shorter length. Fourth quality is totally unsalvageable and consists of the larger felted bits or stained fiber. Third and fourth quality are perfect for cutting up for the birds to use in lining their nests. With daily brushing, felting of the fiber can be avoided, increasing the usable portion of fiber.

Angora wool in popular culture

The director, writer, and actor Edward D. Wood, Jr. was known to have a fetish for angora wool sweaters, referenced in his film "Glen or Glenda?". Director Tim Burton, an admirer of Wood's work, referenced this preference in his 2005 film *Charlie and the*

Chocolate Factory, which shows Willy Wonka (played by Johnny Depp, who had also played Wood in Burton's 1994 biopic *Ed Wood*) passing a room in which pink Angora rabbits are being shorn, saying "I'd rather not talk about that one."

Uses

Angora wool can be used in all sorts of ways. It is commonly used in apparel such as sweaters and suitings, knitting yarn, and felting.

Cashmere wool

Cashmere wool, usually simply known as **cashmere**, is a fiber obtained from the Cashmere goat. The word cashmere derives from an archaic spelling of *Kashmir*.

Cashmere wool is fine in texture, and it is also strong, light, and soft; when it is made into garments, they are extremely warm to wear.

Characteristics

Cashmere is characterized by its soft fibers. It is noted as providing a natural light-weight insulation without bulk. Fibers are highly adaptable and are easily constructed into fine or thick yarns, and light to heavy-weight fabrics. The original undyed or natural colors of cashmere wool are various shades of grey, brown and white.

The Cashmere and Camel Hair Manufacturers Institute defines cashmere as:

- The fine (dehaired) undercoat fibers produced by a Cashmere goat (Capra hircus laniger).
- The fiber is generally non-medullated and has a mean maximum diameter of 19 microns. The co-efficient of variation around the mean shall not exceed 24%. There can be no more than 3% (by weight) of cashmere fibers over 30 microns. (Reference IWTO Test Method 8-89).

In the United States, under the U.S. Wool Products Labeling Act of 1939, as amended, (U.S.C. 15 Section 68b(a)(6)), a textile product may not be labeled as containing cashmere if:

(A) such wool product is not the fine (dehaired) undercoat fibers produced by a cashmere goat (capra hircus laniger);

(B) the average diameter of the fiber of such wool product exceeds 19 microns; or

(C) such wool product contains more than 3 percent (by weight) of cashmere fibers with average diameters that exceed 30 microns. The average fiber diameter may be subject to a coefficient of variation around the mean that shall not exceed 24 percent.

Source of the fiber

Cashmere wool fiber for clothing and other textile articles is obtained from the Cashmere domestic goat. The goat (*Capra hircus laniger*) is a mammal belonging to the subfamily Caprinae of the family Bovidae. The goats produce a double fleece consisting of the fine, soft undercoat or underdown of hair mingled with a straighter and much coarser outer coating of hair called guard hair. In order for the fine under down to be sold and processed further, it must first be de-haired. De-hairing is a mechanical process that separates the coarse hairs from the fine hair and after de-hairing the resulting "cashmere" is ready to be dyed and converted into yarn, fabrics and garments.

Gathering

Cashmere is collected during the spring moulting season when the goats naturally shed their winter coat. In the Northern Hemisphere the goats moult over a period beginning as early as March and as late as May.

In some regions, the mixed mass of down and coarse hair is removed by hand with a coarse comb that pulls tufts of fiber from the animal as the comb is raked through the fleece. The collected fiber then has a higher yield of pure cashmere after the fiber has been washed and dehaired. The long, coarse guard hair is then typically clipped from the animal and is often used for brushes, interlinings and other non-apparel uses. Animals in Iran, Afghanistan, New Zealand and Australia are typically shorn of their fleece, resulting in a higher coarse hair content and lower pure cashmere yield. In America, the most popular method is combing. The process takes up to two weeks but, with a trained eye for when the fiber is releasing, sometimes it is possible to comb the fibers out in about a week.

Production

China has become the largest producer of raw cashmere and their clip is estimated at 10,000 metric tons per year (hair in). Mongolia produces somewhat more than 3,000 tons (hair in), while India, Pakistan, Iran, Afghanistan, Turkey and Central Asian Republics produce significant but lesser amounts. The annual world clip is estimated to be between 15,000 and 20,000 tons (hair in). "Pure cashmere", resulting from removing animal grease, dirt and coarse hairs from the fleece, is estimated at about 6,500 tons. It is estimated that on average yearly production per goat is 150 grams.

Pure cashmere can be dyed and spun into yarns and knit into jumpers (sweaters), hats, gloves, socks and other clothing, or woven into fabrics then cut and assembled into garments such as outer coats, jackets, pants, pajamas, scarves, blankets and other items. Fabric and garment producers in Italy, Scotland, England and Japan have long been known as market leaders.

In the US, the town of Uxbridge, Massachusetts was an incubator for the cashmere wool industry. It had the first power looms for woolens and the first manufacture of "satinets". Capron Mill had the first power looms, in 1820. It burned on July 21, 2007, in the spectacular Bernat Mill fire.

Types of fiber

- Raw — fiber that has not been processed and is essentially straight from the animal
- Processed — fiber that has been through the processes of de-hairing, washing, carding, and is ready either to spin or to knit/crochet/weave
- Virgin — new fiber which has been made into yarns, fabrics or garments for the first time

- Recycled — fibers reclaimed from scraps or fabrics that were previously woven or felted, and which may or may not have been previously used by the consumer.

History

The fiber is also known as *pashm* (Persian word for Wool) or *pashmina* (Persian / Urdu word driven from Pashm) for its use in the handmade shawls of Kashmir. The woolen shawls find written mention between 3rd century BC and the 11th century AD. However, the founder of the cashmere wool industry is traditionally held to be the 15th century ruler of Kashmir, Zayn-ul-Abidin, who introduced weavers from Turkestan.

In the 18th and early 19th century Kashmir (then called Cashmere by the English), had a thriving industry producing shawls from goat down imported from Tibet and Tartary through Ladakh. The down trade was controlled by treaties signed as a result of previous wars. The shawls were introduced into Western Europe when the General in Chief of the French campaign in Egypt (1799-1802) sent one to Paris. The shawls arrival is said to have created an immediate sensation and plans were put in place to start manufacturing the product in France.

Trading in Commercial quantities of raw cashmere between Asia and Europe began with Valerie Audresset SA, Louviers, France claiming to be the first European company to commercially spin cashmere. The down was imported from Tibet through Kasan the capital of the Russian province Volga and was used in France to create imitation woven shawls, unlike the Kashmir shawls the French shawls had a different pattern on either side. The imported cashmere was spread out on large sieves and beaten with sticks to open the fibres and clear away the dirt. After opening the cashmere was washed and children removed the coarse hair. The down was then carded and combed using the same methods used for worsted spinning.

In 1819 several Tibetan and Tartary cross goats where imported into France by Mr M. Jaubert under the auspices of the French government and at the expense of Mr Ternaux. Mr Edward

Riley (nephew of Alexander Riley) saw the herd in 1828 and described it as a mixture of colors from brown to white, covered with course hair with an average of three ounces (84 grams) of down underneath the hair. Mr Riley also saw Mr M. Polonceau's herd, Mr Polonceau selected from the Ternaux herd and crossed his animals with a selected fine Angoras buck. In 1831 Mr Riley went back to France and purchased ten females in kid and two bucks from Mr Polonceau and sent them to Australia, at the time the average production of the Polonceau herd was 16 ounces (500 grams) of down.

By 1830 the weaving of cashmere shawls using yarn produced in France had become an important Scottish industry and the Scottish Board of Trustees for the Encouragement of Arts and Manufactures offered a 300 Pound Sterling reward to the first person who could spin cashmere in Scotland based on the French system. Captain Charles Stuart Cochrane collected the required information while in Paris and received a Scottish patent for the process in 1831. In the autumn of 1831 the patent was sold to Henry Houldsworth and sons of Glasgow. In 1832 Henry Houldsworth and sons commenced the manufacture of yarn and in 1833 received the reward.

Dawson International claim to have invented the first commercial dehairing machine in 1890 and from 1906 they purchased cashmere from China, but were restricted to purchasing fiber from Beijing and Tianjing until 1978. In 1978 trade was liberalised and Dawson International began buying cashmere from many provinces.

Chiengora wool

Chiengora is a yarn or wool spun from dog hair. The word is a portmanteau of "chien", the French word for dog, and "angora." It is up to 80% warmer than wool and is not elastic.

Often chiengora is blended with wool during the carding process. This blend has some give to it, which is preferable when knitting. It is also often blended with wool in order to create a yarn with less heat insulation.

History of chiengora

Spinning dog hair is not a new art form. Dog hair has been found in yarns dating back from pre-historic Scandinavia, and in textiles from the Navajo Indians of North America. It was the main fiber spun on the Northern American continent before the Spaniards introduced sheep.

In modern times it is rarely used. In general it is only used by hand spinners with pet dogs.

Benefits of chiengora

Chiengora is similar in appearance to Angora and is furry and very soft. Chiengora tends to "fluff" with use, creating a halo effect. It is warm, even in frigid temperatures, and it sheds water well.

Llama wool

The **llama** (*Lama glama*) is a South American camelid, widely used as a pack animal by the Incas and other natives of the Andes mountains. In South America llamas are still used as beasts of burden, as well as for the production of fiber and meat.

The height of a full-grown, full-size llama is between 5.5 feet (1.6 meters) to 6 feet (1.8 meters) tall at the top of the head. They can weigh between approximately 280 pounds (127 kilograms) and 450 pounds (204 kilograms). At birth, a baby llama (called a *cria*) can weigh between 20 pounds (9 kilograms) to 30 pounds (14 kilograms). Llamas are very social animals and like to live with other llamas as a herd. Overall, the fiber produced by a llama is very soft and is naturally lanolin free. Llamas are intelligent and can learn simple tasks after a few repetitions. When using a pack, llamas can carry about 25%–30% of their body weight for several miles.

Llamas appear to have originated from the central plains of North America about 40 million years ago. They migrated to South America and Asia about 3 million years ago. By the end of the last ice age (10,000–12,000 years ago) camelids were extinct in North America. As of 2007, there were over 7 million llamas and alpacas in South America and, due to importation from South America in the late 20th century, there are now over 100,000 llamas and 6,500–7,000 alpacas in the US and Canada.

Classification

Although early writers compared llamas to sheep, their similarity to the camel was soon recognized. They were included in the genus *Camelus* in the *Systema Naturae* of Linnaeus. They were, however, separated by Cuvier in 1800 under the name of *llama* along with the guanaco. Alpacas and vicuñas are in genus *Vicugna*. The genera *Lama* and *Vicugna* are, with the two species of true camels, the sole existing representatives of a very distinct section of the Artiodactyla or even-toed ungulates, called Tylopoda, or "bump-footed," from the peculiar bumps on the soles of their feet. The Tylopoda consists of a single family, the Camelidae, and shares the order Artiodactyla with the Suina (pigs), the Tragulina (chevrotains), the Pecora (ruminants), and the Cetancodonta (hippos and cetaceans, which belong to Artiodactyla from a cladistic if not traditional standpoint). The Tylopoda have more or less affinity to each of the sister taxa, standing in some respects in a middle position between them, sharing some characteristics from each, but in others showing special modifications not found in any of the other taxa.

The 19th century discoveries of a vast and previously unexpected extinct Tertiary fauna of North America, as interpreted by palaeontologists Leidy, Cope, and Marsh, aided understanding of the early history of this family. Llamas were not always confined to South America; abundant llama-like remains were found in Pleistocene deposits in the Rocky Mountains and in Central America. Some of the fossil llamas were much larger than current forms. Some species remained in North America during the last ice ages. North American llamas are categorized as a single extinct genus, *Hemiauchenia*. Llama-like animals would have been a common sight in 25,000 years ago, in modern-day California, Texas, New Mexico, Utah, Missouri, and Florida.

The camelid lineage has a good fossil record. Camel-like animals have been traced from the thoroughly differentiated modern species back through early Miocene forms. Their characteristics became more general, and they lost those that distinguished them as camelids; hence they were classified as ancestral artiodactyls. No fossils of these earlier forms have been found in the Old World, indicating that North America was the original home of camelids, and that Old World camels crossed over via the Bering land bridge. The formation of the Isthmus of Panama three million years ago allowed camelids to spread to South America as part of the Great American Interchange, where they evolved further. Meanwhile, North American camelids died out at the end of the Pleistocene.

Characteristics

The following characteristics apply especially to llamas. Dentition of adults:-incisors 1/3 canines 1/1, premolars 2/2, molars 3/2; total 32. In the upper jaw there is a compressed, sharp, pointed laniariform incisor near the hinder edge of the premaxilla, followed in the male at least by a moderate-sized, pointed, curved spank canine in the anterior part of the maxilla. The isolated canine-like premolar which follows in the camels is not present. The teeth of the molar series which are in contact with each other consist of two very small premolars (the first almost rudimentary) and three broad molars, constructed generally like those of *Camelus*. In the lower jaw, the three incisors are long, spatulate, and procumbent; the outer ones are the smallest. Next to these is a curved, suberect canine, followed after an interval by an isolated minute and often deciduous simple conical premolar; then a contiguous series of one premolar and three molars, which differ from those of *Camelus* in having a small accessory column at the anterior outer edge.

The skull generally resembles that of *Camelus*, the relatively larger brain-cavity and orbits and less developed cranial ridges being due to its smaller size. The nasal bones are shorter and broader, and are joined by the premaxilla.

Vertebrae:

- cervical 7,
- dorsal 12,
- lumbar 7,
- sacral 4,

- caudal 15 to 20.

The ears are rather long and slightly curved inward, characteristically known as "banana" shaped. There is no dorsal hump. Feet are narrow, the toes being more separated than in the camels, each having a distinct plantar pad. The tail is short, and fibre is long, woolly and soft.

In essential structural characteristics, as well as in general appearance and habits, all the animals of this genus very closely resemble each other, so that whether they should be considered as belonging to one, two, or more species is a matter of controversy among naturalists.

The question is complicated by the circumstance of the great majority of individuals which have come under observation being either in a completely or partially domesticated state. Many are also descended from ancestors which have previously been domesticated; a state which tends to produce a certain amount of variation from the original type. The four forms commonly distinguished by the inhabitants of South America are recognized as distinct species, though with difficulties in defining their distinctive characteristics.

These are:

- the llama, *Lama glama* (Linnaeus);
- the alpaca, *Vicugna pacos* (Linnaeus);
- the guanaco (from the Quechua "huanaco"), *Lama guanicoe* (Müller); and
- the vicuña, *Vicugna vicugna* (Molina)

The llama and alpaca are only known in the domestic state, and are variable in size and of many colors, being often white, brown, or piebald. Some are grey or black. The guanaco and vicuña are wild, the former being endangered, and of a nearly uniform light-brown color, passing into white below. They certainly differ from each other, the vicuña being smaller, more slender in its proportions, and having a shorter head than the guanaco. The vicuña lives in herds on the bleak and elevated parts of the mountain range bordering the region of perpetual snow, amidst rocks and precipices, occurring in various suitable localities throughout Peru, in the southern part of Ecuador, and as far south as the middle of Bolivia. Its manners very much resemble those of the chamois of the European Alps; it is as vigilant, wild, and timid. The fiber is extremely delicate and soft, and highly valued for the purposes of weaving, but the quantity which each animal produces is minimal. Alpaca are descended from a wild vicuna ancestor while the domesticated llama is descended from a wild guanaco ancestor, though at this point there has been a considerable amount of hybridization between the two species.

Differentiating characteristics between llamas and alpacas include the llama's larger size and longer head. Alpaca fiber is generally more expensive but not always more valuable. Alpacas tend to have a more consistent color throughout the body. The most apparent visual difference between llamas and camels is that camels have a hump or humps and llamas do not.

Commonly unknown, llamas do not have eyelashes. However, their cousin the alpaca does.

Breeding situations

Harem breeding : Male is left with females most of the year.

Field breeding : A female is turned out into a field with a male llama and left there for some period of time. This is the easiest method in terms of labor, but the least useful in terms of prediction of a likely birth date. An ultrasound test can be performed and together with the exposure dates a better idea when the cria is expected can be determined.

Hand breeding : This is the most efficient method, but requires the most work on the part of the human involved. A male and female llama are put into the same pen and breeding is monitored. They are then separated and rebred every other day until one or the other refuses the breeding. Usually one can get in two breedings using this method, though some studs have routinely refused to breed a female more than once. The separation presumably helps to keep the sperm count high for each breeding and also helps to keep the condition of the female llama's reproductive tract more sound. If the breeding is not successful within two to three weeks, the female is rebred once again.

History

One of the main uses for llamas at the time of the Spanish conquest was to bring down ore from the mines in the mountains. Gregory de Bolivar estimated that in his day, as many as three hundred thousand were employed in the transport of produce from the Potosí mines alone, but since the introduction of horses, mules, and donkeys, the importance of the llama as a beast of burden has greatly diminished.

The Inca deity Urcuchillay was depicted in the form of a multicolored llama. The Moche people frequently placed llamas and llama parts in the burials of important people, as offerings or provisions for the afterlife. The Moche culture of pre-Columbian Peru depicted llamas quite realistically in their ceramics.

Fiber

Llamas also have a fine undercoat which can be used for handicrafts and garments. The coarser outer guard hair is used for rugs, wall-hangings and lead ropes. The fiber comes in many different colors ranging from white, grey, redish brown, brown, dark brown and black.

The individual shafts of the wool can be measured in micrometres. 1 micrometre = 1/1000 millimetre.

A table of the average diameter of some of the finest, natural fibers.

Animal	**Fiber diameter(micrometres)**
Vicuña	6 – 10
Alpaca (Suri)	10 - 15
Muskox (Qiviut)	11 - 13
Merino	12 - 20
Angora Rabbit	13
Cashmere	15 - 19

Yak Down	15 - 19
Camel Down	16 - 25
Guanaco	16 - 18
Llama (Tapada)	20 - 30
Chinchilla	21
Mohair	25 - 45
Alpaca (Huacaya)	27.7
Llama (Ccara)	30 - 40

Technically the fiber is not wool as it is hollow with a structure of diagonal 'walls' which makes it strong, light and good insulation. Wool as a word by itself refers to sheep fiber. However, llama fiber is commonly referred to as llama wool or llama fiber.

In popular culture

The name "llama" has been used for a wide variety of descriptions for people and items alike within general computing and gaming industries. Within some computing environments, the label "llama" has been derogatory indicating a person with little knowledge and new to the environment. Acronyms have been spelled similarly to llama and thus pronounced as llama. The llama has proved to be quite popular among some simulation games. Also the llama has been made popular in many movies as well, such as *Napoleon Dynamite* and the Disney film *The Emperor's New Groove*, as well as in several Monty Python sketches and the opening credits of *Monty Python and The Holy Grail*. The label "llama" is also used in game shows as a term for a contestant who leaves the game show with nothing.

A **guard llama** is a llama used in farming to protect sheep, alpacas, goats or other livestock from coyotes, dogs and other predators. Typically a single gelding (castrated male) is used.

Guarding

Your first line of defense is always good fencing. Guard llamas may defend against predators in many ways. Llamas are instinctively alert and aware of their surroundings, and may draw attention to an intruder by making a startling alarm call. They may walk or run toward an intruder, and chase, paw at, or kick it. Some llamas may herd the animals they are guarding into a tight group or lead them away from danger. Others may stand apart from the group and watch the intruder. Although llamas have been known to kill predators (including coyotes, woodchucks, and muskrats), they should not be considered attack animals. They are generally effective against single intruders only, not packs.

Effectiveness

Most research on the effectiveness of guard llamas has been done with sheep. A 1990 study by Iowa State University found that 80 percent of sheep producers with guard llamas rated them as effective or very effective. The study found that average rates of loss to predators fell from 21 to 7 percent after the introduction of a guard llama. In other studies, over half of guard llamas completely eliminated losses due to predators. Dogs and coyotes have been injured and even killed by llamas.

Selection

Females are the most common guard llamas. Because of their nurturing nature they are almost always effective as guards. Intact or gelded males can be a problem because of their attempts to breed smaller livestock they are guarding. Geldings will still at times attempt to breed livestock even if gelded young. When this happens, they smother or kill the livestock they are guarding. With the llama market being level these days, there is an abundance of females available to guard. Guard llamas should be at least 2 years old before they are expected to protect other livestock. This allows them to mature physically and mentally, as well as develop territorial instincts. A potential guard llama may be introduced to the species they are going to guard at a younger age, but this is not necessary for bonding or effective guarding. It also takes a period of time usually for a guardian llama to settle into their new job.

Llamas placed as guardians often have independent personalities and may not be friendly toward people. However, any guard llama should be trained to accept a halter and lead, and to tolerate basic care. A llama that is aggressive toward humans is not a good candidate for guarding livestock, because it may attempt to protect the flock from its human owners. A guard llama needs to be in generally good health. It must be able to see, hear, forage, and move properly. Llamas that are expected to protect large flocks or herds on rougher terrain may need to be in better physical condition than those used to guard smaller areas.

Care

Llamas require regular care like any other animal. They graze and eat hay along with the animals they protect. Depending on the type and quality of forage, grain may be necessary. They also need llama specific minerals. Llamas are resistant to many diseases that affect other livestock. However, they are susceptible to certain parasites and should be wormed regularly, vaccinated annually, and observed for signs of infection or infestation. Llamas should be sheared each spring to keep them cool in summer, and need shelter from the wind in winter. The only other regular care required is toenail trimming 2–4 times per year.

Alpaca fiber

Alpaca fleece is the natural fiber harvested from an Alpaca. It is light weight or heavy weight, depending on how it is spun, soft, durable, luxurious and silky natural fiber. While similar to sheep's wool, it is warmer, not prickly, and has no lanolin which makes it hypoallergenic. However, this lack of lanolin also prevents Alpaca fiber from being naturally water-repellent. It also has less crimp, thus making it much less elastic. Alpaca fleece is made into various exports, from very simple and inexpensive garments made by the aboriginal communities to sophisticated, industrially made and expensive products such as suits. In the United States, groups of smaller alpaca breeders have banded together to create "fiber co-ops," in order to make the manufacture of alpaca fiber products less expensive.

In physical structure, alpaca fiber is somewhat akin to hair, being very glossy. Alpaca fibre is generally coarser than wool fibre, and alpaca yarns are weaker than most wool yarns. In processing, slivers lack fibre cohesion and single alpaca rovings lack strength. More twisting is necessary to improve strength, but this reduces yarn softness.

Alpaca has generally higher medullated fibre than wool. These are fibres with a central core, which may be continuous, interrupted, or fragmented. The cells of the central core may contract or disappear, forming air pockets which assist insulation. However the higher incidence of medullated fibres in alpaca, compared to wool and mohair, can be an objectionable trait. They can take less dye, standing out in the finished garment, and are weaker. The proportion of medullated fibres is higher in the coarser, unwanted guard hairs: there is less or no medullation in the finer, lower micrometre fibres.

Good quality alpaca fiber is approximately 18 to 25 micrometres in diameter. Whilst breeders report fibre can sell for 2 to 4 dollars per ounce, the world wholesale price for processed pre-spun alpaca "tops" is only between about \$10 to \$24 US/kg (according to quality), i.e. about \$0.28 to \$0.68 per oz. Finer fleeces, ones with a smaller diameter, are preferred, and thus are more expensive. As an alpaca gets older the width of the fibers gets thicker, at between 1 μm and 5 μm per year. This is often caused by over nutrition; if fed too much nutritious food the animal doesn't get fat, instead the fiber gets thicker. Any alpaca fiber exceeding 34μ is classified as llama.

As with all fleece-producing animals, quality varies from animal to animal, and some alpacas produce fiber which is less than ideal. Fiber and conformation are the two most important factors in determining an alpaca's value.

Alpacas come in many shades from a true-blue black through browns-black, browns, fawns, white, silver-greys, and rose-greys.

However, white is predominant, because of selective breeding: the white fiber can be dyed in the largest ranges of colors. In South America, the preference is for white as they generally have better fleece than the darker-colored animals. This is because the dark colors had been all but bred out of the animals. The demand for darker fiber sprung up in the United States and elsewhere, however in order to reintroduce the colors, the quality of the darker fiber has decreased slightly. Breeders have been diligently working on breeding dark animals with exceptional fiber, and much progress has been made in these areas over the last 5-7 years.

The preparing, carding, spinning, weaving and finishing process of alpaca is very similar to the process used for wool.

Types of alpacas

There are two types of alpaca: Huacaya (which produce a dense, soft, crimpy sheep-like fiber), and the mop-like Suri (with silky pencil-like locks, resembling dread-locks but not actually matted fibers). Suris are prized for their longer and silkier fibers, and estimated to make up between 19-20% of the Alpaca population. Since its import into the United States, the number of Suri alpacas has grown substantially and become more color diverse. The Suri is thought to be rarer, possibly because it is less hardy in the harsh South American mountain climates, as its fleece offers less insulation against the cold.

History of alpacas

Alpaca have been bred in South America for thousands of years. Vicuñas were first domesticated and bred into alpacas by the ancient tribes of the Andean highlands of Peru, Chile and Bolivia. In recent years alpacas have also been exported to other countries. In countries such as the USA, Australia and New Zealand breeders shear their animals annually, weigh the fleeces and test them for fineness. With the resulting knowledge they are able to breed heavier-fleeced animals with finer fiber. Fleece weights vary, with the top stud males reaching annual shear weights up to 7 kg total fleece and 3 kg good quality fleece. The discrepancy in weight is because an alpaca has guard hair which is often removed before spinning.

History of fiber industry

The Amerindians of Peru used this fiber in the manufacture of many styles of fabrics for thousands of years before its introduction into Europe as a commercial product. The alpaca was a crucial component of ancient life in the Andes, as it provided not only warm clothing but also meat. Many rituals revolved around the alpaca, perhaps most notably the method of killing it: An alpaca was restrained by one or more people, and a specially-trained person plunged his bare hand into the chest cavity of the animal, ripping out its heart. Today, this ritual is viewed by most as barbaric, but there are still some tribes in the Andes which practice it.

The first European importations of alpaca fiber were into Spain. Spain transferred that fiber to Germany and France. Apparently alpaca yarn was spun in England for the first time about the year 1808 but the fiber was condemned as an unworkable material. In 1830 Benjamin Outram, of Greetland, near Halifax, appears to have reattempted spinning it, and again it was condemned. These two attempts failed due to the style of fabric into which the yarn was woven — a type of camlet. It was not until the introduction of cotton warps into Bradford trade about 1836 that the true qualities of alpaca could be developed into fabric. It is not known where the cotton warp and mohair or alpaca weft plain-cloth came from, but it was this simple and ingenious structure which enabled Titus Salt, then a young Bradford manufacturer, to use alpaca successfully. Bradford is still the great spinning and manufacturing center for alpaca. Large quantities of yarns and cloths are exported annually to the European continent and the US, although the quantities vary with the fashions in vogue. The typical "alpaca-fabric" is a very characteristic "dress-fabric."

Due to the successful manufacture of various alpaca cloths by Sir Titus Salt and other Bradford manufacturers, a great demand for alpaca wool arose which could not be met by the native product.

Apparently, the number of alpacas available never increased appreciably. Unsuccessful attempts were made to acclimatize alpaca in England, on the European continent and in Australia, and even to cross English breeds of sheep with alpaca. There is a cross between alpaca and llama — a true hybrid in every sense — producing a material placed upon the Liverpool market under the name "Huarizo". Crosses between the alpaca and vicuña have not proved satisfactory. Current attempts to cross these two breeds are underway at farms in the US. According to the Alpaca Owners and Breeders Association, alpacas are now being bred in the US, Canada, Australia, New Zealand, UK, and numerous other places.

In recent years, interest in alpaca fiber clothing has surged, perhaps partly because alpaca ranching has a reasonably low impact on the environment. Outdoor sports enthusiasts recognize that its lighter weight and better warmth provides them more comfort in colder weather, so outfitters such as R.E.I. and others are beginning to stock more alpaca products. Using an alpaca and wool blend such as merino is common to the alpaca fibre industry in order to improve processing and the qualities of the final product.

In December 2006 the General Assembly of the United Nations proclaimed 2009 to be the International Year of Natural Fibres, so as to raise the profile of alpaca and other natural fibres.

Sheep and Wool Production

The total world wool production in 1992/93 was 1.664 million tonnes on a clean basis. Production in Australia, the world's largest producer was 561 thousand tonnes clean in 1992/93. New Zealand's production of wool was the lowest level for 30 years at 193 thousand tonnes clean. Estimated production in the Commonwealth of Independent States (C.I.S), the third largest producer in the world, was 170 thousand tonnes clean, while the production estimated for China, the fourth largest producer, was 124 thousand tonnes clean. Production in Argentina was 68 thousand tonnes, while Uruguay's production was 55 thousand tonnes. Production in the United Kingdom was 47 thousand tonnes clean while production in South Africa was 44 thousand tonnes clean.

Table World wool production
(thousand tonnes clean)

Country or Region	1987/88	1988/89	1989/90	1990/91	1991/92	1992/93
Country						
Australia	594	626	725	699	574	561
New Zealand	260	254	233	227	221	193
Soviet Union/CIS	207	215	216	212	188	170
China	105	111	119	120	120	124
Argentina	94	98	89	82	73	68
Uruguay	63	58	65	63	57	55
United Kingdom	42	44	47	48	47	47
South Africa	54	57	59	63	49	44
Turkey	43	43	43	42	40	38
Pakistan	22	23	25	26	27	28
India	16	18	21	21	21	21
United States of America	21	22	22	22	21	20
Spain	15	17	18	19	18	18
Brazil	18	18	18	19	17	17
Morocco	14	14	14	14	14	14

Iran	14	14	14	14	14	14
Romania	18	17	16	15	14	12
France	13	13	13	13	12	12
Mongolia	10	11	11	11	12	12
Chile	11	12	12	12	11	11
Bulgaria	14	13	12	12	11	9
Region						
Other Western Europe	34	36	38	46	44	37
Other Eastern Europe	30	29	29	20	18	16
Other Asia	34	37	36	41	38	38
Other Africa	49	50	51	51	53	53
Other America	18	20	19	18	18	21
World Total	1,813	1,869	1,965	1,928	1,727	1,664
of which:						
Merino	805	846	926	939	804	784
Halfbred	473	487	510	461	408	413
Crossbred	535	536	529	528	515	467

Source : *International Wool Textile Organisation (IWTO)*

p - figures are provisional for the latest season.

Table shows world wool production by major wool producing countries and regions for the period 1987/88 to 1992/93 season. World wool production is broken up into three breed groups: Merino, Halfbred and Crossbred.

Table shows world woolled sheep populations by major producing countries and regions for the period 1986/87 to 1991/92 according to three breed groups. Australian wool is predominantly Merino and Halfbred while New Zealand is the world's largest producer of Crossbred wools. Graph 1.3 illustrates shares of world wool production in 1992/93 by the major producer countries.

Table World woolled sheep population (millions)

Year ending Sept. of second year shown	**Census Month**	**Average 1980-81/ 1984/85**	**1986/87**	**1987/88**	**1988/89**	**1989/90**	**1990/91**	**1991/92**	**1992/93**
Albania	Dec	1.7	1.4	1.4	1.5	1.5	1.6	1.6	1.6
Argentina	June	32.4	28.8	29.2	29.3	28.6	27.6	25.7	
Australia a	Mar	132.9	153.2	156.6	165.2	175.2	166.6	150.7	141.4
Brazil	Dec	18.3	19.7	19.9	20.1	20.0	20.1	20.3	
Bulgaria	Jan	10.7	9.6	8.9	8.6	8.1	7.9	6.7	
Canada	June	0.8	0.7	0.7	0.7	0.8	0.8	0.8	0.8

Chile	June	6.1	5.5	5.6	5.7	5.2	4.7	4.6	
China	Dec	104.8	99.0	102.7	110.6	113.5	112.8	110.9	110.9
Czechoslovakia	Jan	1.0	1.1	1.0	1.1	1.0	0.9	0.9	
Falkland Is.	May	0.7	0.7	0.7	0.7	0.7	0.7	0.7	
France	Dec	12.6	10.8	12.1	11.5	11.2	11.1	10.6	
E. Germany	Dec	2.2	2.6	2.7	2.6	2.6	}3.2	}2.5	
W. Germany	Dec	1.2	1.4	1.4	1.5	1.5	}	}	
Greece	Dec	8.8	11.0	10.8	10.4	10.4	10.2	9.8	
Hungary	Dec	3.1	2.3	2.3	2.2	2.1	1.9	2.3	
India	May	40.0	39.0	39.0	39.0	40.0	40.0	40.0	40.0
Iran	Oct	34.2	45.0	45.0	45.0	45.0	45.0	45.0	
Iraq	Mar	11.8	9.0	9.0	9.5	9.6	7.8	9.0	0
Irish Republic	June	3.5	5.6	6.7	7.7	8.7	8.9	8.9	
Italy	Dec	10.1	11.5	11.5	11.6	11.6	10.8	10.8	
Lesotho	Aug	1.2	1.4	1.4	1.4	1.5	1.5	1.5	
Mongolia	Dec	14.5	13.2	13.2	13.5	14.3	15.1	15.1	
Morocco	Mar	15.2	13.8	13.8	13.8	13.8	13.5	14.0	14.1
Namibia	Aug	5.3	6.2	6.3	6.4	6.5	6.7	6.7	
New Zealand	June	70.0	64.2	64.6	60.6	57.9	55.2	52.5	50.3
Pakistan	May	22.6	26.6	27.5	28.3	29.2	30.2	30.8	
Peru	Dec	14.7	13.1	13.2	12.9	13.0	12.3	12.2	

Poland	June	4.1	4.7	4.4	4.4	4.2	3.2	2.4	
Portugal	Dec	4.4	3.0	3.0	3.2	3.3	3.4	3.4	3.3
Romania	Jan	16.9	(17.0)	16.8	16.2	15.4	14.1	13.5	
South Africa b	Aug	27.3	23.8	24.2	25.9	25.6	24.4	23.2	22.3
Former Soviet Union c	Jan	143.0	142.2	140.8	141.0	138.9	134.6	119.8	117.4
Spain	Dec	16.3	17.9	20.3	23.1	22.7	24.0	24.3	
Turkey	Dec	48.3	48.7	48.8	49.0	48.8	47.5	47.3	
U.K.	June	33.1	38.7	40.9	43.0	43.8	43.6	44.0	
U.S.A.	Jan	12.4	10.6	10.9	10.9	11.4	11.2	10.8	10.2
Uruguay	June	20.6	24.4	24.1	24.9	25.2	25.9	25.6	25.0
Yugoslavia	Jan	7.4	7.8	7.8	7.6	7.6	7.4	7.5	
Other Africa c		113.8	119.0	121.3	123.9	121.8	126.9	125.7	
Other America c		22.9	23.4	23.7	24.3	24.6	24.7	24.9	
Other Asia c		48.0	45.9	45.3	48.2	49.9	50.8	50.2	
Other Western Europe c			5.8	5.5	5.8	5.7	6.1	6.3	6.4
World Total of which:		**1104.7**	**1.129.0**	**1145.3**	**1.172.7**	**1172.7**	**1.165.1**	**1.123.6**	
Soviet Union, China, Eastern Europe		299.8	290.5	291.6	299.0	299.1	292.1	273.1	

Source: International Wool Textile Organisation (IWTO)

a Covers all farms.

b Official series plus fixed estimate for woolled sheep in Bantu areas.

c See note below for country coverage.

Introduction to Mohair

Somewhat confusingly, mohair comes from the angora goat, a species indigenous to Turkey but said to have originated in the mountains of Tibet - although its true origins are subject to speculation. The evidence, however, suggests that angora goats arrived in Turkey by way of Palestine and the desert regions further north. The breed is thought to be at least 3,000 years old, and there is little doubt that for many centuries these unusually frail and beautiful creatures have been highly prized.

The breed takes its name from Angora in Turkey, better known today as Ankara. The hair of the goat - which is white, long and very fine and silky - is called "mohair" which is a corruption of the ancient Arabic word "mukhyar" meaning the "best of selected fleece". It was noted for its softness, brightness and receptiveness to rich dyes.

Today, the best raw material comes from South Africa where there are strict guidelines and standards, and the industry is well organised. The focus in breeding programmes is to obtain goats that produce less kemp fibre.

Despite its historic connections with mohair, Turkish mohair production lags behind the industries in South Africa and Texas. Turkish quality control leaves much to be desired by modern standards and Turkish fleeces are considered too kempy. The amount of mohair obtained per goat is much lower than South African and Texan goats, as animals raised in Turkey are shorn only once a year.

Australia currently contributes 4 per cent and New Zealand only 2 per cent of world mohair production, although the fibre produced is more lustrous than that obtained in more arid climates. It is also reported that genetic breeding programmes in Australasia are resulting in a dramatic reduction in the level of kemp.

Angora goats are not a sturdy breed and thrive best under certain conditions. The angora goat's demands are exact: they thrive at altitude in a warm, dry climate. If exposed to cold or wet, they may die of pneumonia, and this provides a sharp contrast to the much hardier cashmere goat.

The best fleece is produced in high altitude where the animals can forage for a variety of shrubs and aromatic plants. It is important for the goats to lead an active life, constantly on the move.

More attention must be paid to the fragile angora goat than to any other livestock. The amount of mohair that the angora goat produces (unlike the cashmere goat) is mainly dependent on the nutritive value of its feed, rather than upon seasonal or climatic effects, although mohair production obviously falls during drought periods.

Production of Mohair

Mohair accounts for only 0.1 per cent of world natural fibre production. Annual world mohair production amounts to 15 thousand tonnes compared with 15 thousand tonnes of cotton and 1.7 million tonnes of wool. The major producers are Southern Africa (South Africa and Lesotho), followed by the USA (Texas), Turkey, Argentina, Australia and New Zealand. Australian and New Zealand production is still very small as breeders in both countries are trying to develop a breed of angora goat suitable for their particular environment, but it is hoped that production will expand. Small amounts of mohair are also produced in Zimbabwe; by the Navajo Indians in Arizona, USA and Mexico; and on many small angora goat farm operations in the UK, Spain and France. However, the quantities from these sources are negligible compared with the major producing countries.

The latest figures suggest that the total production of mohair in 1993 was 14.95 thousand tonnes.

Table World mohair production by main producing countries (thousand tonnes)

Year	South Africa	Fusa	Fturkey	Fargentina	Flesotho	Faustralia	New Zealand	Miscproduction	Total
1970	4.1	7.8	4.1	1.1	0.9	-	-	-	18.0

1971	4.3	6.8	4.5	1.0	0.9	-	-	-	17.5
1972	3.7	4.6	4.1	1.0	0.8	-	-	-	14.2
1973	3.4	4.5	4.1	1.0	0.6	-	-	-	13.6
1974	3.7	3.8	4.1	1.0.	0.6	-	-	-	13.2
1975	3.8	3.9	3.9	1.0	0.6	-	-	-	13.2
1976	4.1	3.6	4.0	1.0	0.6	-	-	-	13.3
1977	4.5	3.6	4.1	1.0	0.4	-	-	-	13.6
1978	4.9	3.7	4.5	1.0	0.5	-	-	-	14.6
1979	5.4	4.2	4.5	1.0	0.5	-	-	-	15.6
1980	6.1	4.0	4.5	1.0	0.5	-	-	-	16.1
1981	6.9	4.5	4.5	1.0	0.5	-	-	-	17.4
1982	7.6	4.5	4.5	1.0	0.5	-	-	-	18.1
1983	7.5	4.8	4.5	1.3	0.67	-	-	-	18.77
1984	8.1	5.1	3.5	1.0	0.75	0.5	0.05	0.05	19.05
1985	9.1	5.4	3.5	1.1	0.8	0.5	0.07	0.06	20.53
1986	11.0	5.6	3.5	1.25	0.8	0.6	0.14	0.07	22.26
1987	12.0	6.8	3.5	1.5	0.8	0.8	0.25	0.08	25.73
1988	12.5	7.0	3.0	1.5	0.6	1.0	0.35	0.1	25.95
1989	11.6	6.8	2.0	1.2	0.6	1.0	0.5	0.2	23.9
1990	10.8	6.8	1.8	1.0	0.5	1.0	0.5	0.2	22.6
1991	7.6	6.8	1.5	0.8	0.5	0.6	0.4	-	18.2
1992	6.7	6.8	1.2	0.6	0.5	0.5	0.3	-	16.6
1993*	5.8	6.6	1.0	0.5	0.4	0.5	0.15	-	14.95

Source: International Mohair Association

Fibre Characteristics of Mohair

The Mohair fleece of the angora goat is white, smooth and lustrous and has a high tensile strength. The smooth lustrous appearance is caused by the flat, overlapping scales covering the fibre. Although mohair - like wool - consists of the protein keratin, it nevertheless differs from wool in certain respects. The cross-section of wool is slightly elliptical, whereas the very fine mohair fibre is round. The scales are larger than wool and lie flatter, making a smoother fibre surface. The resultant greater reflection of light gives mohair its characteristic lustre.

The value of a fleece is determined by fibre diameter, lustre, softness, freedom or near freedom from kemps, and clean yield. Kemps are short, heavily medullated, coarse fibres. Kemp fibres contain air spaces (medulla) which reduce the effectiveness of dye and in a finished cloth show up as being much lighter in colour than the other fibres. Although in certain end uses kemp can be used to create a special effect, in mohair kemp is undesirable - too much kemp will cause serious problems in spinning and dyeing. The presence of any foreign material in the fleece will affect the quality of the final product and will have to be removed prior to processing, adding to the cost of manufacture. Kemp can be controlled or reduced by genetic selection.

Grading is primarily related to fibre diameter. The age of the goat is probably the most important determinant in the quality and quantity of mohair produced. Fleece production increases from birth and peaks at approximately three or four years of age. The average peak production in South Africa is about 4-5 kg a year for females and 5-6 kg for males. Over the goat's lifespan, the fibre diameter increases from an average of 24 microns for kids up to 46 microns for strong adults. Kids normally produce fibre with a diameter of 24-28 microns at their first shearing, approximately 29-30 at one year, 31-34 at 18 months, and from 36 to 46 microns as adults. Staple length shows little change with age and grows at an average rate of 20-25 mm/month. The first three shearings produce the most sought-after fibre and subsequently the fibre becomes coarser. Kid mohair fetches the highest price but only represents 16 per cent of the clip.

End Uses of Mohair

Mohair is a lustrous fibre with a silky, luxurious appearance but it is also very hard wearing. One of the advantages of this fibre is its tremendous versatility. It can be used both for clothing and furnishing and, within these, its end uses are wide ranging. Individual fibres are strong and make a finished fabric that is non-crushable, soil resistant and does not pill. Mohair has an affinity for dyes and is able to absorb them completely and indelibly. It provides warmth during the winter months but also makes a cool suiting fabric for the humidity of summer, hence its popularity in the Far East, particularly Japan.

Mohair is used to manufacture many products - including knitting yarn for hand or machine knitwear, lightweight suitings, fabric for stoles, scarves and warm blankets and durable upholstery velours. It is often blended with wool for top quality blankets where the mohair content makes the fabric warmer, and at the same time lighter.

About 12 per cent of total mohair production goes into furnishing fabrics, such as upholstery velours and moquettes. Such fabrics are often used for upholstery, particularly in prestige locations - including the first class areas of ships such as the QE2. Mohair upholstery velours are chosen because, although expensive, the fabric is extremely hard wearing and easy to clean while creating a feeling of quality.

One of the challenges facing the mohair industry - particularly the knitting sector - is that the fibre has been imitated by much cheaper acrylic yarns, developed to have similar properties and described as "mohair-like". These products are seen to have done genuine mohair a disservice, adulterating its high quality image.

Introduction to Cashmere

The appeal of cashmere and its unrivalled status as a luxury fibre hinges on three key factors:

- its visual appeal and its extreme softness;
- its scarcity, and
- its image or mystique.

As a luxury fibre, Cashmere commands some of the highest prices in the world of textiles. Only vicuna and musk ox - neither of which is available in anything approaching commercial quantities - achieve higher prices than cashmere. Another key feature of its attraction is its scarcity in comparison with other well known fibres, both natural and man-made. The uncertainty and speculation which surround the production and availability of cashmere have increased its appeal, sometimes sending prices soaring upwards. Also, the geographical remoteness of cashmere production, the dependence on manual skills in the early stages of processing and the fibre's association with exotic peoples following a traditional rural way of life add to the attraction of cashmere fibre in highly industrialised western urban markets.

Cashmere is one of the alternative - and lesser used - spellings of Kashmir, a region, partly in India and partly in Pakistan, in the western Himalayas. This wild and mountainous area gave its name to the fine soft goat's wool, or down, which first came to the West in the form of intricately woven cashmere shawls. In fact the fibre came not from Kashmir but from Tibet where it was gathered by herdsmen from their goats during the animals' spring moult. Cashmere fibre took its name from Kashmir as it was there that it was spun, woven and sold as a finished item. Today in Kashmir and Tibet - where the fibre is still produced and processed by hand - it is known locally as pashmina.

Production of Cashmere

Detailed information on cashmere production, particularly that in China, is not easy to obtain. Accurate figures on national cashmere production are difficult - if not impossible - to acquire. One source of information is the IWS China Branch which estimates that in 1988 there were 67 million goats in China, of which 40 million were producing cashmere.

However, in 1988, world production of cashmere was estimated at about 5,000 tonnes. This compares with an annual availability of wool in the same year of 1.8 million tonnes. World cashmere production is thought to have declined since then.

Estimates of the volume of cashmere produced in China, Mongolia, Iran and Afghanistan vary considerably. An estimate of current world production of cashmere raw material is 4,500 tonnes, which represents a 10 per cent decline from a figure quoted in 1987 of 5,000 tonnes.

China itself produces roughly 60 per cent of the total volume of raw cashmere, with Inner Mongolia contributing up to 70 per cent of this amount. The remainder is thought to be split roughly equally between Mongolia (20-25 per cent) and Iran and Afghanistan (20-25 per cent). Iranian and Afghan cashmere is of a lower quality to the cashmere from China and is spun into yarn principally for woven cloth.

As well as being by far the world's largest supplier, China produces the best quality cashmere. The Chinese claim that the very finest cashmere is produced north of the 40th parallel in Inner Mongolia (north of the Yangtse River).

Fibre Characteristics of Cashmere

Chinese cashmere has a fibre diameter of between 12.5 and 16.0 microns. A diameter of 15.5 microns is considered a standard for cashmere. The longer the fibre the better the quality. The Chinese Commodity Inspection Bureau (CCIB) specifies that the hair should be longer than 32 mm. A fibre length of 46 mm is considered long.

White breeds are most desirable, as white down commands the best prices. White fibre is preferred since it is easiest to dye, producing the purest colours. This is particularly important for cashmere knitwear where soft pastel shades are perennial favourites. Cross-breeding can result in undesirable coloured fibre.

Cashmere produced in Mongolia is generally slightly coarser, between 16.0 and 17.5 microns, but longer. It is used in knitwear and weaving. Cashmere produced in Iran and Afghanistan has a diameter of 17-21 microns and is chiefly used for weaving.

End Uses of Cashmere

The knitwear industry is the largest consumer of cashmere.

Traditionally, Scotland has been the home of the cashmere knitwear industry, producing collections known to prestigious markets all over the world. Many knitwear producers use cashmere from time to time, often using blended yarns. Few specialise in 100 per cent cashmere knitwear, however. The Scottish knitters still constitute one of the biggest markets for cashmere fibre outside China.

The weaving sector is a smaller consumer of cashmere than is the knitwear industry. Nevertheless, significant amounts of cashmere go into accessories (scarves, shawls, stoles), rugs (especially travel rugs and "throws") and cloth for luxury coats, jackets and suits for the menswear trade.

The hair which is removed from the down in the debarring process is used in carpets, underfelts, and interlinings for men's suits and jackets.

Introduction to Camel Hair

The *Camelus* is part of the *Camelidae Gray* family, as is the South American *Auckenidi* (which includes Llama, alpaca, vicuna and guanaco). The *Camelus* is made up of two sub-species: the one humped and the two humped.

The one humped dromedary or Arabian camel is found throughout Africa, Arabia, the Near East and, to a lesser extent, in other areas of Asia. It was imported into the Canary Islands, Spain, the former USSR, and to various Central and South American countries and Australia, where it adapted to local conditions.

The two humped species, known as the Bactrian camel, is bred in Eastern and Central Asia. Surviving in extremely cold climates, the Bactrian camel has been used throughout history by the Tartars, the Mongols and the Chinese. It is not a particularly intelligent animal, having a difficult and capricious character. Both species are used as pack animals, for riding, and sometimes for sport. Camel hair raw material is largely obtained from the double humped Bactrian camel.

The double humped camel is bred mainly in the northern areas of China and Mongolia. In Inner Mongolia (China) breeding areas are concentrated in Alxa Megn prefecture, bordering on the Gobi

Desert and in Mongolia. This is an area where the predominantly desert conditions yield only shrubs, on which camels alone can survive. In Mongolia most camels are raised in the Gobi Desert which makes up the southern third of the country. Over half the camel hair produced by China comes from Inner Mongolia, with the remainder from Xinjiang, Gansu, Qinghai and Ningxia. Some camel hair also comes from Afghanistan and Iran, but this is generally of an inferior quality.

Production of Camel Hair

Details on the production of camel hair are very limited.

In 1987, China recorded national production of 1800 tonnes of camel hair, of which 56% came from Inner Mongolia. In this same period, China exported 546 tonnes.

Fibre Characteristics of Camel Hair

Camel hair, like cashmere, comprises two qualities: relatively coarse outer hair and inner down fibre. The underdown produced by animals living in the hottest desert climates tends to be coarser and sparser than from those living in a more temperate climate. The best fibre is found in Inner Mongolia and Mongolia. The fine down fibre varies from 19-24 microns - about 2 microns coarser than Iranian cashmere - and varies between 2.5 and 12.5 cm in length. This fibre is the result of many years of selective breeding.

The outer hair of the camel is coarse and can be up to 37.5 cm in length with a diameter of 20-120 microns. The average weight of the adult female under hair is 3.5 kg while that of the male is double this amount. The fibres are obtained by shearing and also by collecting the hair during the moulting season.

Like cashmere, only the soft underwool or down hair is used in the production of yarn. When the camel moults it does not lose its hair all at once: first the neck hair falls off, then the mane and finally the body hair. This process takes place over a six to eight week period starting in late spring. The hair covering the humps is not shorn since, without it, the animals would be more susceptible to disease in the summer months. The hair is obtained by a number of methods: by combing, by shearing and simply by collecting the clumps of hair shed naturally during the moulting season.

Varying from reddish to light brown, the hair is sorted according to shade and age of the animal. Baby camel hair, which has an average diameter of about 19 microns and a length of 2.5-12.5 cm, is the finest and softest. It holds greater cachet but it is not currently in greater demand than adult hair as its high premium is beyond its economic value.

During the winter the Bactrian camel produces long, thick hair. A type of mane grows around the neck and a long tuft extends from the muzzle. Long hair is also found on the joints of the elbows, knees and on the limbs. The most common colour is reddish brown, with variants from brown to grey. The white fleece is the most valued but is very rare.

End Uses of Camel Hair

Fabrics containing camel's hair are left in the natural state or dyed to a darker shade of brown. The fine fur fibres are woven or blended with fine wool for overcoating, top coating, sportswear and sports hosiery.

The long hair removed by the dehairing process is used to make felt for the Mongolian yurts or tents and for the herdsmen's winter coats, which are very warm and completely waterproof. It is also used for carpet backing. The strong, springy hair of the camel mane is used for interlinings and the outer hair is traditionally used in bedding as it is said to have properties beneficial to rheumatism and arthritis.

Introduction to the Llama

The South American camelids are in four existing forms: all of which live in the high altitudes of the Andes: the Llama (*Lama glama*), the alpaca (*Lama pacos*), the vicuna (*Vicugna vicugna*), the guanaco or huanaco (*Lama hunchus* or *Lama guanicoe*). These animals can endure the climate of the highest Andean altitudes - from 2,500m up to 5,500m - from tropical areas to sub-polar regions, adapting to the rarefied atmosphere and are able to survive on the tough natural vegetation of the steppes. Like the Afro-Asian camel, they are pseudo-ruminants; unlike true ruminants they have three stomachs rather than four. The Llamas' tendency to kick and spit saliva and the remains of undigested food has been exaggerated; they will only do so if badly irritated.

The Llama and alpaca are domestic animals and have lived with man since time immemorial. Llama males in particular, are used as a beast of burden and have been since the times of the ancient Incas. The alpaca is the species most famous for its fibre production. The vicuna and guanaco, however, are wild animals and have a more aggressive nature. As a result, the fibre from these is seldom harvested.

Today, although less significant than in its heyday, alpaca production remains one of Peru's staple industries. In areas where little or no crops can be cultivated for subsistence, the breeding of animals is the peasants' only means of livelihood. Alpaca is also still in a small way connected to traditional ceremonies of the peasant Indian population. Weaving, although modified following the introduction of the European treadle loom in the early years of the Colombian period, is still carried out in some parts of the Andes in much the same way as it always has been.

Much of Peru's population lives in the Altiplano grasslands of the Andes at altitudes where the perpetual cold inhibits growth of trees and crops. The local Indians' livelihood depends predominantly on animals. The camelids, in contrast, are adapted to the high altitudes where they are able to convert the poor highland forage and bear young. Their soft padded feet, unlike sheep's cloven hooves, do not break the ground.

Production of Alpaca Fibre

It is estimated that there are some four million alpaca in South America, three million *Lama glama* (or domestic Llama) and 125,000 vicuna. The wildest of the Llama group, the guanaco, is in a state of great danger; the entire South American herd is thought to number fewer than 50,000.

During the early 1970's stocks of alpaca and llama were significantly reduced, seriously affecting the livelihoods of the local population. Subsequently efforts have been made, through education and research, to restore the level of the camelid population. But the fibre industry is erratic and highly dependent on world demand. It is also subject to the political and economic events that characterise life in Peru, which has also variously affected the level of the population of these animals.

A further factor affecting the breeding of the animals is the physiognomy of the land itself. The central Andean region - and particularly the vulnerable highlands - have been overgrazed in recent years by sheep and cattle forcing the alpaca back into the more remote and impoverished areas of the Altiplano.

Fibre production has been low in the last two years, dropping by as much as 40 per cent. This has been partly a result of drought.

Alpaca raw material is not exported. All raw material is processed in Peru into products for export, in the form of tops, yarns and knitwear - although some is still used for domestic consumption, for knitwear and woven fabrics, and also for the craft industry for products sold in the tourist trade.

There are about three million alpacas worldwide. Roughly 80 per cent are found in Peru, chiefly in the southern regions of Puno, Arequipa and Cuzco, where the animals have been domesticated since the ninth century. The most important areas in Bolivia are Pacejes, Carangas and Omasuyos.

Fibre Characteristics of Alpaca

There are two types of alpaca; the huacaya, which accounts for 80 per cent of the total, and the suri which makes up the remaining 20 per cent. The fibre obtained from the suri is the longest and most highly prized.

The hair of the alpaca is fine and silky, between 20 and 34 microns in diameter and 8-12 cm in length. The fleece comes in a wide variety of shades, which is a special characteristic of the alpaca. Colours range from pure white and various shades of white - which represent about 80-85 per cent of the clip and have the highest value - to warm fawns, reddish browns and a variety of greys and black.

The animals are shorn. With the encouragement of the research stations and major merchants, shearing is carried out with modern equipment, an advance on the pieces of glass or rusty knives used in the past.

End Uses of Alpaca

The fleece from the alpaca is now the only fibre from the South American camelid used in any quantity for spinning yarns for fashion applications. The primary end use for alpaca is knitwear but it also goes into woven cloth for clothing, accessories - such as shawls and stoles - and rugs.

More recently there have been attempts to promote in Europe blends of alpaca with wool, cotton and silk for both knitwear and woven cloth as a means of widening its use.

Llama hair is used for ropes or sacking and other tough applications, sometimes for export when the price is depressed. The hair from the vicuna and guanaco are almost completely unavailable.

Introduction to the Angora Rabbit

The origin of the angora breed is not known. It is believed to be a mutation which developed among wild rabbits in France in the late 18th century.

Angora rabbit hair is very fine, soft hair used principally in the production of high quality knitwear, although currently there is a trend towards incorporating small quantities of angora in woven cloth. It is also used in blends with other natural fibres for the production of yarns for both knitwear and woven cloth for apparel.

Rabbits are farmed on a highly intensive "factory farm" system or by individual farmers producing on a smaller scale. China has a large number of individual farmers and farming of rabbits is highly labour intensive. Rabbits are bred in hutches with a grid floor, constructed so as to avoid the animals damaging their coats. Because angora rabbits are albino, the hutches have to be kept in semi-darkness. The angora rabbit is generally shorn every three months. The fibre on the French type is sometimes pulled. This method offers the advantage that new hair grows after each harvest, but it is not generally favoured as the animal can suffer from shock. The hair from the female is considered to be better than that of the uncastrated male.

Production of Angora Fibre

China is by far the world's leading producer of angora rabbit hair, contributing about 90 per cent of global production. Chile is the world's second biggest, followed by Argentina. Small amounts of angora are produced in East European countries, including Czechoslovakia and Hungary, and very small amounts in France.

World production figures for angora rabbit hair are difficult to obtain as there is no group or association specific to the fibre. In 1986 world production of angora rabbit hair raw material was estimated at 7,000 - 8,000 tonnes. Chinese production peaked in 1984, reaching 5,000 - 7,000 tonnes. Production has since declined considerably worldwide. One trade estimate puts current annual Chinese production at only 2,000 -3,000 tonnes and Chilean production at 150 - 200 tonnes.

Fibre Characteristics of Angora

The weight of the rabbit is between 2 and 4 kg and its body is covered with an abundance of white silky hairs. The average growth of hair is 0.7 mm per day; the coat grows more rapidly in winter than summer.

Maximum production is obtained with the third and fourth shearing. Some rabbits yield a satisfactory amount until they are eight or even ten years old. Individual yields are in the range of 200 - 500 gm and average about 300 gm. Average length of hair is approximately 36 mm and diameters are between 11 and 13 microns. But there is a large differential between short and long hair. Super grade angora can be as much as 70 mm in length. China specifies that the length of super grade should be a minimum of 38 mm.

End Uses of Angora

The angora fibre has a smooth, silky texture which makes it

difficult to spin, and the fibres tend to slip out of the yarn and shed from the fabric; nevertheless, the fibre is desired for its texture, warmth, light weight and pure white colour, although it is sometimes dyed in pastel shades. Angora rabbit hair is used primarily for items such as sweaters, mittens, baby clothes, and millinery.

There are basically two types of hair. The first, known as the "French type", is longer and spikier and contains guard hair which is hollow and does not take dye. Used in garments, this type of hair shows up as contrasting pale fibre and is often used to create a fine, brushed appearance. The second type of hair is finer and is produced by an angora rabbit with German origins. It is less spiky in character, and can be used to make a softer yarn which is sometimes viewed as an alternative to cashmere. It is used in very fine yarns for high fashion knitwear and thermal underwear. A typical angora blend yarn is a 70/20/10 woollen spun blend of lambs wool/angora/nylon. This would use a shorter fibre from the middle of the range. A high fashion garment, on the other hand, would have a larger percentage of angora made from longer fibre.

Introduction to the Yak

Yak hair is regarded by some as being an acceptable alternative to cashmere, although it is not produced in commercial quantities.

Although a member of the hoofed *bovidae* family, the yak is actually a unique species in itself, weighing 700-800 lb (315-360 kg). It differs from other bovines in several of its characteristics - for instance, its tail is similar to that of the horse but is less mobile, having long, thick/wavy hair.

Production of Yak Hair

Each yak only produces an average of 100 gm of hair a year, which is pulled or combed in the spring moult. The outer hair needs to be separated from the down hair. One estimate reported in *Wool Record* in 1989 put the numbers of domestic yaks on the plateau flanking the Himalayas at 13 million with the majority in China: in Qinghai province, which borders on Tibet; in the adjoining provinces of Sichuan and Gansu; and in the autonomous region of Tibet itself.

The output from Qinghai province was estimated in 1989 at a steady 500 tonnes a year.

Note: The Wool Record is a journal published monthly in the UK and covers a wide range of topics of interest to the world's textile industry.

Fibre Characteristics of Yak Hair

Yak are widely used in the mountainous regions of the Qinghai-Tibet Plateau as beasts of burden and for subsistence through its milk and meat. The hides are used by the local people and in more recent years herdsmen have earned money from selling the hair. The animal, which lives above the snowline, has developed a thick coat of long hair reaching almost to the ground.

Wild yaks tend to have black hair, but domestic yaks have hair which is often piebald, predominantly black and brown with white markings. White hair is inevitably the most precious, as it can be dyed. However, only about 10 per cent of yaks grow white hair. The underhair of the one year old calf has a diameter of 15-17 microns and is 4-5 cm in length. Adult underhair is 18-20 microns in diameter and 3.0-3.5 cm long.

End Use of Yak Hair

The hair is used locally for weaving coverings for huts, blankets, mats and sacks. Strong ropes are made from the tail hair, and felted fabrics from the down hair. Once dehaired, the fine down hair can be made into yarn comparable to cashmere.

Beaver

The largest amphibious member of the rodent family, it is found in Europe and America. Beaver fur, like muskrat, is considered the best for felt hat manufacture. Coming from an animal which weights about 20 kgs, the fur has an average fibre diameter of 15.8 microns. It is soft and silky and lends itself to textile use, but the hair is used only when certain shiny effects are desired in blends. Considerable demand exists for beaver pelts in the fur industry. They are plucked and shorn and because of the light belly portion, they appear to be striped. Canadian beaver has a blue-brown fur fibre while other animals vary in shading from light brown to pale tawny. Today, the pelt is used in fur coats and in trimming fur and fabric garments.

Weasel

There are about 175 species in existence. They have a long cylindrical body and walk on their toes, not on the soles of their feet. Some species are well known, the mink and the ermine for example are ferocious and bloodthirsty animals. Larger than these two is the wolverine which is found in Europe, Asia and America. Other members with valuable fur are the marten and the sable. Still another group includes the badger. The fur industry uses nearly all the species of the weasel family in making coats, trimmings, capes, etc. The textile industry uses large amounts of their fine fibres, but only those with names that will add to the dignity and glamour of the fabrics. The accent is on luxury.

Sheep shearing

Sheep shearing, **shearing** or **clipping** is the process by which the woollen fleece of a sheep is cut off. The person who removes the sheep's wool is called a *shearer*. Typically each adult sheep is shorn once each year (a sheep may be said to have been "shorn" or "sheared", depending upon dialect). The annual shearing most often occurs in a shearing shed, a facility especially designed to process often hundreds and sometimes more than 3,000 sheep per day. Sheep shearing is an essential part of sheep rearing in countries around the world.

History of Sheep Shearing

Up until the 1870s Australian sheep were washed prior to shearing and in the later years this process included the use of hot water and soap. Sheep washing in Australia in the nineteenth century was influenced by the Saxony sheep breeders in Germany who washed their sheep and by the Spanish practice of washing the wool after shearing. There were three main reasons for the custom in Australia:

1. The English manufacturers demanded that Australian woolgrowers provide their fleeces free from vegetable matter, burrs, soil etc.
2. The dirty fleeces were hard to shear and demanded that the metal blades shears be sharpened more often.
3. Wool in Australia was carted by bullock team or horse teams and charged by weight. Washed wool was lighter and did not cost as much.

The practice of washing the wool rather than the sheep evolved from the fact that hotter water could be used to wash the wool, than that used to wash the sheep. When the practice of selling wool in the grease occurred in the 1890's wool washing and scouring became obsolete.

Australia and New Zealand had to discard the old methods of wool harvesting and evolve more efficient systems to cope with the huge numbers of sheep involved. By 1915 most large sheep station sheds in Australia had installed machines, driven by steam or later by internal combustion engines. Shearing tables were invented in the 1950's, but have not proved popular, although some are still used for crutching.

Modern shearing

Today, large flocks of sheep are shorn by professional shearing teams working eight hour days, most often in spring, by machine shearing. These contractor teams will consist of shearers, shed hands and a cook (in the more isolated areas). The shed staff working hours and wages are regulated by industry awards. A working day starts at 7.30 am and the day is divided into 4 "runs" of 2 hours each. "Smoko" breaks of a half hour each are at 9.30am and again at 3pm. The lunch break is taken at 12 midday for one hour. Most shearers are paid on a piece rate, i.e., per sheep. Shearers who "tally" more than 200 sheep per day are known as "gun shearers". Typical mass shearing of sheep today follows a well-defined workflow: remove the wool, throw the fleece onto the wool table, skirt, roll and class the fleece, place it in the appropriate wool bin, press and store the wool until it is transported. In 1984 Australia became the last country in the world to permit the use of wide combs, due to previous Australian Workers Union rules. Although they were rare in sheds, women now take a large part in the shearing industry by working as wool rollers, rouseabouts, wool classers and also shearing, too.

Removing the wool

A sheep is caught by the shearer from the catching pen and taken to his "stand" on the shearing board. It is then shorn using mechanical handpiece. The wool is removed by following an efficient set of movements, devised by Godfrey Bowen in c. 1950, (the *Bowen Technique*) or the *Tally-Hi* method. In 1963 the Tally-hi shearing system was developed by the Australian Wool Corporation and promoted using synchronised shearing demonstrations. Sheep struggle less using the Tally-Hi method, reducing strain on the shearer and there is a saving of about 30 seconds shearing each sheep. The shearer begins by removing the sheep's belly wool, which is separated from the main fleece by a rouseabout, while the sheep is still being shorn. A professional or "gun" shearer typically removes a fleece without badly marking or cutting the sheep in two to three minutes, depending on the size and condition of the sheep, or less than two in elite competitive shearing. The shorn sheep is moved from the board via a chute in the floor, or wall, to a counting out pen, efficiently removing it from the shed.

The CSIRO in Australia has developed a non-mechanical method of shearing sheep using an injected protein that creates a natural break in the wool fibres. After fitting a retaining net to enclose the wool, sheep are injected with the protein. When the net is removed after a week, the fleece has separated and is removed by hand. In some breeds a similar process occurs naturally.

Skirting the fleece

Once the entire fleece has been removed from the sheep, the fleece is *thrown*, clean side down, on to a wool table by a shed hand (commonly known in New Zealand and Australian sheds as a *rouseabout* or *roustie*). The wool table top consists of slats spaced approximately 12 cm apart. This enables short pieces of wool, the *locks* and other debris, to gather beneath the table separately from the fleece. The fleece is then *skirted* by one or more wool rollers to remove the sweat fribs and other less desirable parts of the fleece. The removed pieces largely consist of shorter, seeded, burry or dusty wool etc. which is still useful in the industry. As such they are placed in separate containers and sold along with fleece wool. Other items removed from the fleece on the table, such as faeces, skin fragments or twigs and leaves, are discarded a short distance from the wool table so as not to contaminate the wool and fleece.

Wool classing

Following the skirting of the fleece, it is folded, rolled and examined for its quality in a process known as wool classing, which is performed by a registered and qualified wool classer. Based on its type, the fleece is placed into the relevant wool bin ready to be pressed (mechanically compressed) when there is sufficient wool to make a wool bale.

Shearing devices

Blade shears : Blade shears consist of two blades arranged similarly to scissors except that the hinge is at the end farthest from the point (not in the middle). The cutting edges pass each other as the shearer squeezes them together and shear the wool close to the animal's skin. Blade shears are still used today but in a more limited way. Blade shears leave some wool on a sheep and this is more suitable for cold climates where the sheep needs some protection from the elements. For those areas where no powered-machinery is available blade shears are the only option. Blades are more commonly used to shear stud rams.

Machine shears : Machine shears, known as handpieces, operate in a similar manner to human hair-clippers in that a power-driven toothed blade, known as a cutter, is driven back and forth over the surface of a comb and the wool is cut from the animal. The original machine shears were powered by a fixed hand-crank linked to the handpiece by a shaft with only two universal joints, which afforded a very limited range of motion. Later models have more joints to allow easier positioning of the handpiece on the animal. Electric motors on each stand have generally replaced overhead gear for driving the handpieces. The jointed arm is replaced in many instances with a flexible shaft. Smaller motors allowed the production of shears in which the motor is in the handpiece; these are generally not used by professional shearers as the weight and heat of the motor becomes bothersome with long use.

Preparing Sheep for Shearing : It is very important that wool looks its best when displayed for sale. To ensure this occurs, the following preparation measures should be practised.

- Shearing is stressful for sheep. To reduce this, move sheep from the grazing area to the shearing shed quietly and always handle sheep with care.
- Dag the sheep at least seven days before shearing.
- In between dagging and shearing, keep sheep on a maintenance ration - unless the ewes have lambs at foot.
- Avoid penstain. Penstain is caused by sheep defecating on each other through being penned too closely. Penstain will affect the way the wool takes up dye. To avoid this fault, hold the sheep in a bare paddock for at least six hours and preferably 12 hours before penning up for shearing. The shearing yards should be well drained. If a mob is pen stained, don't mix it with a clean mob. Never tightly pen sheep with full stomachs into yards.
- If there are sheep with different lengths of wool, breeds or sex, draft them into separate mobs.
- If possible, keep sheep out of undeveloped and/or seedy areas in the weeks before shearing.
- Never shear wet sheep, as wool which is shorn wet will discolour very quickly.

Once the sheep are shorn it is important to provide plenty of feed and shelter, particularly if shearing is close to lambing. Shorn sheep feel the cold and shelter from wind and rain is essential for the first week after shearing.

Preparing Angora Goats for Shearing : The preparation of the mohair clip for sale is the culmination of the year's work. The fibre shorn reflects the "total environment" experienced throughout the growing period. The total environment includes the physical environment and the husbandry practices of the grower.

As shearing approaches every effort should be made to protect the long mohair from the possibility of contamination from vegetable matter, dust and pigmented fibres. Such contamination will depreciate the value of the mohair. It is advisable to keep the goats in clean, well grassed, open paddocks to avoid contamination from dust and vegetable matter. Avoid crowding or yarding the mohair producing goats with coloured grade animals. The pigmented fibre from such animals often contaminates otherwise clean mohair.

Some animals particularly crossbreeds, shed hair in the spring. It is good management to shear before this occurs. As the fleece sheds it also mats and these fleeces must be kept separate to prevent their discounted price affecting other fleeces.

Fineness of fibre to a large extent is determined by the age of the animals, and therefore it is advisable to draft the herd into age groups, eg. kids - 2-4 tooths and mature aged goats, prior to shearing. The various age groups should then be shorn separately.

Preparing Alpaca for Shearing : Alpacas should be grouped separately before shearing for sex, age (ie. adult, Tui and Cria) and coat colour, each grouped being shorn separately. The recommended shearing sequence is from white, grey, brown, black and lastly, mixed colours to minimise colour contamination. Likewise, the Cria should be shorn first, then the Tui and followed by the adult.

Apart from this separation prior to shearing, Alpacas do not require any other pre-shearing preparation.

Preparing Cashmere, Camels and Yaks for Shearing : There appears to be no special pre-shearing treatment required for these animals prior to harvesting the fibre owing to the manner in which the fibre is harvested.

Preparing Angora Rabbits for Shearing : Provided the angora rabbits have been kept in clean cages and on proper rations, there should be no special pre-shearing treatment of the rabbit. However, if some animals are dirty or their fur is contaminated with vegetable matter, these should be kept separate to prevent cross contamination of the faulty fibre with clean fault free fibre.

Pashmina

Pashmina refers to a type of fine cashmere wool and the textiles made from it. The name comes from *Pashmineh*, made from Persian *pashm* ("wool"). The wool comes from changthangi or pashmina goat, which is a special breed of goat indigenous to high altitudes of the Himalayas. Pashmina shawls are hand spun, woven and embroidered in Kashmir, and made from fine cashmere fiber.

History

The fiber is also known as *pashm* or *pashmina* for its use in the handmade shawls of Kashmir. The woolen shawls made from wool in Kashmir find written mention between 3rd century BC and the 11th century AD. However, the founder of the cashmere wool industry is traditionally held to be the 15th century ruler of Kashmir, *Zayn-ul-Abidin*, who introduced weavers from Central Asia.

Cashmere shawls have been manufactured in Nepal and Kashmir for thousands of years. The test for a quality pashmina is warmth and feel.

Production

The goat sheds its winter coat every spring. One goat sheds approximately 3-8 ounces of the fiber. See also Cashmere wool

To meet the demand, the goats are now commercially reared in the Gobi Desert area in Inner and Outer Mongolia. The region has identical harsh weather conditions to those of the Himalayan region, and is thereby apt for the goats to grow this inner wool, but also has acres of grazing ground to produce cashmere economically and commercially. During spring (the molting season) the goats shed this inner wool, which regrows in winter. The inner wool is collected and spun to produce cashmere. The quality of the cashmere produced in the Gobi Desert is just as high as that produced in the Himalayas, while the costs are less.

Pashmina Products

Pashmina accessories are available in a range of sizes, from "scarf" (12" x 60") to "wrap" or "stole" (28" x 80") to full sized shawl (36" x 80"). Pure pashmina is a rather gauzy, open weave, as the fiber cannot tolerate high tension. The most popular pashmina fabric is a 70% pashmina/30% silk blend, but 50/50 is also common. The 70/30 is tightly woven, has an elegant sheen and drapes nicely, but is still quite soft and light-weight.

A pashmina shawl can range in cost from as little as about $35US for a pure pashmina scarf or up to thousands of $US for a super high-quality pure pashmina shawl. They are known for their softness and warmth. A craze for pashminas in the mid-1990s resulted in high demand for pashminas, so demand exceeded supply.

When pashmina shawls rose into fashion prominence during the mid-'90s, they were marketed dubiously. Cashmere used for pashmina shawls was claimed to be of a superior quality, which was really due to the enhanced sheen and softness that the fabric (cashmere blended with silk) had. In the consuming markets, pashmina shawls were redefined as a shawl/wrap with cashmere and silk, notwithstanding the actual meaning of pashmina. Some shawls marketed as pashmina shawls contain wool, while other unscrupulous companies marketed the man-made fabric viscose as "pashmina" with deceptive marketing statements such as "authentic viscose pashmina".

6

History of Wool

Wool is one of our most versatile fibers. It is such a complex blend of properties that modern science still cannot duplicate it or create a synthetic clone. Textiles created from wool range from thick and coarse carpets to extremely fine merino underwear suitable for a baby's skin.

Because they live in extreme climates, sheep have managed to evolve a highly sophisticated covering for themselves. Their fleece, with its tightly crimped fibers, contains many air pockets that insulate them, and us, from the cold. In scientific terms, the outer cells of the fiber repel water while the inner cells absorb moisture, which is the property that makes wool such a warm material. Wool is highly absorbent, capable of retaining up to 25 percent of its weight in moisture. It becomes warmer to the wearer as it slowly absorbs moisture from the air. Also wool is slow to feel damp, and it dries as slowly, and so does not chill the wearer by drying too fast as cotton and silk can. Wool is naturally flame-retardant, owing to its tendency to retain moisture. Also its absorbency makes wool ideal for dyes-wool takes on richer, deeper, purer colors than vegetable fibers can.

Today, the main areas of wool production are Australia, New Zealand, South Africa and Argentina.

History

It is, alas, uncertain who was responsible for looking at a sheep and realizing that its fleece might be useful. The earliest dated surviving textile, found in a Danish bog, originates from 1500 BC, while the oldest fine woolen fabric dates to the fifth century BC and was found in a Greek colony.

Eventually, sheep destined for mutton roasts and sheep destined for fine woven rugs were distinguished, as good eating does not necessarily mean good quality wool. Early wild species of sheep had long, coarse outer hair protecting their short fleece undercoats. It is this underlayer that is desirable for textile use and has been selectively bred into modern sheep.

A somewhat ghastly fact is that "wool grease" a fatty substance which covers the fibers sheared off the sheep, is purified and the resulting lanolin is mixed into cosmetics.

Like human civilizations, the story of wool begins in Asia Minor during the Stone Age about 10.000 years ago. Primitive man living in the Mesopotamianlain used sheep for three basic needs: food, clothing shelter. Later on man learned to spin and weave. As primitive as they must have been, woolens became part of the riches of Babylon. The warmth of wool clothing and the mobility of sheep allowed mankind to spread civilization far beyond the warm climate of Mesopotamia.

Between 3000 and 1000 BC the Persians, Greeks and Romans distributed sheep and wool throughout Europe as they continued to improve breeds. The Romans took sheep everywhere as they built their Empire in what is now Spain, North Africa, and on the British Isles. They established a wool plant in what is now Winchester, England as early as 50 AD. The Saracens, nomadic people of the Syrian-Arabian deserts, conquered Spain in the eighth century and established a widespread wool export trade with North Africa, Greece, Egypt and Constantinople.

During the twelfth century, weaving in Florence, Genoa and Venice was stimulated by the Norman conquest of Greece. The conquerors sent about a hundred Greek weavers to Palermo as slaves, and their extraordinary work was copied at once by Italian weavers. Back in Spain a thriving wool trade helped finance the voyages of Columbus and the Conquistadors. Guarding its wealth closely, Spain levied the death penalty or anyone exporting sheep until 1786. That year King Louis XVI imported 386 Merino ewes to cross with sheep on his estate at Rambouillet in Northern France. The resulting Rambouillet breed is highly desirable today because of its fine and long-staple wool.

Just like Spain, England froze its borders to raw wool exports. In 1377 England's King Edward III, "the royal wool merchant," stopped woven-goods imports and the domestic weaving of foreign wools and invited Flemish weavers fleeing the Spanish invasion to settle in England where the industry thrived.

By 1660 wool textile exports were two-thirds of England's foreign commerce. Columbus brought sheep to Cuba and Santo Domingo on his second voyage in 1493, and Cortez took their descendants along when he explored what is now Mexico and the southwestern United States, Navajo and other Southwest Indian tribes are famous yet today for their magnificent woolen rugs and colorful wall hangings. Although pelts may have been worn in Britain as early as the late Bronze Age (3000 BC) England's "empire of wool" peaked during the 1509-47 reign of King Henry VIII. He seized the flocks of the monasteries and redistributed then to court favorites. This caused unemployed shepherds to be sent to prison for non-payment of debts and was one of the unfair treatments which incited immigration to America. Despite the fact that England tried to discourage a wool industry in North America, a few smuggled sheep had multiplied to about 1,000,000 by 1665. Massachusetts even passed a law requiring young people to spin and weave.

Traditions and folklore grew with the industry. Spinning duties fell to the eldest unmarried daughter in the family, hence the term spinster. Spun yarn was wound on a reel (weasel) which made a popping sound when a given yardage was reached. Pop goes the weasel! King George III of England made wool trading in the Colonies a punishable offense. Cutting off the offender's right hand was the chosen punishment. This policy, together with other oppressive actions including the Stamp Act of 1765, which required that revenue stamps be affixed to all printed matter and official documents in the Colonies, helped incite the Revolutionary War. Despite the King's attempts to disrupt wool commerce, the wool industry flourished in America. Both Washington and Jefferson maintained flocks of sheep; both were inaugurated in woolen suits. New inventions like the spinning jenny, combing machines and water-powered looms, expanded the industry rapidly. Sheep moved West with civilization and beyond; at the turn of the 18th century small flocks in the hands of pioneers started the industry in Australia, New Zealand and South Africa.

Sheep are as versatile as the fiber they produce. All parts are used; they provide tender, delicious meat…and wool is a renewable resource. Sheep thrive in all 50 states and most nations of the world, often in rough, barren ranges, or high altitudes where other animals cannot survive because of lack of vegetation. Sheep can survive and flourish on weeds and vegetation other animals will not eat, therefore they convert to protein a group of natural resources, which would otherwise be wasted. Sheep fill our food and fiber needs today just as they have for centuries.

Introduction

Astronauts wear wool for comfort in the confines of their spacecraft. Wool protects mountain climbers and polar scientists, the sailors who navigate single-handed the oceans of the world and men 'who strike oil in Alaska. It is a fibre fit for heroes-and for more ordinary folk. As modern as moonflight, and as ancient as the hills. The story of wool began long ago, before recorded history when primitive man first clothed himself in the woolly skins, of the wild sheep he killed for food. He had discovered a durable fabric which gave him what nothing else could give: protection alike from heat and cold, from wind and rain. A versatile fabric which kept him cool in the heat of the day and warm in the cold of the night, which could absorb moisture without feeling wet.

Man can never match it. No other material, natural or man-made, has all its qualities. But man can refine and improve wool. He has done so by selective breeding of sheep and by incorporating in wool fabrics such qualities as shrink resistance, durable creasing and pleating, mothproofing, shower-proofing and stain-proofing.

Science and technology have kept wool in the forefront of fabrics, adapting to modern needs without impairing its virtues. Wool is part of Britain's history and heritage, more so than any other commodity ever produced in these islands. It was woven into cloth here in the Bronze Age which began about 1900 BC. But in historical terms this is comparatively recent. Elsewhere in the world, primitive man had domesticated the sheep in 10 000 BC.

Wool in History

The sheep could be milked (and still is, in many parts of the world). When it shed its fleece this could be spun and woven into cloth. Man soon realized that to kill the sheep for its meat alone was a waste of food and material. And once he became a shepherd with the help of his friend the dog- probably the only animal to be domesticated before the sheep- he soon devised a method of producing clothing from the fleece.

Even before 10,000 BC wool cloth was being spun and woven by the tribes of northern Europe. To spin it they took the wool in one hand and drew it out, twisting it into a thread with the fingers of the other hand. The result was a thick uneven yarn. Later, a crude spindle was developed by fitting a stone or clay ring to the end of a short wooden stick. The ring acted as a flywheel and enabled the drawn-out yarn to be wound on to the spindle. This method of spinning was used for thousands of years and is still used by peasant communities in various parts of the world.

Weaving is the criss-crossing of threads of wool to make cloth. The first loom consisted of a beam from which lengths of yarn (warps) were hung and weighted at the lower end by stones. The 'weft' yarn was threaded to and fro across the suspended 'warp' yarns in an over-and-under action, like darning a sock. As with spinning, this system was used for thousands of years.

There were now two implements: one for spinning, and one for weaving spun wool. The loom was the first to be improved. The warp threads were laid out horizontally across a frame instead of being suspended vertically from a beam. Then alternate warp threads were tied to sticks (healds) which were raised and lowered in turn. Through the aperture formed between the two sets of warp threads the wooden needle carrying the weft thread could be passed in one motion, thus avoiding the laborious 'over- and- under' action. Later still, the needle was hollowed out into a 'shuttle' so that it could carry within itself a reel of weft thread, as it does in a modern loom.

By the time the Romans invaded these islands in 55 BC the Britons had developed a wool industry and this was encouraged by their new masters. Roman emperors cherished British woollen cloth-'so fine it was comparable with a spider's web'.

The Saxon invasions in the fifth century nearly destroyed the industry. But it is known that in the eighth century Britain was exporting woollen fabrics to the Continent and after the arrival of the Norman conquerors in 1066 the industry expanded. By the twelfth century wool was becoming England's greatest national asset. Cloth making was widespread, particularly in the large towns of southern and eastern England nearest the Continent.

But the greatest wealth came from exports of raw wool. Kings and their ministers keenly appreciated the revenue that resulted from exports and export taxes-and for the power it gave to the king who could grant, or withdraw, concessions to the wool towns and to the industry.

Weaver's trade guilds, powerful for hundreds of years, were founded to guarantee good work by experienced craftsmen. The 'Staple' was established-a mart where raw wool for sale abroad had, by law, to be sent and where the export tax levied by the king could be collected. The Staple was originally located in Flanders-an important textile manufacturing area-but was later withdrawn to England where a number of ports became Staple towns.

The peak of production was reached in the thirteenth century. Then the wool trade declined for a long period because of political strife. In 1331 King Edward III encouraged Flemish master weavers to settle here. They and their descendants were to play a part in the final ascendancy of English cloth.

The export trade in raw wool recovered and the first half of the fourteenth century was a time of prosperity for English wool farmers But it was overshadowed by the long war with France (export taxes on wool were one of the principal means of financing the war) and by bubonic plague (the Black Death) which in 1349 decimated the population. In many villages as much as three-quarters of the population died. This led to an increase of the sheep flocks, for there were not enough people left to cultivate the land for arable crops.

'Sheep have eaten up our meadows and our downs, Our corn, our wood, whole villages and towns.' ...wrote a poet at the time.

Despite setbacks, raw wool exporting expanded, and so also did manufacturing of wool fabrics. This was becoming both specialized and localized. The West Country had three advantages-extensive sheep pastures, a supply of soft water for washing, scouring and dyeing, and water-power to drive milling machinery. Similarly, the Pennine districts of Yorkshire and Lancashire had soft water, and water power from steeply graded streams.

In East Anglia there was soft water but no hills or fast-running streams to provide power for 'fulling' mills. Fulling, or milling, is a shrinking process which makes the fabric firmer and its surface more compact. Instead, East Anglia used the long, fine wool from its native sheep breeds to produce a cloth which did not require the fulling process. This was the type of cloth we today call 'worsted'- after the Norfolk village of Worstead. For four hundred years East Anglia dominated the worsted trade, with skills inherited from the Flemish settlers of 1331. Cloth from English looms quickly achieved an international reputation. From being primarily a raw wool exporter, England became in the fourteenth and fifteenth centuries a manufacturer and exporter of cloth. At the end of the fifteenth century England was 'largely a nation of sheep farmers and cloth manufacturers'. The next two centuries saw continued expansion of the industry despite conflicts at home and abroad.

In the sixteenth century Huguenot weavers, persecuted in France, sought refuge here and brought their skills with them. England began to surpass Flanders in woollen manufacture which, by the end of the seventeenth century, comprised two-thirds of the value of her exports.

Radical changes lay ahead, in the geographical disposition of the industry, in labour use and in manufacturing processes. By 1770 output of worsted from the West Riding of Yorkshire equaled that of East Anglia. The cloth manufacturing 'conurbation' began to take shape-Leeds, Bradford, Halifax, Huddersfield, Wakefield.

The Industrial Revolution of 1750-1850 caused upheaval. It ushered in new inventions stemming from the Lancashire cotton industry, to mechanize and speed dramatically the processes of spinning and weaving. Manufacturing methods, unchanged Since the revival of the trade in the fourteenth century, were now superseded. Mechanization had been opposed in the past and it was again. In the Luddite riots of 1812 equipment was destroyed by organized bands of workers, who feared they would lose employment.

But machinery won the day. The older industries in such areas as East Anglia, where opposition had been most bitter, declined and never recovered. They were overtaken by Yorkshire where machinery was more readily accepted. The younger industry jumped ahead and never lost its lead, supported by abundant supplies of cheap coal to generate steam and, later, electrical power. Other important manufacturing centres developed in Scotland, famed for its tweeds; and in the West Country which specialized in production of high quality woven carpets.

Growing wool

There are nearly one thousand million sheep in the world and some thirty million are in the United Kingdom. But these figures tell only part of the story, for the influence of British breeds is world wide.

Sheep can adapt themselves to an extraordinarily wide range of environment. In this country there are about forty recognized breeds, suited to the varieties of climate, soil, herbage and terrain encountered here. Some of the more famous of these breeds form the foundation stock in all those parts of the world where sheep are significant-notably in the great grassland countries of the southern hemisphere.

So the skill of British breeders has had widespread effect, stemming from the eighteenth century when the great Robert Bakewell of Leicestershire pioneered new techniques not only in breeding but also in husbandry. Bakewell's work represented a great leap forward, but he was not the first in the field. It has taken centuries of selective breeding and cross-breeding to produce the sheep of today.

A first requirement was to improve the natural coat of the sheep. This contained not only wool fibre but hair and 'kemp'-a fibre unsuitable for dyeing. These had to be eliminated or minimized by selective breeding. Early sheep also grew both coarse and fine wool in the same fleece so here was another requirement-to breed sheep which grew one or the other kind of wool. British breeds produce mostly coarser quality wool-not to be regarded as inferior to fine wool but merely different. It is ideally suited for certain products such as carpets, tweeds and knitting yarns.

Our flocks may be roughly grouped into three main groups-short-wool and down; longwool and lustre; and mountain and hill. Hill and lowland sheep are complementary to each other. The flocks on hill and upland grazing (comprising three-quarters of the land mass of the United Kingdom) provide lambs for fattening in the lowlands and crossbred ewes to produce future fat lambs.

Meat production from fat lambs is more important to the lowland man but the hill producer can derive as much as a third of his income from wool. Breeders strive for the ideal-the animal that will meet the requirements both of the butcher and the wool manufacturer; one that will rear more lambs and have the milk to feed them.

Despite the demands of the meat trade, British wool today is better than it has ever been. Between one-third and one-half of the home wool clip is exported annually. There are about 90,000 wool producers in the United Kingdom producing nearly 40 million kg of fleece wool a year. All of it is sold through our own, producer-operated British Wool Marketing Board which can carry out for the individual sheep farmer what he is unable to do by himself-programmes and policies for fleece improvement, better presentation, organized marketing and wool sales promotion.

The Board arranges for the wool sent in by farmers to be graded into national grades suited to particular manufacturing requirements. Farmers are paid according to the grading of their wool, which the Board sells to the trade at auction. It is a tribute both to the excellence of our wool and to the efficiency of our marketing system that British wool regularly commands the highest price in the world for its type.

Wool manufacturing

The two main types of woven cloth are woollen and worsted. The yarn for woollen cloth is usually made from short-fibred wool and during processing the individual fibres are thoroughly intermingled. In the worsted process, which uses the longer-fibred wools, the individual fibres are separated and laid approximately parallel to each other.

Weaving is not involved in all types of wool fabrics. Knitted fabrics are made with a single, continuous yarn (instead of two-warp and weft-as in woven cloth) and the threads are interlooped. Felt-probably the first-ever wool fabric-is made by intermingling the wool fibres and compressing them into a sheet.

Because of the different purposes for which it is suited, raw wool must first be graded and sorted-long wools for the worsted trade, short wools mainly for the woollen trade, the tough springy wools for carpets and so on. Whatever the final requirement, wool must next be cleaned in a soap solution to remove its natural grease and dirt. Machinery is then employed to extract seeds and burrs and other foreign matter which may remain.

Short wools are passed through 'scribbling' and 'carding' machinery which produces 'slivers'-thin continuous ropes of wool-which in the spinning process are drawn out and twisted into yarn. The longer wools for worsted production are put through a 'comb' which produces ropes of parallel fibres known as 'tops'. These are then drawn out into finer and finer threads in the spinning process.

Before weaving, the yarn which is to form coloured cloths is dyed. Then on to the modern, high-speed power loom which can create an inexhaustible variety of weaves and patterns. There are a number of finishing processes. Woollen cloth must be shrunk and felted by being passed through rollers and soap solutions. The nap (surface) is raised by passing the cloth through drums set with the heads of teasels (spiky plants) and then cropped by a kind of mowing machine. Raising and cropping are not needed for worsted where the aim is to display, rather than conceal, the weave pattern. Despite the development of complex and elaborate machinery, the basic principles of spinning and weaving machines are the same as when primitive man first twisted raw wool into yarn between his fingers and then, on his crude loom, wove it into cloth.

The medieval loom remained substantially unchanged until, in 1733, John Kay invented his 'flying shuttle' which was driven mechanically to and fro across the warp without having to be thrown 'by the weaver. Automatic spinning followed. Sir Richard ArkWright's roller-spinning machine was horse-driven at first and later, by water power, when it became known as the waterframe. In 1767 James Hargreaves, a Blackburn weaver, invented the spinning jenny, with multiple spindles mounted side by side. With this development one spinner could operate as many as 120 spindles at a time.

Samuel Crompton's spinning mule combined the principles of both the water-frame and the jenny. The spindles were no longer stationary but mounted on a movable carriage. This travelled away from the rollers, drawing-out the wool threads which at the same time were twisted by the spindles to impart strength—a principle still used on spindles all over the world.

Other machines were invented for preparing wool for weaving. They included the combing machine, used in the worsted industry for combing the long wool fibres parallel and removing the short fibres; and the carding machine for opening out, blending and straightening the wool fibres after cleansing.

Eventually power was applied to all the mechanical processes. By the beginning of the nineteenth century Watt's steam engine was in the Yorkshire mills. By the end of the century hand loom weaving had practically disappeared. The way now lay ahead for continuing development-added refinements, improved quality and increased speed of manufacture which have made wool today, as in the past, the most valued fabric in the world.

The Modern Wonders of Wool

Wool is the most versatile textile fibre known to man and its uses are legion. Apart from its inherent natural virtues, it is also a really ,easy care' fabric thanks to modern scientific achievements. Similarly, wool garments and fabrics can now be permanently shower-proofed and stain-proofed. Shower-proofing, while allowing the fabric to shed water from the outside of the garment also allows the skin to breathe and exude water vapour. It is achieved through the use of waxes and silicones applied by various methods to the wool.

Stain-proofing does not make it impossible for grease and other stains to mark the fabric. But the stains can be removed with a household solvent cleaner without leaving the usual unsightly ring.

All-wool fabrics can now be durably creased or pleated-men's wool trousers and women's wool slacks and skirts can keep smart creases in all conditions of wear and weather. Another process enables wool fabrics to be washed and drip-dried with only the minimum of ironing.

7

Introduction of Silk

Silk is a natural protein fiber, some forms of which can be woven into textiles. The best-known type of silk is obtained from cocoons made by the larvae of the mulberry silkworm *Bombyx mori* reared in captivity (sericulture). The shimmering appearance for which silk is prized comes from the fibers' triangular prism-like structure which allows silk cloth to refract incoming light at different angles.

Wild silks are produced by caterpillars other than the mulberry silkworm and can be artificially cultivated. A variety of wild silks have been known and used in China, South Asia, and Europe since early times, but the scale of production was always far smaller than that of cultivated silks. They differ from the domesticated varieties in color and texture, and cocoons gathered in the wild usually have been damaged by the emerging moth before the cocoons are gathered, so the silk thread that makes up the cocoon has been torn into shorter lengths. Commercially reared silkworm pupae are killed by dipping them in boiling water before the adult moths emerge, or by piercing them with a needle, allowing the whole cocoon to be unraveled as one continuous thread. This permits a much stronger cloth to be woven from the silk. Wild silks also tend to be more difficult to dye than silk from the cultivated silkworm.

Silks are produced by several other insects, but only the silk of moth caterpillars has been used for textile manufacture. There has been some research into other silks, which differ at the molecular level. Silks are mainly produced by the larvae of insects that complete metamorphosis, but also by some adult insects such as webspinners. Silk production is especially common in the Hymenoptera (bees, wasps, and ants), and is sometimes used in nest construction. Other types of arthropod produce silk, most notably various arachnids such as spiders.

Wild silks

Wild silks have been known and used in many countries from early times, although the scale of production is far smaller than that from cultivated silkworms.

Wild silk should not be confused with the very rare sea silk which is produced from the fibres or byssus produced by the seashell *Pinna noblis* and related species.

Commercially reared silkworms *Bombyx mori* (Linnaeus, 1758), are normally killed before the pupae emerge either by pricking them with a needle or dipping the cocoons into boiling water, thus allowing the whole cocoon to be unravelled as one continuous thread. This allows a much finer cloth to be woven from the silk.

There are more than 500 species of wild silkworms in the world although only a few are used to produce cloth. They usually produce a tougher and rougher silk than that from domesticated *Bombyx mori* silkworms. Wild silks are usually harvested after the moths have left the cocoons, cutting the threads in the process so that there is not one long thread as with domesticated silkworms.

Wild silks tend to be more difficult to bleach and dye than silk from *Bombyx mori*, but most have naturally attractive colours, particularly the rich golden sheen of the silk produced by the muga silkworm from Assam and is often known as Assam silk. The eri silkworm from India feeds on the leaves of the castor plant. It is the only completely domesticated silkworm other than *Bombyx mori*. The silk is extremely durable, but cannot be easily reeled off the cocoon and is thus spun like cotton or wool.

History of wild silk

Wild silk threads have been found and identified from two Indus River sites, Harappa and Chanhu-daro, dating to c. 2450-2000 BCE. This is roughly the same period as the earliest evidence of silk use in China, previously thought to have had the oldest silk industry in the world. The specimens of threads from Harappa appear on Scanning electron microscope analysis to be from two different species of silk moth, *Antheraea mylitta* and *A. assamensis*, while the silk from Chanhu-daro may be from a *Philosamia* species, (Eri silk), and this silk appears to have been reeled.

Wild silks were also in use in China from early times. Moreover, the Chinese were aware of their use in the Roman Empire and apparently imported goods made from them by the time of the Han dynasty.

There are significant indications in the literature that wild silks were in use in Persia and in Greece by the late 5th century BCE, apparently referred to as "Amorgina" or "Amorgian garments" in Greece.

Pliny the Elder, in the 1st century CE, obviously had some knowledge of how wild silkworms' cocoons were produced and utilised on the island of Cos, even though his account included some fanciful ideas.

List of some wild silk moths and their silk

- *Bombyx mandarina* (Moore). Possible wild form of *B. mori*.
- *Bombyx sinensis* - from China. Prolific but small cocoons.
- *Antheraea pernyi* (Guénerin-Méneville, 1855). - the Chinese Tussah Moth. The colour and quality of the silk depends on the climate and soil.
- *Antherraea yamamai* (Guénerin-Méneville, 1861). - The "tensan" silk moth. Has been cultivated in Japan for more than 1000 years. It is a naturally white silk but does not dye well,

though it is very strong and elastic. It is now very rare and expensive.

- *Antheraea mylitta* (Drury, 1773). - The "tasar" silkworm.,
- *Antheraea assamensis* (Helfer, 1837). - From Assam. Has a beautiful glossy golden hue which improves with age and washing. Is never bleached or dyed and is stain resistant. Was reserved for the exclusive use of royal families in Assam for 600 years.
- *Samia cynthia* (Drury, 1773). - The Ailanthus Silkmoth
- *Anisota senatoria* (J. E. Smith, 1797). - "Orange-tipped oakworm moth." North American moth.
- *Philosamia rinini*. - The eri silkmoth from Assam. Produces a white silk which resembles wool mixed with cotton, but feels like silk.
- *Gonometa postica* Walker. - From the Kalahari region.
- *Gonometa rufobrunnae* Aurivillius. - Feeds on the Mopane tree in southern Africa
- *Attacus cynthia*. - Somewhat domesticated silkworm from China. Introduced into North America.
- *Telea polyphemus*. - Has the most potential of any North American silkworms.
- *Hyalphora cercropia*. - North American. Quality of the silk depends on food source.
- *Calasoma promethia*. - North American
- *Automeris io*. - (Fabricius, 1775). North American moth.

Artificial silk or (as the term is used in the textile industry) **art silk** is a synthetic manufactured fiber which resembles silk but costs less to produce. Frequently, *art silk* is just a synonym for rayon.

The first successful artificial silks were developed in the 1890s of cellulose (wood) fiber and marketed as *art silk* or *viscose*, a trade name for a specific manufacture. In 1924, the name of the fiber was officially changed in the U.S. to rayon, although the term *viscose* continued to be used in Europe and currently the material is referred to in the industry as *viscose rayon*.

Although not sold under the name *art silk* initially, nylon, the first synthetic fiber, was developed in the United States in the late

1930s and used as a replacement for Japanese silk during World War II. Its properties are far superior to rayon and silk when wet, and so it was used for many military applications, such as parachutes. Although nylon is not a good substitute for silk fabric in appearance, it is a successful functional alternative. Du Pont's original plans for nylon to become a cheaper and superior replacement for silk stockings were soon realized, then redirected for military use just two years later during World War II. Nylon became a prominent industrial fiber in a short time frame, permanently replacing silk in many applications. In the present day, imitation silk may be made with rayon, mercerized cotton, polyester, a blend of these materials, or a blend of rayon and silk.

Despite a generally similar appearance, genuine silk has unique features that are distinguishable from artificial silk. However, in some cases art silk can be passed off as real silk to unwary buyers. A number of tests are available to determine a fabric's basic fiber makeup, some of which can be performed prior to purchasing a fabric whose composition is questionable.

Assam silk

Assam silk denotes the three major types of indigenous wild silks produced in Assam—golden Muga, white Pat and warm Eri silk. The Assam silk industry, now centered in Sualkuchi, is a labor intensive industry.

Muga silk

Muga silk is the product of the silkworm *Antherea assamensis* endemic to Assam. The pupa of these silkworms feed on *som* (*Machilus bombycina*) and *sualu* (*Litsaea polyantha*) leaves. The silk produced is known for its glossy fine texture and durability. Due to its low porosity the Muga yarn cannot be bleached nor dyed and its natural golden color is retained. This silk can be hand-washed with its luster increasing after every wash. Very often the silk outlives its owner. Assam has received a Geographical indication for the production of Muga.

Pat Silk

Pat silk is produced by silkworms which feed on mulberry leaves. It is usually brilliant white or off-white in colour. It's cloth can dry in shadow.

Eri Silk

Eri silk is made by "Philosamia ricini" which feed on leaves of Castor oil plant. It is also known as Endi or Errandi silk. Due to the fact that manufacturing process of Eri allows the pupae to develop into adults and only the open ended cocoons are used for turning into silk , it is also popularly known as non-violent silk. This silk is soft and warm and is popular as shawls and quilts.

Thai Silk

Thai silk is produced from the cocoons of Thai silkworms. Thai weavers, mainly from the Khorat Plateau in the northeast region of Thailand, raise the caterpillars on a steady diet of mulberry leaves. Khorat is the center of the silk industry in Thailand and a steady supplier of rose Thai silk for many generations.

Today, Thai silk is considered to be one of the finest fabrics in the world, a product of a unique manufacturing process and bearing unique patterns and colours.

Origin of Thai Silk

After silk originated in ancient China where the practice of weaving silk began around 2,640 BCE, Chinese merchants spread the use of silk to different regions throughout Asia through trade. Some accounts indicate that archaeologists found the first fibers of silk in Thailand to be over 3,000 years old in the ruins of Baan Chiang, the site is considered by many to be Southeast Asia's oldest civilization.

Weaving

The production of Thai silk begins with the Bombyx mori, a

small silk worm that comes from the eggs of a silk moth. For their first year, these worms feast on the leaves of mulberry trees before building a cocoon from their spittle.

In its original cocoon form, raw silk is bumpy and irregular. Thai weavers separate the completed cocoons from the mulberry bush and soak them in a vat of hot boiling water to separate the silk thread from the caterpillar inside the cocoon.

The Bombyx mori usually produces silk thread of varying colors, ranging from light gold to very light green, with lengths varying from 500 to 1,500 yards per cocoon.

A single thread filament is too thin to use on its own so Thai women combine many threads to produce a thicker, usable fiber. They do this by hand-reeling the threads onto a wooden spindle to produce a uniform strand of raw silk. The process is a tedious one as it takes nearly 40 hours to produce a half kilogram of Thai silk.

Many local operations use a reeling machine for this task, but the majority of most silk thread is still hand-reeled. The difference is that hand-reeled threads produce three grades of silk: two fine grades that are ideal for lightweight fabrics and a thick grade for heavier material.

The silk fabric is then soaked in hot water and bleached before dyeing in order to remove the natural yellow coloring of Thai silk yarn. To do this, skeins of silk thread are immersed in large tubs of hydrogen peroxide. Once washed and dried, the silk is then woven using a traditional hand operated loom.

Identification

Since traditional Thai silk is hand woven, each silk fabric is unique and cannot be duplicated through commercial means. In contrast, artificial silk is machine woven, which means that every part of the fabric is identical and has the same color.

In addition, Thai silk has a unique luster, with a sheen that has two unique blends: one color for the warp and another for the weft. Color changes as you hold the Thai silk fabric at varying angles against light.

Moreover, Thai silk smells like hair when burned, a testament to the natural fiber that comes from the silk worm, which is similar to the fiber of human hair and fingernails. If you move the flame, Thai silk immediately stops burning. On the other hand, artificial silk smells like plastic when burned.

In terms of price, Thai silk is usually 10 times more expensive than artificial silk.

Types of Thai Silk

To be able to identify genuine Thai silk easily, Thailand's Agriculture Ministry uses a peacock emblem to authenticate Thai silk and protect it from imitations. The peacock emblem serves as a guarantee of quality and it comes in four different colors based on specific silk types and production process. These are the following:

Gold peacock : Indicates the premium Royal Thai Silk, a product of native Thai silkworm breeds and traditional hand-made production.

Silver peacock : Indicates Classic Thai Silk, developed from specific silkworm breeds and hand-made production.

Blue peacock : Indicates Thai Silk, a product of pure silk threads and with no specific production method (allows chemical dyes).

Green peacock : Indicates Thai Silk Blend, a product of silk blended with other fabrics and with no specific production method.

Exports : In 2006, $14,540,325 worth of silk was exported from Thailand. The predominant markets are the U.S., and the U.K. Silk fabric accounts for about half of the silk exported from Thailand (the rest being raw silk, yarn, cocoons, and silk waste). However, Thai producers remain only a small contributor to the global trade in silk

Spider Silk

Spider silk, also known as **gossamer**, is a protein fiber spun by spiders. Spiders use their silk to make webs or other structures, which function as nets to catch other creatures, or as nests or cocoons for protection for their offspring. They can also suspend themselves using their silk, normally for the same reasons.

Many small spiders use silk threads for ballooning, the scientific term for the dynamic kiting spiderlings (mostly) use for dispersal. They extrude several threads into the air and let themselves become carried away with upward winds. Although most rides will end a few meters later, it seems to be a common way for spiders to invade islands. Many sailors have reported that spiders have been caught in their ship's sails, even when far from land.

In some cases, spiders may even use silk as a source of food. Methods have been developed to silk a spider forcibly.

Properties

Spider silk is a remarkably strong material. Its tensile strength is superior to that of high-grade steel, and as strong as Aramid filaments, such as Twaron or Kevlar. Most importantly, spider silk is extremely lightweight: a strand of spider silk long enough to circle the earth would weigh less than 16 ounces (450 g).

Spider silk is also especially ductile, able to stretch up to 40% of its length without breaking. This gives it a very high toughness (or work to fracture), which "equals that of commercial polyaramid (aromatic nylon) filaments, which themselves are benchmarks of modern polymer fiber technology."

Composition

Spider silk is composed of complex protein molecules. This, coupled with the isolation stemming from the spider's predatory nature, has made the study and replication of the substance quite challenging. Because of the repetitive nature of the DNA encoding the silk protein, it is difficult to determine its sequence and to date, silk-producing sequences have only been decoded for fourteen species of spider. In 2005, independent researchers in the University of Wyoming (Tian and Lewis), University of the Pacific (Hu and Vierra), the University of California at Riverside (Garb and Hayashi) and Shinshu University (Zhao and Nakagaki) have uncovered the molecular structure of the gene for the protein that various female spider species use to make their silken egg cases.

Although different species of spider, and different types of silk, have different protein sequences, a general trend in spider silk structure is a sequence of amino acids (usually alternating glycine and alanine, or alanine alone) that self-assemble into a beta sheet conformation. These "Ala rich" blocks are separated by segments of amino acids with bulky side-groups. The beta sheets stack to form crystals, whereas the other segments form amorphous domains. It is the interplay between the hard crystalline segments, and the elastic semi amorphous regions, that gives spider silk its extraordinary properties.

Various compounds other than protein are used to enhance the fiber's properties. Pyrrolidine has hygroscopic properties and helps to keep the thread moist. It occurs in especially high concentration in glue threads. Potassium hydrogen phosphate releases protons in aqueous solution, resulting in a pH of about 4, making the silk acidic and thus protecting it from fungus and bacteria that would otherwise digest the protein. Potassium nitrate is believed to prevent the protein from denaturating in the acidic milieu.

Types of silk

Many species of spider have different glands to produce silk for different jobs, such as housing and web construction, defense, capturing and detaining prey, or mobility. Thus, different specialized silks have evolved with material properties optimized for their intended use. For example, *Argiope argentata* has five different types of silk, each for a different purpose:

- **dragline silk**: Used for the web's outer rim and spokes, as well as for the lifeline. As strong as steel, but much tougher.
- **capture-spiral silk**: Used for the capturing lines of the web. Sticky, extremely stretchy and tough.
- **tubiliform silk**: Used for protective egg sacs. Stiffest silk.
- **aciniform silk**: Used to wrap and secure freshly captured prey. Two to three times as tough as the other silks, including dragline.
- **minor-ampullate silk**: Used for temporary scaffolding during web construction

Biosynthesis

The unspun silk dope is pulled through silk glands, resulting in a transition from stored gel to final solid fiber.

The gland's visible, or external, part is termed the spinneret. Depending on the species, spiders will have anything from two to eight spinnerets, usually in pairs. The beginning of the gland is rich in thiol and tyrosine groups. After this beginning process, the ampulla acts as a storage sac for the newly created fibers. From there, the spinning duct effectively removes water from the fiber and through fine channels also assists in its formation. Lipid secretions take place just at the end of the distal limb of the duct, and proceeds to the valve. The valve is believed to assist in rejoining broken fibers, acting much in the way of a helical pump.

The spinneret apparatus of a *Araneus diadematus* consists of the following glands:

- 500 Glandulae piriformes for attachment points
- 4 Glandulae ampullaceae for the web frame
- about 300 Glandulae aciniformes for the outer lining of egg sacs, and for ensnaring prey
- 4 Glandulae tubuliformes for egg sac silk
- 4 Glandulae aggregatae for glue
- 2 Glandulae coronatae for the thread of glue lines

Human uses

Peasants in the southern Carpathian Mountains used to cut up tubes built by *Atypus* and cover wounds with the inner lining. It reportedly facilitated healing, and even connected with the skin. This is believed to be due to antiseptic properties of spider silk.

Some fishermen in the indo-pacific ocean use the web of *Nephila* to catch small fish. The silk of *Nephila clavipes* has recently been used to help in mammalian neuronal regeneration. At one time, it was common to use spider silk as a thread for crosshairs in telescopes, microscopes and similar optical instruments.

Artificial spider silk

Spider silk is as strong as many industrial fibers. There is commercial interest in duplicating spider silk artificially, since spiders use renewable materials as input and operate at room temperature, low pressures and using water as a solvent. However, it has been difficult to find a commercially viable process to mass-produce spider silk.

It is generally considered not possible to use spiders themselves to produce industrially useful quantities of spider silk, due to the difficulties of managing large quantities of small spiders (although this was tried with *Nephila* silk). Compared with silkworms, spiders are aggressive and will eat one another, making it inadvisable to keep many spiders together in the same space. Other efforts have involved extracting the spider silk gene and using other organisms to produce the required amount of spider silk. In 2000, Nexia, a Canadian biotechnology company, was successful in producing spider silk protein in transgenic goats. These goats carried the gene for spider silk protein, and the milk produced by the goats contained significant quantities of the protein (1-2 grams of silk proteins / litre of milk). Attempts to spin the protein into a fiber similar to natural spider silk resulted in fibers with tenacities of 2-3 grams/denier.

Extrusion of protein fibers in an aqueous environment is known as 'wet-spinning'. This process has so far produced silk fi*bers of diameters ranging from 10-60 μm, compared to diameters of 2.5-4 μm seen in natural spider silk.*

The spider's highly sophisticated spinneret is instrumental in organizing the silk proteins into strong domains. Specifically, the spinneret creates a gradient of protein concentration, pH, and pressure, which drive the protein solution through liquid crystalline phase transitions, ultimately generating the required silk structure (which is a mixture of crystalline and amorphous biopolymer regions). Replicating these complex conditions in lab environment has proved difficult. Nexia used wet spinning and squeezed the silk protein solution through small extrusion holes in order to simulate the behavior of the spinneret, but this has so far not been sufficient to replicate the exact properties of the native spider silk.

Sericulture

Sericulture, or **silk farming**, is the rearing of silkworms for the production of raw silk. Although there are several commercial species of silkworms, *Bombyx mori* is the most widely used and intensively studied. According to Confucian texts, the discovery of silk production from *B. mori* about 2700 BC, although archaeological records point to silk cultivation as early as the Yangshao period (5000 - 10,000 BC). Later it was introduced in Europe, the Mediterranean and other Asiatic countries. Sericulture has become one of the most important cottage industries in a number of countries like China, Republic of Korea, Japan, India, Brazil, Russia, Italy and France. Today, China and Japan are the two main producers, together manufacturing more than 50% of the world production each year.

Production

Silkworm larvae are fed cut-up mulberry leaves, and, after the fourth molt, climb a twig placed near them and spin their silken cocoons. The silk is a continuous-filament fiber consisting of fibroin protein, secreted from two salivary glands in the head of each larva, and a gum called sericin, which cements the two filaments together. The sericin is removed by placing the cocoons in hot water, which frees silk filaments and readies them for reeling. The immersion in hot water also kills the silkworm larvae.

Single filaments are combined to form yarn. This yarn is drawn under tension through several guides and wound onto reels. Finally, the yarn is dried, and the now raw silk is packed according to quality.

Stages of production

The stages of production are as follows:

1. The silk moth lays eggs.
2. When the eggs hatch, the caterpillars are fed mulberry leaves.
3. When the silkworms are about 25 days old, they are 10,000 times heavier than when they hatched. They are now ready to spin a silk cocoon.

4. The silk is produced in two glands in the silkworm's head and then forced out in liquid form through openings called spinnerets.
5. The silk solidifies when it comes in contact with the air.
6. The silkworm spins approximately 1 mile of filament and completely encloses itself in a cocoon in about two or three days but due to quality restrictions, the amount of usable silk in each cocoon is small. As a result, 5500 silkworms are required to produce 1 kg of silk.
7. The silkworm then metamorphoses and changes into a moth; however, the silkworm is usually killed with heat before it reaches this stage. The silkworms are killed, because once they reach the moth stage, the moth secretes a fluid to dissolve the silk so it can emerge from the cocoon. This damages the cocoon and the silk then becomes a lower quality. Some silkworms are allowed to live to be used for breeding.
8. The silk is obtained from the undamaged cocoons by brushing the cocoon to find the outside ends of the filament.
9. The silk filaments are then wound on a reel. One cocoon contains approximately 1,000 yards of silk filament. The silk at this stage is known as raw silk. Just one thread consists of 48 individual silk filaments. This could lead to at least 4000 yards in a whole cocoon.
10. A yarn can now be formed by combining several threads of silk.

Silk waste

Silk waste includes all kinds of raw silk which may be unwindable, and therefore unsuited to the throwing process. Before the introduction of machinery applicable to the spinning of silk waste, the refuse from cocoon reeling, and also from silk winding, which is now used in producing spun silk fabrics, was nearly all destroyed as being useless, with the exception of that which could be hand-combed and spun by means of the distaff and spinning wheel, a method which is still practised by some of the peasantry in India and other countries in Asia.

Sources

The supply of waste silk is drawn from the following sources:

- The silkworm, when commencing to spin, emits a dull, lustreless and uneven thread with which it suspends itself to the twigs and leaves of the tree upon which it has been feeding, or to the straws provided for it by attendants in the worm-rearing establishments: this first thread is unreelable, and, moreover, is often mixed with straw, leaves and twigs.
- The outside layers of the true cocoon are too coarse and uneven for reeling; and as the worm completes its task of spinning, the thread becomes finer and weaker, so both the extreme outside and inside layers are put aside as waste.
- Pierced cocoons, that is, those from which the moth of the silkworm has emerged-and damaged cocoons.
- During the process of reeling from the cocoon the silk often breaks; and both in finding a true and reelable thread, and in joining the ends, there is unavoidable waste.
- Raw silk skeins are often re-reeled; and in this process part has to be discarded: this being known to the trade as gum-waste. The same term — gum-waste — is applied to " waste " made in the various processes of silk throwing; but manufacturers using threads known technically as organzines and trams call the surplus "manufacturer's waste."

Processing

A silk "throwster" receives his silk in skein form, the thread of which consists of a number of silk fibres wound together to make a certain diameter or size, the separate fibre having actually been spun by the worm. The silk-waste spinner receives his silk in quite a different form: merely the raw material, packed in bales of various sizes and weights, the contents being a much-tangled mass of all lengths of fibre mixed with much foreign matter, such as ends of straws, twigs, leaves, worms and chrysalis. It is the spinner's business to straighten out these fibres, with the aid of machinery, and then to so join them that they become a thread, which is known as spun silk.

There are two distinct kinds of spun silk: one called *schappe* and the other *spun silk* or *discharged spun silk*. All silk produced by the worm is composed of two substances: fibroin, the true thread, and sericin, which is a hard, gummy coating of the fibroin. Before the silk can be manipulated by machinery to any advantage, the gum coating must be removed, really dissolved and washed away - and according to the method used in achieving this operation the result is either a schappe or a discharged yarn. The former, schapping, is the French, Italian and Swiss method, from which the silk when finished is neither so bright nor so good in colour as the discharged silk; but it is very clean and level, and for some purposes absolutely essential, as, for instance, in velvet manufacture.

Velvet

Velvet is a type of tufted fabric in which the cut threads are very evenly distributed, with a short dense pile, giving it a distinct feel.

Composition

Velvet can be made from many different kinds of fibers. It is woven on a special loom that weaves two pieces of velvet at the same time. The two pieces are then cut apart and the two lengths of fabric are wound on separate take-up rolls. Velvet was very expensive and was among the luxury goods. Velvet is difficult to clean, but in modern times, dry cleaning is used.

Velvet is made, ideally, from silk. Cotton can also be used, though this often results in a slightly less luxurious fabric. More recently, synthetic velvets have been developed, mostly polyester, nylon, viscose, acetate and mixtures of different synthetics, or synthetics and natural fibers (eg. viscose and silk). Velvet can also be made from fibers such as linen, mohair and wool. A cloth made by the Kuba people of the Democratic Republic of Congo from raffia is often referred to as “Kuba velvet”. A small percentage of lycra is used sometimes to give stretch.

History of Velvet

The art of velvet-weaving probably originated in ancient Kashmir around the beginning of the fourteenth century.

King Richard II of England directed in his will that his body should be clothed *in velveto* in 1399.

The earliest sources of European artistic velvets were Lucca, Genoa, Florence and Venice, and Genoa continues to send out rich velvet textures. Somewhat later the art was taken up by Flemish weavers, and in the 16th century Bruges attained a reputation for velvets which was not inferior to that of the great Italian cities.

Silk in India

Silk in India as elsewhere, is an item of luxury. For more than four thousand years, this cloth produced from the cocoons of caterpillers, has been associated with crowned heads and riches throughout the different ages. As a designer once said "Silk does for the body what diamonds do for the hand".

It was China that was the birth place of the production of raw silk and silk weaving. The fiber produced was so treasured that it became a measure of currency and reward. The imperial courts in China even established factories to weave silk fabrics for ceremonial use and for gifts to foreign powers.

China was exporting silk to countries as far away as Rome, as early as the second century B.C. China remained the major silk producer for centuries. The Chinese silk industry was highly organized and supported by the state which made silk into a veritable cash crop. Thus, silk became the industrial wealth for China, and its production was a jealously guarded secret so that it could retain its monopoly of the trade. Imperial law decreed a death penalty for those who disclosed the secrets.

Through The Silk Route: The Sassanids, realizing the trade potential in silk, became intermediaries for the Chinese silk trade. Sassanids were mainly responsible for the export of silk from the East to the West. Silk both woven and raw was traded to Mediterranean countries via Parthia and Syria, from where it made its way to Europe. Silk fabrics, influenced by Chinese prototypes, were also woven in the Sassanian weaving centers of Khurasan, Kashan and other places. Soon these silk brocades became known for their beauty and were exported to other countries.

Sassasian polychrome silk became very famous during this time. These were the most sought-after gifts, presented to Emperors by envoys and traders. Khurasan was renowned for this fabric. These later would also influence Indian silk brocades.

Sericulture was taken outside China in the second century A.D. According to legend, it was smuggled out by a Chinese princess who was married to a prince of Khotan in Central Asia. She hid the silk cocoons in her coiffure and took them to her adopted country. The introduction of sericulture made Khotan prosperous.

Over the centuries, silk weaving also became popular in other areas as well, particularly in Persia, and in the region around Syr Darya and Oxus rivers. Khotan, Bulkh, Kashgar, Bukhara, Khurasan, Kashan, Damascus and Gujarat in India became the known centers.

Persia especially was a dominant center early on and Persian weavers were in great demand. Damascus became particularly famous for making such highly coveted patterned satin fabrics known as "Damask satin". Later Timur, the central Asian conqueror, deported the weavers of the damask cloth from Damascus to Samarkand and Bukhara.

One such group of Persian Zoroastrians migrated from Southern Persia (Faristan) to Saurashtra in Gujarat and are called *Parsis* in India. The weavers among them must have introduced to this region the Sassanian motifs and techniques popular in their own country. Since they came from the area around the Persian Gulf, known for its high quality pearls, their beautiful embroided borders use real pearls. The influence of these Gujarati fabrics greatly affected the rest of the Indian brocade industry as far as technique and design were concerned – migrating Gujarati weavers were responsible for setting up many new weaving centers and re-enforcing existing ones.

Silk Goes to India

The brocade weaving centers of India developed in and around the capitals of kingdoms or holy cities because of the demand for expensive fabrics by the royal families and temples. Rich merchants of the trading ports or centers also contributed to the development of these fabrics. Besides trading in the finished product, they advanced money to the weavers to buy the costly raw materials that is silk and zari. The ancient centers were situated mainly in Gujarat, Malwa and South India. In the North, Delhi, Lahore, Agra, Fatehpur Sikri, Veranasi, Mau, Azamgarh and Murshidabad were the main centers for brocade weaving. Northern weavers were greatly influenced by the brocade weaving regions of eastern and southern Persia, Turkey, Central Asia and Afghanistan.

Gujrati masons and weavers were brought by Akbar to the royal workshops in AD 1572. Akbar took an active role in overseeing the royal textile workshops, established at Lahore, Agra and Fatehpur Sikri where skilled weavers from different backgrounds worked. Expert weavers from those distant lands worked with the local weavers and imparted their skills to the locals. This intermingling of creative techniques brought about a great transformation in the textile weaving industry. The exquisite latifa (beautiful) buti was the outcome of the fusion of Persian and Indian designs. Brocades produced at the royal workshops of other well known Muslim centers in Syria, Egypt, Turkey and Persia were also exported to India. Under the Mughals, sericulture and silk-weaving received special encouragement and silk cloth produced in the Punjab came to be prized throughout the world. Lahore and Multan developed into major centers of silk industry. The tradition continues.

Silk Weaving in Pakistan – A Contemporary Review

The Pakistan territory has been known for excellent silk weaves since the first millennium B.C. In the Middle Ages, silk, gold and silver brocades made there found ready buyers in Europe, the Middle East, and even China.

After independence a large number of weavers migrated from Delhi and Banaras and set up workshops in Lahore, Karachi and

Khairpur. However, after the partition of Bangladesh in 1971, the majority of the weavers have deserted Khairpur. One of the reasons for this was language and state rights that were promised but never given to those who migrated. Thus the people belonging to Indian origin migrated to Karachi and settled in Orangi town which has emerged as one of the biggest Khadi hand loom markets of Pakistan. These weavers have continued to weave these brocades in traditional patterns, but have also introduced newer ones and while taking inspiration from the old Mughal silks.

The weavers' raw material, the silk cocoons are imported from China and the silk thread is cultivated at these centers only. They mostly fulfill demands of cities like Lahore and Karachi (the two major cities) and to some extent of Hyderabad. The major centers continue to be Orangi town and Shershah where the fabrics are woven on a large scale.

Silk brocades, texturally, are divided mainly into two groups.

- *Kinkhwab*
- *Pot-thans*

Kinkhwab (Brocade)

Kam means little or scarcely. *Khwab* means a dream and it's said that even with such a name 'Its beauty, splendor and elegance can be hardly dreamt of'. *Kinkhwabs* are heavy fabrics or several layers of warp threads with an elaborate all-over pattern of extra weft, which may be of silk, gold and / or silver threads or combinations. There may be three to seven layers of warp threads. (*Tipara* means three layers and *Chaupara* means four layers to *Satpara* meaning seven layers). Kin means golden in Chinese. Its specialty is in profusely using the gold and silver thread in a manner that sometimes leaves the silk background hardly visible.

When the figure work is in silver threads with a background of gold threads it is called 'Tashi Kinkhwab'. This is a variety of 'Kinkhwab' which has a ground worked with an extra warp of gold [badla (flat wire) zari] and the pattern created with an extra weft of silver badla zari or vice versa. A satin weave is very often used, resulting in a smooth ground for the fabric. The heavy fabric appears to be in layers, as the warp ends are crammed drawing three, four and up to seven ends per dent for the Tipara, Chaupara up to Satpara respectively.

Zari is generally of two types Badla and Kala batto. Badla Zari was made of flattened gold or silver wire with the ancient method of making zari from pure metal without any core thread. This accounted for its peculiar stiffness. Sometimes cracks would develop in the metal during the process of weaving which resulted in the loss of its natural luster and smoothness. Therefore weaving with Badla Zari was difficult and required great skill. Often a touch of Badla was given to floral motives to enhance the beauty. This type of zari has mostly gone out of favor amongst the contemporary weavers and they mostly depend on polyester or pure silk as a substitute.

Origin : Kinkhwab was originally an elegant, heavy silk fabric with a floral or figured pattern known most for its butis and jals woven with silk as the warp and tilla as the weft, produced in China and Japan. Tilla in the earlier times was known as kasab. It was a combination of silver and tamba (copper) which was coated with a veneer of gold and silver.

Silk brocade of Banaras, Ahmedabad and Surat were well known in the seventeenth century. While Banaras continues to be a center of production of Silk Brocades, Ahmedabad and Surat have practically nothing to show today. On the other hand, Silk Brocade weaving has gained ground in the South of India.

Kinkhwabs have also been known as 'Kimkhabs', 'Kamkhwabs', 'Kincobs', 'Zar-baft' (Gold Woven), zartari, zarkashi, mushaiar.

Pot-thans

These are called *Katan* (a thread prepared by twisting a different number of silk filaments) brocades. Pot-thans are lighter in textures (lower thread count) than Kinkhwabs but closely woven in silk and all or certain portions of the pattern are in gold or silver zaris. These fabrics are mostly used for making expensive garments and saris. Very often the satin ground weave is particularly used for garments fabrics. These fabrics are characterized by their jals which are normally made out of silk & tilla.

Bafta poth : Bafta refers to a kind of wool that was used in Kashmiri shawls. When this wool became thinner and began to be used in a fabric, the fabric was known to be bafta-poth.

Mashru : The cloth was distinguished by its butis woven in circular shapes that gave an impression of ashrafis (gold coins). The ashrafis were usually woven in gold zari.

This is a mixed fabric with a woven stripe or zigzag pattern. The warp and weft used were of two different materials (silk and cotton, cotton and linen, silk and wool or wool and cotton) in different colors. It was used mostly for lower garments such as trousers, the lining of the heavy brocade garments or as furnishing.

Gul Badan (the literal meaning of which is 'flower like body') was a known variety of mushru (cotton and silk) popular in the late 19th century. Sangi, Ganta, Ilaycha were types of mushru too. These were popular since ancient times and were known to be woven at all leading silk centers. One reason for their popularity was Islam. Since Islam does not allow men to wear pure silk, mashru (literally meaning permitted) became very popular amongst Muslims.

Himru or Amru : A type of Indian brocade is the *Himru*, a specialty of Hyderabad and Aurangabad, which is woven from silk and zari on silk to produce variegated designs, woven on the principle of extra weft. Himru can be very pretty with a pseudo-rich effect in general. It continued to be in popular demand on the account of its low price as compared to the pure silk brocades. Another point in its favor is that it can be woven very fine so as to give it a soft feel, thus making it more suitable as a fabric for personal wear than the true brocade.

The cloth is distinguished by its intricate *char-khana* (four squares) jal. These are woven like kinkhwabs, but without the use of kala battu (zari) instead badla zari is used.

Contemporary Trends

Kinkhwabs fabrics of India have earned a great reputation for their craftsmanship and grandeur. By and large, still continue to do so, even in the face of fierce competition from other types of woven and printed fabrics.

Kinkhwabs today are typically ornate, jacquard-woven fabrics. The pattern is usually emphasized by contrasting surfaces and colours and appears on the face of the fabric, which is distinguished easily from the back. Uses include apparel, draperies, upholstery and other decorative purposes.

Gyasar : Gyasar is a silk fabric of a Kinkhwab structure with ground, in which the gold thread is profusely used with Tibetan designs. The fabric is especially popular with Tibetans and used extensively in their dresses as well as in decorative hangings, prayer mats, etc.

Gyanta : Gyanta is a silk fabric of Kinkhwab structure of a satin body with or without the use of gold thread. These sometimes have a tantric design (which is also known as Tchingo) of human heads with three eyes woven in gold and silver threads on a black satin ground.

Jamawar

"Jama" means robe and "war" is yard. The base of the jamawar is mostly resham, with perhaps an addition of a little polyester. The brocaded parts are woven in similar threads of silk and polyester. Most of the designs seen today are floral, with the kairy (i.e. the paisley) as the predominant motif.

Today, the best jamavar is woven in Pakistan. This fabric is widely used in that country for bridal and special occasion outfits. The texture and weave of patterns is such that the fabric often gets caught when rubbed against rough surfaces (metallic embroidery, jewellery etc.) it must therefore be handled delicately when worn.

Banarasi

Origin : Banaras is situated on the Calcutta / Delhi rail route 760 km (475 miles) from Calcutta. It has always been a big textile center of silk weaving. European travelers like Marco Polo (1271-

1295) and Tavernier (1665) do not mention the manufacture of Brocades in Banaras. Ralph Fitch (1583-91) describes Banaras as a thriving sector of the cotton textile industry. The earliest mention of the brocade and Zari textiles of Banaras is found in the 19th century. With the migration of silk weavers from Gujrat during the famine of 1603, it is likely that silk brocade weaving started in Banaras in the seventeenth century and developed in excellence during the 18th and 19th century.

Distinguishing Characteristics : The following are considered to be the main characteristics of the brocade fabrics of Banaras.

1. Heavy gold work.
2. Compact weaving
3. Figures have small details.
4. Metallic visual effects.
5. Pallus
6. Jal (A net like pattern)
7. Mina work.

Banarasi brocade produced two sub-variants from its original structure namely:

- Katan
- Tanchoi

Katan

Katan, a thread, prepared by twisting a different number of silk filaments according to requirement gives a firm structure to the background fabric. Katan is a plain woven fabric with pure silk threads. It consists of two threads twisted together and is mostly used for the warp of light fabrics.

Katan can be further classified into the following:

1. Katan Butidar: Fabric with Katan warp and weft with butis (designs and patterns) in gold or resham (untwisted silk).
2. Katan Butidar Mina: Katan Butidar with Mina work (design made out of zari thread) in butis.
3. Katan Butidar Paga Saree: Saree with Katan warp, resham weft, small butis all over body, closely spaced (about 10 cm

(4") apart), about 5 cm (2") wide border and 30-55 cm (12-22") wide *pallu*.

4. Katan Brocade: This is a fabric with Katan Warp and Katan weft with figures in gold thread with or without mina, with the traditional styles being 'katrawan', 'kardhwan' and 'Fekva'.
1. Katrawan: A technique or design in which the floating portions of the extra weft (laid from selvege to selvege) at the back of the fabric is cut.
2. Kardhwan:
3. Fekva
5. Jangla: Plain fabric of Katan warp and Katan weft, with all-over floral designs in an extra weft of either silk or zari.
6. Katan Katrawan Mina: A fabric in Katrawan style with Mina.

Katan Motifs and designs

These days the currently used designs & motifs involving Katan are:

- Katan Jal Set: Over the years with minor innovations and influences from other materials, Jangla is now known as 'Katan Jal Set'.
- Katan Buti Zari Resham: Katan Butidar has evolved over time to become Katan Buti Zari Resham.
- Katan Stripe and Katan Check are also popular variants found in the markets.

Tanchoi

Plain woven body with one color extra weft, one color weft and one color warp. Relative to the jamawar, it is lighter and softer. Tanchoi could be further classified into the following:

Satan Tanchoi is the satin weave (four ends and eight picks or five ends and five picks satin) with the warp in one color and the weft in one or more colors. The extra weft in the design may also be used as body weft.

1. Satan Jari Tanchoi: Satan Tanchoi with weft in the order of one silk and one gold thread (Jari), or two silk (double) and one gold thread.

2. Satan Jari Katrawan Tanchoi: Satan Jari tanchoi in which the floating, extra weft, gold thread at the back is cut and removed.
3. Atlas: Atlas is a pure satin body. Relative to other fabrics, Atlas is thicker, heavier and is shinier than other fabrics because of the extra use of zari. It is also known as gilt, because it is even shinier than the katan.
4. Mushabbar: The cloth is distinguished by its jal woven as bushes and branches of trees. The normal association with the design was that of a jungle.

Concluding Remarks : The most common & popular fabrics remains the banarasi, jamawar, pot-thans, atlas and katans. These are the fabrics that a person can usually find in our local markets and have a high level of demand. However the other materials like tanchoi, mushabbar, himru / amru, mushru, etc. have been relegated to selective niches in the market. Most people even after coming across these fabrics usually refer to them directly as jamawar due to the absence of such materials in popular use and lack of awareness in general of the availability of these fabrics.

Awareness of these materials will have to be started at the top with the elite of the society (since they are the ones who have the resources to buy these expensive clothing). Thus, we will require special exhibitions of designers who work with these materials, displaying of these materials at fashion shows, promotion of the clothing designed in the materials with the high end boutiques and awareness creation through experts & designers talk shows on television, radio, etc.

Jamawar

Origin : Traders introduced this Chinese silk cloth to India, mainly from Samarkand and Bukhara and it gained immense popularity among the royalty and the aristocracy. King and nobles bought the woven fabric by the yard, wearing it as a gown or using it as a wrap or shawl. Jamawar weaving centres in India developed in the holy cities and the trade centres. The most well known jamawar weaving centres were in Assam, Gujrat, Malwa and South India.

Due to its rich and fine raw materials, the rich and powerful merchants used jamawar and noblemen of the time, who could not only afford it but could even commission the weavers to make the fabric for them, as in the case of the Mughals. Emperor Akbar was one of its greatest patrons. He brought many weavers from East Turkestan to Kashmir.

One of the main reasons for the diversity in the designs of the jamawar cloth was the migratory nature of its weavers. Ideas from almost all parts of the world influenced these designs.

The Indian motifs were greatly influenced by nature like the sun, moon, stars, rivers, trees, flowers, birds etc. The figural and geometrical motifs such as trees, lotus flower, bulls, horses, lions, elephants, peacocks, swans, eagles, the sun, stars, diagonal or zigzag lines, squares, round shapes, etc. can be traced through the entire history of jamawar and are still being used but in a rather different form in terms of intricacy and compositions, thus creating new patterns.

Indian weaver predominantly used a wide variety of classical motifs such as the swan (hamsa), the Lotus (kamala), The Tree Of Life (kulpa, vriksha), the Vase of Plenty (purna, kumbha), the Elephant (hathi), the Lion (simha), flowing floral creepers (lata patra), Peacocks (mayur) and many more. Mythical creatures such as winged lions, centaurs, griffins, decorative of ferocious animals, animals formally in profile or with turned heads, animals with human figures in combat or represented in roundels were also commonly used motifs. These motifs have remained in existence for more than two thousand years. However, new patterns have consistently been introduced; sometimes some of these are even an amalgamation of the existing patterns. Such attempts at evolving new designs were particularly noticeable from the 10th century onwards, when patterns were altered to meet the specific demands of the Muslim rulers.

The bull or the swan, arranged between vertical and diagonal stripes can still be found in the silk jamawar saris of India. Patterns with small flowers and two-coloured squares (chess board design) are seen, used both as a garment and as furnishing material – bed spreads with same kind of pattern are still woven in some parts of Gujarat.

Jamawar dating back to the Mughal era however contained big, bold and realistic patterns, which were rather simple with ample space between the motifs. The designs stood out prominently against the background of the cloth.

Complex patterns were developed only when additional decorative elements were included in the basic pattern. During later periods, the gap between the motives was also filled with smaller motives or geometrical forms. The iris and narcissus flowers became the most celebrated motifs of this era and were combined with tulips, poppies, primulas, roses and lilies. A lot of figurative motives were also used in the Mughal era such as deers, horses, butterflies, peacocks and insects. The Mughal kings played a vital role in the enhancement of jamawar by putting their inspirations into the cloth's designing and visiting the weavers on a regular basis to supervise its making. Shining, decorative pallus were jals were the main designs of this time. The borders were usually woven with silk and zari.

After the Mughal period, the figurative motifs were discouraged by the Muslims and more floral and paisleys were introduced. However, inspiration was taken from these figurative motives and put into designs as in the case of using only the peacock feathers instead of the complete figure.

Another big change was brought about in 1985, where the source of inspiration was the Chinese Shanghai cloth. The patterns of the Chinese Shanghai were amended in accordance to the weave construction of the jamawar cloth and introduced in the cloth. This proved to be a very successful change and is still appreciated by many.

In recent years, the Indian government has attempted a modest revival of this art by setting up a shawl-weaving centre at Kanihama in Kashmir. Efforts to revive this art have also been made by bringing in innovations like the creation of jamawar saris by craftsmen in Varanasi. Each sari is a shimmering tapestry of intricate design, in colours that range from the traditionally deep, rich shades to delicate pastels. A minimum of four months of patient effort goes into the creation of each jamawar sari. Many of the jamawar saris now have matching silk shawls attached to them, creating elegant ensembles fit for royalty.

The Process Involved In the Making of Jamawar in Pakistan : It is woven on the jacquard loom. Joseph-Marie Jacquard, improving on the original punched-card design of Jacques De Vaucanson's loom of 1745 developed the Jacquard system in France in 1804-05. The pattas, which are the punched cards, controlled the actions of the loom, allowing automatic production of intricate woven patterns . The bigger the motif, the greater the number of cards required to make them.

Pakistan makes its own yarn from the imported cocoons that come from China. The yarn is cultivated in areas like Orangi town & Shershah which is then sold to the weavers. The pure silk yarn, before it can be used, has to undergo treatment such as bleaching or washing (in soap) and then dyeing. In its raw state, the silk is hard due to the sericlan ; therefore it has to be removed. A single filament of the silk yarn is not strong enough to be woven on its own; therefore, it needs to be twisted in order to give it strength and hold.

A specific person who is called a naqsha-bandh first draws the patterns or designs on paper which are then transferred on a graph paper on a comparatively much bigger scale. Every square in the graph signifies a specific number of threads on the loom. The unfinished, rough ideas and sketches are provided to these naqsha-bandhs by the wholesalers and are thus plotted on the graph. The use of various threads in the pattern such as, zari, resham, polyester etc. are separated on the graph with the help of colours indicated on a key chart. The wholesalers later decide the main colours and this information are forwarded to the weavers. The naqsha-bandhs do not have say in the designing of the motifs and patterns. They do what they are told to do.

In this way, the pattern or motif is drawn on the graph paper to provide the weaver with the exact picture of each thread making up the design in the process of weaving. The designs and patterns are then transferred from the graph paper on a wooden frame and are referred to as the naqsha. The naqsha that is made with cotton threads is a smaller sample of the actual design, which is to be woven on the loom. The warp is then taken for the weaving process, which is carried out, on various looms such as the pit loom, jacquard loom and power loom. There is a vast difference between the outputs of the three types of looms. The power looms cannot match the intricacy that can be achieved using the pit or jacquard loom. This is the reason for the far superior workmanship that can be found in the earlier designs dating back to the Mughal era.

Nowadays brocade is being produced on the power looms for its wide-scale production for the market. Several kannis or little wooden shuttles of different colors are used for a single weft line of the fabric. Up to 50 colours could be worked into one shawl made of the jamawar cloth. The most popular colours being zard, sufed, mushki, ferozi, ingari, uda gulnar and kirmiz.

This thread can also be twisted with gold threads in order to make zari . The zari fibre is doubled with the yarn to prepare it for the process of weaving. Another reason for twisting the zari fibre is to reduce its excessive shine. The zari fibre is wrapped on reels and is doubled with the yarn with the help of a machine, on cones. These fibres are then wrapped on reels with the help of a doubling machine. The threads are then steamed and wrapped on the final spools . The required threads (silk, zari, etc.) are then taken to the charkha, which is a machine used to make the warp for the weaving process.

Current Scenario in Karachi: Designs & Motifs of today: The effect achieved after the cloth is woven resembles that of embroidery. Therefore, the jamawar weaving technique is often defined as ‘embroidery weaving’ or ‘loom embroidery’. This technique can also be applied on other fibres but jamawar is generally restricted to rich silk threads. Currently, any of the major textile fibres may be used in a wide range of quality and price.

Currently, two kinds of Kinkhwab (Jamawar) are available in the markets. Mughal Jamawar and Self Jamawar. Mughal Jamawar has a distinct characteristic of the use of gold and silver zari with silk, the use of gold zari with silver zari and the use of zari with polyester. Self Jamawar does not involve zari and basically is either silk on silk or silk with polyester.

Currently, the motifs and patterns of jamawar have evolved tremendously from the old times. The big size and the bold motifs that are the remnant of the past civilizations are missing in today's jamawar designs. The currently used motifs and patterns (floral, paisleys, butis, etc.) display greater intricacy as compared to the boldness observed in previous times. Even the compositions have changed as less space between the motifs is observed compared to the past designs. According to the wholesalers for the local market, the removal of figurative motifs diminishes all risks in its sales. However, even though old jamawar motifs have changed, the concept of incorporating gold and silver threads in the construction of the jamawar cloth can still be seen, though on a smaller scale.

In order to maintain harmony and correlation between motifs, certain geometrical patterns are common. The most common of them being chevron, checks, straight or diagonal lines, mothra (a double line containing a simple or running pattern inside) and so forth. The natural forms are woven in a highly decorative and stylize manner. After assimilating the essence of a pattern, the designer implements their own interpretation of it. Thus, a leaf can evolve into a flower or a bird form. Decorative motifs like the leaf, flower, fruits, creeper, etc. are used to maintain the symmetry of the pattern.

The market for pure silk has also gotten limited due to ever increasing prices of the raw materials, thus primarily only designers use pure silk in their work (importing cocoons from China and then weaving the cloth). Modern Power looms have replaced much of the hand-made craftsmanship of the weavers and while they can easily satisfy the demands of the times, the quality that jamawar was once famous for is not the same anymore because of this mass production method.

The quality of jamawar has decreased due to the modern pressures of cost benefits and mass production. Pure silk is no longer a feasible option for most weavers, who now employ a mix thread of silk combined with other mixed yarns including silk and wool, silk and cotton, silk and viscose. In areas even where these weavers still employ pure silk, they are making only razor thin profits and thus most have discontinued the work by not training new workers and letting the family owned businesses die out, as offspring choose alternative professions to follow. The reason for the low profits of weavers has to do with the supply chain. Makers of Jamawar have to keep their costs low to sell to the majority of the consumers who cannot afford the cloth at higher prices. This means that the weaver suffers most, since they come last in the supply chain and cannot afford to be out of work and plus cannot dictate the price at which they will weave the cloth due to the almost monopoly of the few fixed designers cum wholesalers who dictate the market.

The design aspect has also suffered in modern times. As compared to the traditional designs dating back hundreds of years, when religion, culture, area, stories etc. had profound influence on the weavers and lead to symbols & verses being woven into the fabrics themselves e.g. the Persian Ashrafi design, the Hindu Ramnami dupattas, Muslim kalima & ayahs, the Indian symbols of the Vase of Plenty for fullness, Tree of Life as the wish fulfilling tree, a Lotus for purity and perfection, Elephant symbolizing influence, Lion denoting power, etc., modern day designs woven in Karachi no longer have an identity of their own.

Most of the modern day designs are restricted to flowers & paisleys and replicated endlessly. They also have not experimented or taken risks with other patterns or designs and that is why there has been no innovation in this industry for many years.

However it is interesting to note here that the graduates of the art schools have been found experimenting and producing new forms of woven textiles.This trend has resulted in the production of various design houses like Khaadi, NoorJehan Bilgerami, Gultex etc. The awareness for the revival of hand woven silk and Jamawar is ascending, thus beniting the craft school and resulting in the manufacture of some new experimental contemporary fabrics.

8

History of Silk

According to Chinese tradition, the **history of silk** begins in the 27th century BCE. Its use was confined to China until the Silk Road opened at some point during the latter half of the first millennium BC. China maintained its virtual monopoly over silk for another thousand years. Not confined to clothing, silk was also used for a number of other applications, including writing, and the colour of silk worn was an important indicator of social class during the Tang Dynasty.

Silk cultivation spread to Japan in around 300 CE, and by 522 the Byzantines managed to obtain silkworm eggs and were able to begin silkworm cultivation. The Arabs also began to manufacture silk during this same time. As a result of the spread of sericulture, Chinese silk exports became less important, although they still maintained dominance over the luxury silk market. The Crusades brought silk production to Western Europe, in particular to many Italian states, which saw an economic boom exporting silk to the rest of Europe. Changes in manufacturing techniques also began to take place during the Middle Ages, with devices such as the spinning wheel first appearing. During the 16th century France joined Italy in developing a successful silk trade, though the efforts of most other nations to develop a silk industry of their own were unsuccessful.

The Industrial Revolution changed much of Europe's silk industry. Due to innovations in spinning cotton, it became much cheaper to manufacture and therefore caused more expensive silk production to become less mainstream. New weaving technologies, however, increased the efficiency of production. Among these was the Jacquard loom, a precursor to modern computers, developed for silk embroidery. An epidemic of several silkworm diseases caused production to fall, especially in France, where the industry never recovered. In the 20th century Japan and China regained their earlier role in silk production, and China is now once again the world's largest producer of silk. The rise of new fabrics such as nylon reduced the prevalence of silk throughout the world, and silk is now once again a somewhat rare luxury good, much less important than in its heyday.

Origin of the Silk – Legend of Lady (HSI-LING-SHIH)

Chinese legend gives the title Goddess of Silk to Lady Hsi-Ling-Shih, wife of the mythical Yellow Emperor, who was said to have ruled China in about 3000 BC. She is credited with the introduction of silkworm rearing and the invention of the loom. Half a silkworm cocoon unearthed in 1927 from the loess soil astride the Yellow River in Shanxi Province, in northern China, has been dated between 2600 and 2300 BC. Another example is a group of ribbons, threads and woven fragments, dated about 3000 BC, and found at Qianshanyang in Zhejiang province. More recent archeological finds - a small ivory cup carved with a silkworm design and thought to be between 6000 and 7000 years old, and spinning tools, silk thread and fabric fragments from sites along the lower Yangzi River – reveal the origins of sericulture to be even earlier.

Silkworm and the Family

There are many indigenous varieties of wild silk moths found in a number of different countries. The key to understanding the great mystery and magic of silk, and China's domination of its production and promotion, lies with one species: the blind, flightless moth, Bombyx mori. It lays 500 or more eggs in four to six days and dies soon after. The eggs are like pinpoints – one hundred of them weigh only one gram. From one ounce of eggs come about 30,000 worms which eat a ton of mulberry leaves and produce twelve pounds of raw silk. The original wild ancestor of this cultivated species is believed to be Bombyx mandarina Moore, a silk moth living on the white mulberry tree and unique to China. The silkworm of this particular moth produces a thread whose filament is smoother, finer and rounder than that of other silk moths. Over thousands of years, during which the Chinese practiced sericulture utilizing all the different types of silk moths known to them, Bombyx mori evolved into the specialized silk producer it is today; a moth which has lost its power to fly, only capable of mating and producing eggs for the next generation of silk producers.

Early History

The appearance of silk

The earliest evidence of silk was found at the sites of Yangshao culture in Xia County, Shanxi, where a silk cocoon was found cut in half by a sharp knife, dating back to between 5,000 and 3,000 BCE. The species was identified as bombyx mori, the domesticated silkworm. Fragments of primitive loom can also be seen from the sites of Hemudu culture in Yuyao, Zhejiang, dated to about 4,000 BCE. Scraps of silk were found in a Liangzhu culture site at Qianshanyang in Huzhou, Zhejiang, dating back to 2,700 BCE. Other fragments have been recovered from royal tombs in the Shang Dynasty (ca. 1600 BCE - ca. 1046 BCE).

During the later epoch, the Chinese lost their secret as the Koreans, the Japanese, and later the Indians succeeded in discovering how to make silk. Allusions to the fabric in the Old Testament show that it was known in western Asia in biblical times. Scholars believe that starting in the 2nd century BC the Chinese established a commercial network aimed at exporting silk to the West. Silk was used, for example, by the Persian court and its king, Darius III, when Alexander the Great conquered the empire. Even though silk spread rapidly across Eurasia, with the possible exception of Japan its production remained exclusively Chinese for three millennia.

Myths and legends

The writings of Confucius and Chinese tradition recount that in the 27th century BCE a silk worm's cocoon fell into the tea cup of the empress Leizu. Wishing to extract it from her drink, the young girl of fourteen began to unroll the thread of the cocoon. She then had the idea to weave it. Having observed the life of the silk worm on the recommendation of her husband, the Yellow Emperor, she began to instruct her entourage the art of raising silk worms, sericulture. From this point on, the girl became the goddess of silk in Chinese mythology. Silk would eventually leave China in the hair of a princess promised to a prince of Khotan. This probably occurred in the early 1st century CE. The princess, refusing to go without the fabric she loved, would finally break the imperial ban on silk worm exportation.

Though silk was exported to foreign countries in great amounts, sericulture remained a secret that the Chinese guarded carefully. Consequently, other peoples invented wildly varying accounts of the source of the incredible fabric. In classical antiquity, most Romans, great admirers of the cloth, were convinced that the Chinese took the fabric from tree leaves. This belief was affirmed by Seneca the Younger in his Phaedra and by Virgil in his Georgics. Notably, Pliny the Elder knew better. Speaking of the *bombyx* or silk moth, he wrote in his Natural Histories "They weave webs, like spiders, that become a luxurious clothing material for women, called silk."

Silk usage in Ancient and Medieval China

In China, silk worm farming was originally restricted to women, and many women were employed in the silk-making industry. Even though some saw the development of a luxury product as useless, silk provoked such a craze among high society that the rules in the *Li Ji* were used to regulate and limit its use to the members of the imperial family. For approximately a millennium, the right to wear silk was reserved for the emperor and the highest dignitaries. Later, it gradually extended to other classes of Chinese society. Silk began to be used for decorative means and also in less luxurious ways: musical instruments, fishing, and bow-making. Peasants did not have the right to wear silk until the Qing dynasty (1644-1911).

Paper was one of the greatest discoveries of ancient China. Beginning in the 3rd century BCE paper was made in all sizes with various materials. Silk was no exception, and silk workers had been making paper since the 2nd century BCE. Silk, bamboo, linen, wheat and rice straw were all used differently, and paper made with silk became the first type of luxury paper. Researchers have found an early example of writing done on silk paper in the tomb of a Marchioness who died around 168, in Mawangdui, Hunan. The material was certainly more expensive, but also more practical than bamboo. Treatises on many subjects, including meteorology, medicine, astrology, divinity, and even maps written on silk have been discovered.

During the Han Dynasty, silk became progressively more valuable in its own right, and became more than simply a material. It was used to pay government officials and compensate citizens who were particularly worthy. By the same token that one would sometimes estimate the price of products according to a certain weight of gold, the length of the silk cloth became a monetary standard in China (in addition to bronze coins). The wealth that silk brought to China stirred up envy in neighbouring peoples. Beginning in the 2nd century BC the Xiongnu, regularly pillaged the provinces of the Han Chinese for around 250 years. Silk was a common offering by the emperor to these tribes in exchange for peace. For more than a millennium, silk remained the principal diplomatic gift of the emperor of China to his neighbours or to his vassals. The use of silk became so important that "silk" (Ÿ~) soon constituted one of the principal radicals of the Chinese alphabet.

Broadly speaking, the use of silk was regulated by a very precise code in China. For example, the Tang Dynasty and Song Dynasty imposed upon bureaucrats the use of a particular colour according to their different functions in society. Under the Ming, silk began to be used in a series of accessories: handkerchiefs, wallets, belts, or even an embroidered piece of fabric displaying dozens of animals, real or mythical. These fashion accessories remained associated with a particular position: there was a specific bonnet for warriors, for judges, for nobles, and others for religious use. The women of high Chinese society heeded codified practices and used silk in their garments to which they added countless motifs. A 13th century work, the *Jinpingmei*, gives a description of one such motif:

"Golden lotus having a quilted backgammon pattern, double-folded, adorned with savage geese pecking at a landscape of flowers and roses; the dress' right figure had a floral border with buttons in the form of bees or chrysanthemums."

Chinese silk and its commerce

A number of archaeological discoveries showed that silk had become a luxury material appreciated in foreign countries well before the opening of the Silk Road by the Chinese. For example, silk has been found in the Valley of Kings in a tomb of a mummy dating from 1070 BC. First the Greeks, then the Romans began to speak of the Seres (people of silk), a term to designate the inhabitants of the far-off kingdom, China. According to certain historians, the first Roman contact with silk was that of the legions of the governor of Syria, Crassus. At the Battle of Carrhae, near to the Euphrates, the legions were said to be so surprised by the brilliance of the banners of Parthia that they fled.

The silk road toward the west was opened by the Chinese in the 2nd century AD. The main road left from Beijing, going either to the north or south of the Taklamakan desert, one of the most arid in the world, before crossing the Pamir Mountains. The caravans that employed this method to exchange silk with other merchants were generally quite large, including from 100 to 500 people as well as camels and yaks carrying around 140 kg (300 lb) of merchandise. They linked to Antioch and the coasts of the Mediterranean, about one year's travel from Beijing. In the South, a second route went by Yemen, Burma, and India before rejoining the northern route.

Not long after the conquest of Egypt in 30 BCE regular commerce began between the Romans and Asia, marked by the Roman appetite for silk cloth coming from the Far East, which was then resold to the Romans by the Parthians. The Roman Senate tried in vain to prohibit the wearing of silk, for economic reasons as well as moral ones.

Spread of Production

Although silk was well known in Europe and most of Asia, China was able to keep a near monopoly on silk production. The monopoly was defended by an imperial decree, condemning to death anyone attempting to export silkworms or their eggs. Only around the year 300 CE did a Japanese expedition succeed in taking some silkworm eggs and four young Chinese girls, who were forced to teach their captors the art of sericulture. Techniques of sericulture were subsequently introduced to Japan on a larger scale by frequent diplomatic exchanges between the 8th century and 9th centuries.

Starting in the 4th century BC silk began to reach the West by merchants who would exchange it for gold, ivory, horses or precious stones. Up to the frontiers of the Roman Empire, silk became a monetary standard for estimating the value of different products. Hellenistic Greece appreciated the high quality of the Chinese goods and made efforts to plant mulberry trees and breed silkworms in the Mediterranean basin. Sassanid Persia controlled the trade of silk destined for Europe and Byzantium.

It was not until 552 CE that the Byzantine emperor Justinian obtained the first silkworm eggs. He had sent two Nestorian monks to Central Asia, and they were able to smuggle silkworm eggs to him hidden in rods of bamboo. While under the monks' care, the eggs hatched, though they did not cocoon before arrival. The Byzantine church was thus able to make fabrics for the emperor, with the intention of developing a large silk industry in the Eastern Roman Empire, using techniques learned from the Sassanids. These gynecia had a legal monopoly on the fabric, but the empire continued to import silk from other major urban centres on the Mediterranean. The magnificence of the Byzantine techniques was not a result of the manufacturing process, but instead of the meticulous attention paid to the execution and decorations. The weaving techniques they used were taken from Egypt. The first diagrams of semple looms appeared in the 5th century.

The Arabs, with their widening conquests, spread sericulture across the shores of the Mediterranean. Included in these were Africa, Spain and Sicily, all of which developed an important silk industry.

Since the Chinese lost their monopoly on silk production, there was no longer a market for the most basic of their silk products. They did, however, maintain dominance in the luxury silk item market, and China continued to export high-quality fabric to Europe and the Near East along the silk road.

Much later, following the Crusades, techniques of silk production began to spread across Western Europe. In 1147 while Byzantine emperor Manuel I Komnenos was focusing all his efforts on the Second Crusade, the Norman king Roger II of Sicily attacked Corinth and Thebes, two important centres of Byzantine silk production. They took the crops and silk production infrastructure, and deported all the workers to Palermo, thereby causing the Norman silk industry to flourish. The sack of Constantinople by the Fourth Crusade in 1204 brought decline to the city and its silk industry, and many artisans left the city in the early thirteenth century. Italy developed a large domestic silk industry after 2000 skilled weavers came from Constantinople. Many also chose to settle in Avignon to furnish the popes of Avignon.

The sudden boom of the silk industry in the Italian state of Lucca, starting in the 11th and 12th centuries was due to much

Sicilian, Jewish, and Greek settlement, alongside many other immigrants from neighbouring cities in southern Italy. With the loss of many Italian trading posts in the Orient, the import of Chinese styles drastically declined. Gaining momentum, in order to satisfy the rich and powerful bourgeoisie's demands for luxury fabrics, the cities of Lucca, Genoa, Venice and Florence were soon exporting silk to all of Europe. In 1472 there were 84 workshops and at least 7000 craftsmen in Florence alone.

Reciprocal influences

Silk, which had a reputation of being a Chinese textile, was in fact made throughout the region of Eurasia, using various breeds of lepidopterans, both wild and domestic. While wild silks were produced in many countries, there is no doubt that the Chinese were the first to begin production on such a large scale, having the most effective breed for silk production, the bombyx mori. Chinese sources claim the existence of a machine to unwind silkworm cocoons in 1090. The cocoons were placed in a large basin of hot water, the silk would leave the cauldron by tiny guiding rings, and would be wound onto a large spool, thanks to a backwards and forward motion. Little information exists about spinning techniques in use in China. The spinning wheel, in all likelihood moved by hand, was known by the beginning of the Christian era. The first accepted image of a spinning wheel appears in 1210. There is an image of a silk spinning machine powered by a water wheel that dates to 1313.

More information is known about the looms used. The *Nung Sang Chi Yao*, or *Fundamentals of Agriculture and Sericulture*, compiled around 1210, is rich with pictures and descriptions, many pertaining to silk. It repeatedly claims the Chinese looms to be far superior to all others. It speaks of two types of loom that leave the worker's arms free: the draw loom, which could have either a Chinese or European origin, and the pedal loom which is attributed to the Chinese. The many diagrams originate in the 12th and 13th centuries. When examined closely, many similarities with European machines of that epoch can be seen. Since the Jin dynasty, the existence of silk damasks has been well recorded, and since the 2nd century BCE, four-shafted looms and other innovations allowed the creation of silk brocades.

Silk in the medieval world

A more abundant luxury

The high Middle Ages saw continued use of established techniques for silk manufacture without any changes to speak of, neither in materials nor in tools used. Between the 10th and 12th centuries, small changes began to appear, though the changes of the thirteenth century were much larger and more radical. In a short time, new fabrics began to appear; hemp and cotton each also had their own particular techniques of manufacture. Known since Roman times, silk remained a rare and expensive material. Byzantine magnaneries in Greece and Syria (6th to 8th century), and those of the Arabs in Sicily and Spain (8th to 10th century) were able to supply the luxury material in a much greater abundance.

Improved technology

The 13th century saw an already changing technology undergo many dramatic changes. It is possible that, as with in England at the end of the 18th century, advances in the textile industry were a driving force behind advances in technology as a whole. Silk indeed occupies a privileged place in history on account of this.

At the start of the thirteenth century, a primitive form of milling the silk threads was already in use. In 1221 Jean de Garlande's dictionary, and in 1226, Étienne Boileau's *Livre des métiers* (*Tradesman's Handbook*) enumerated many types of devices which can only have been doubling machines. The instruments used were further perfected in Bologna between 1270 and 1280. From the start of the fourteenth century, many documents allude to the use of devices that were quite complex.

The reel, originally developed for the silk industry, now has multiple uses. The earliest surviving depiction of a spinning wheel is a panel of stained glass in the Cathedral of Chartres. Bobbins and warping machines appear together in the stained glass at Chartres and in a fresco in the Cologne Kunkelhaus (ca 1300). It is possible that the toothed warping machine was created by the silk industry; it allowed the warp to be more uniform and allowed the warp to be of a longer length.

Starting at the end of the 14th century, no doubt on account of the devastation caused mid-century by the Black Death, there was a general shift towards less expensive techniques. Many things which would have earlier been completely forbidden by the guilds were now commonplace (using low quality wool, carding, etc.). In the silk industry, the use of water-powered mills grew, and by the 15th century, the loom designed by Jean le Calabrais saw nearly universal use.

The silk industry in France

Italian silk cloth was very expensive, as much a result of the cost of the raw material as of the production costs. The craftsmen in Italy proved unable to keep up with the exigencies of French fashion, which continuously demanded lighter and less expensive materials. These materials were used for clothing, and garment production began to be done locally. Nevertheless, Italian silk long remained among the most prized, mostly for furnishings and the brilliant colours of the dyes.

Following the example of the wealthy Italian city-states of the era (Venice, Florence, Lucca, etc.), which had become the centre of the luxury textile industry, Lyon obtained a similar function in the French market. In 1466 King Louis XI decided to develop a national silk industry in Lyon. In the face of protests by the Lyonnais, he conceded and moved the silk fabrication to Tours, but the industry in Tours stayed relatively marginal. His main objective was to reduce France's trade deficit with Italy, which caused France to lose 400,000 to 500,000 golden écus a year. It was under Francis I in around 1535 that a royal charter was granted to two merchants, Étienne Turquet and Barthélemy Naris, to develop a silk trade in Lyon. In 1540 the king granted a monopoly on silk production to the city of Lyon. Starting in the 16th century Lyon became the capital of the European silk trade, notably producing many reputable fashions. Gaining confidence, the silks produced in the city little by little began to abandon the original oriental styles and moved towards their own distinctive style, with an emphasis on landscapes. Thousand of workers, the canuts, devoted themselves to the flourishing industry. In the middle of the 17th century over 14,000 looms were in use in Lyon, and the silk industry fed a third of the city's population.

In the 18th and 19th centuries Provence experienced a boom in sericulture that would last until the First World War, with much of the silk produced being shipped north to Lyon. Viens and La Bastide-des-Jourdans are two of the *communes* of Luberon that profited the most from mulberry plantations that have since disappeared. Working at home under the domestic system, silk spinning and silk treatment employed many people and increased the income of the working class.

Spread to other countries

England under Henry IV was also looking to develop a silk industry, but no opportunity arose until the revocation of the Edict of Nantes in the 1680s when hundreds of thousands of French Huguenots, many of which were skilled weavers and experts in sericulture, began immigrating to England to escape religious persecution. Some areas, including Spitalfields saw many high-quality silk workshops spring up, their products distinct from continental silk largely by the colours used. Nonetheless, the British climate prevented England's domestic silk trade from becoming globally dominant.

Many envisioned starting a silk industry in the British colonies in America starting in 1619 under the reign of King James I of England. The silk industry in the Colonies never became very large. Likewise, silk was introduced to numerous other countries, including Mexico, where it was brought by Cortez in 1522. Only rarely did these new silk industries grow to any significant size.

Silk since the Industrial Revolution

The start of the Industrial Revolution

The start of the Industrial Revolution was marked by a massive boom in the textile industry, with remarkable technological innovations made, led by the cotton industry of Great Britain. In its early years, there were often disparities in technological innovation between different stages of fabric manufacture, which encouraged complementary innovations. For example, spinning progressed much more rapidly than weaving.

The silk industry, however, did not gain any benefit from innovations in spinning, as silk is naturally already a thread. Making silk, silver, and gold brocades is a very delicate and precise process, with each colour needing its own dedicated shuttle. In the 17th century and 18th centuries progress began to be made in the simplification and standardization of silk manufacture, with many advances following one after another. Bouchon and Falcon's punchcard loom appeared in 1775, later improved on by Jacques de Vaucanson. Later, Joseph-Marie Jacquard improved on the designs of Falcon and Vaucanson, introducing the revolutionary Jacquard loom, which allowed a string of punchcards to be processed mechanically in the correct sequence. The punchcards of the Jacquard loom were a direct precursor to the modern computer, in that they gave a (limited) form of programmability. Punchcards themselves were carried over to computers, and were ubiquitous until their obsolescence in the 1970s. From 1801 embroidery became highly mechanized due to the effectiveness of the Jacquard loom. The mechanism behind the Jacquard loom even allowed complex designs to be mass produced.

The Jacquard loom was immediately denounced by workers, who accused it of causing unemployment, but soon it had become vital to the industry. The loom was declared public property in 1806, and Jacquard was rewarded with a pension and a royalty on each machine. In 1834 there were a total of 2885 Jacquard looms in Lyon alone. The Canut revolt in 1831 foreshadowed many of the larger worker uprisings of the Industrial Revolution. The canuts occupied the city of Lyon, and would not relinquish it until a bloody repression by the army, led by Marshal Soult. A second revolt, similar to the first, took place in 1834.

Decline in the European silk industry

The first silkworm diseases began to appear in 1845, creating an epidemic. Among them are pébrine, caused by the microsporidia *Nosema bombycis*, grasserie, caused by a virus, flacherie, caused by eating infected mulberry leaves or white muscardine disease, caused by the fungus *Beauveria bassiana*. The epidemic grew to a massive scale, and after having attacked the silkworms, other viruses began to infect the mulberry trees. The chemist Jean-Baptiste Dumas, French minister of agriculture, was charged with stopping the epidemic. In face of sericulturers' call for help, he asked Louis Pasteur to study the disease, starting in 1865. For many years, Pasteur thought that pébrine was not a contagious disease. In 1870 he changed his view, and measures were enacted that caused the disease to decline.

Nevertheless, the increase in the price of silkworm cocoons and the reduction in importance of silk in the garments of the bourgeoisie in the 19th century caused the decline of the silk industry in Europe. The opening of the Suez Canal in 1869 and the silk shortage in France reduced the price of importing Asian silk, particularly from China and Japan.

Starting from the Long Depression (1873 – 1896), Lyonnais silk production had become totally industrialized, and hand looms were rapidly disappearing. The 19th century saw the textile industry's progress caused by advances in chemistry. The synthesis of aniline was used to make mauveine (aniline purple) dye and the synthesis of quinine was used to make indigo dye. In 1884 Count Hilaire de Chardonnet invented artificial silk and in 1891 opened a factory dedicated to the production of artificial silk (viscose), which cost much less and in part replaced natural silk.

Silk in Modern Times

Following the crisis in Europe, the modernization of sericulture in Japan made it the world's foremost silk producer. Italy managed to rebound from the crisis, but France was never able to. Urbanization in Europe saw many French and Italian agricultural workers leave silk growing for more lucrative factory work. Raw silk was imported from Japan to fill the void. Asian countries, formerly exporters of raw materials (cocoons and raw silk), progressively began to export more and more finished garments.

During the Second World War, silk supplies from Japan were cut off, so western countries were forced to find substitutes. Synthetic fibres such as nylon were used in products such as parachutes and stockings, replacing silk. Even after the war, silk was not able to regain many of the markets lost, though it remained an expensive luxury product. Postwar Japan, through improvements in technology and a protectionist market policy, became the world's foremost exporter of raw silk, a position it held until the 1970s. The continued rise in importance of synthetic fibres and loosening of the protectionist economy contributed to the decline of Japan's silk industry, and by 1975 it was no longer a net exporter of silk.

With its recent economic reforms, the People's Republic of China has become the world's largest silk producer. In 1996 it produced 58,000 tonnes out of a world production of 81,000, followed by India at 13,000 tonnes. Japanese production is now marginal, at only 2500 tonnes. Between 1995 and 1997 Chinese silk production went down 40% in an effort to raise prices, reminiscent of earlier shortages. World demand for silk in the 1990s stayed fairly low with the exception of a few markets, including India and the United Kingdom. Silk's image suffered on account of distribution of low quality fabric, though it has improved recently. Today the silk trade is largely dependent on a few consuming countries, including India and Japan.

In December 2006 the General Assembly of the United Nations proclaimed 2009 to be the International Year of Natural Fibres, so as to raise the profile of silk and other natural fibres.

Variation of silk with various countries

China

Silk fabric was first developed in ancient China, possibly as early as 6000 BC and definitely by 3000 BC. Legend gives credit for developing silk to a Chinese empress, Xi Ling-Shi (Hsi-Ling-Shih, Lei-tzu). Silks were originally reserved for the Kings of China for their own use and gifts to others, but spread gradually through Chinese culture and trade both geographically and socially, and then to many regions of Asia. Silk rapidly became a popular luxury fabric in the many areas accessible to Chinese merchants because of its texture and luster. Silk was in great demand, and became a staple of pre-industrial international trade. In July 2007, archeologists discovered intricately woven and dyed silk textiles in a tomb in Jiangxi province, are dated to the Eastern Zhou Dynasty, roughly 2,500 years ago. Although historians have suspected a long history of a formative textile industry in ancient China, this find of silk textiles employing "complicated techniques" of weaving and dyeing provides direct and concrete evidence for silks dating before the Mawangdui-discovery and other silks dating to the Han Dynasty (202 BC-220 AD).

The first evidence of the silk trade is the finding of silk in the hair of an Egyptian mummy of the 21st dynasty, c.1070 BC. Ultimately the silk trade reached as far as the Indian subcontinent, the Middle East, Europe, and North Africa. This trade was so extensive that the major set of trade routes between Europe and Asia has become known as the Silk Road.

The Emperors of China strove to keep knowledge of sericulture secret to maintain the Chinese monopoly. Nonetheless sericulture reached Korea around 200 BC, about the first half of the 1st century AD had reached ancient Khotan, and by AD 300 the practice had been established in India.

Thailand

Silk is produced in Thailand by two types of silkworms, the cultured Bombycidae and wild Saturniidae, all the year round, mostly after the rice harvest by villagers from the southern and northeast parts of the country. Women traditionally weave silk on hand looms, and pass the skill on to their daughters as weaving is considered to be a sign of maturity and eligibility for marriage. Thai silk textiles often use complicated patterns in various colors and styles. Most regions of Thailand have their own typical silks. A single thread filament is too thin to use on its own so women combine many threads to produce a thicker, usable fiber. They do this by hand-reeling the threads onto a wooden spindle to produce a uniform strand of raw silk. The process takes around 40 hours to produce a half kilogram of Thai silk.

Many local operations use a reeling machine for this task, but there are silk threads that are still hand-reeled. The difference is that hand-reeled threads produce three grades of silk: two fine grades that are ideal for lightweight fabrics and a thick grade for heavier material.

The silk fabric is soaked in hot water and bleached before dyeing in order to remove the natural yellow coloring of Thai silk yarn. To do this, skeins of silk thread are immersed in large tubs of hydrogen peroxide. Once washed and dried, the silk is then woven using a traditional hand operated loom.

India

Silk, known as *Pattu* in southern parts of India and *Resham* in Hindi/Urdu (from Persian), has a long history in India. Recent archaeological discoveries in Harappa and Chanhu-daro suggest that sericulture, employing wild silk threads from native silkworm species, existed in South Asia during the time of the Indus Valley Civilisation, roughly contemporaneous with the earliest known silk use in China. Silk is widely produced today. India is also the largest consumer of silk in the world. The tradition of wearing silk sarees in marriages by the brides is followed in southern parts of india. Silk is worn by people as a symbol of royalty while attending functions and during festivals. Historically silk was used by the upper classes, while cotton was used by the poorer classes. Today silk is mainly used in Bhoodhan Pochampally (also known as Silk City), Kanchipuram, Dharmavaram, Mysore, etc. in South India and Banaras in the North for manufacturing garments and sarees. "Murshidabad silk", famous from historical times, is mainly produced in Malda and Murshidabad district of West Bengal and woven with hand looms in Birbhum and Murshidabad district. Another place famous for production of silk is Bhagalpur. The silk from Kanchi is particularly well-known for its classic designs and enduring quality. The silk is traditionally hand-woven and hand-dyed and usually also has silver threads woven into the cloth. Most of this silk is used to make saris. The saris usually are very expensive and vibrant in color. Garments made from silk form an integral part of Indian weddings and other celebrations. In the northeastern state of Assam, three different types of silk are produced, collectively called Assam silk: Muga, Eri and Pat silk. Muga, the golden silk, and Eri are produced by silkworms that are native only to Assam. The heritage of silk rearing and weaving is very old and continues today especially with the production of Muga and Pat *riha* and *mekhela chador*, the three-piece silk saris woven with traditional motifs. *Mysore Silk Sarees*, which are known for their soft texture, last many years if carefully maintained.

Ancient Mediterranean

In the Odyssey, 19.233, when Odysseus, while pretending to be someone else, is questioned by Penelope about her husband's clothing, he says that he wore a shirt "gleaming like the skin of a dried onion" (varies with translations, literal translation here). The Roman Empire knew of and traded in silk. During the reign of emperor Tiberius, sumptuary laws were passed that forbade men from wearing silk garments, but these proved ineffectual. Despite the popularity of silk, the secret of silk-making only reached Europe around AD 550, via the Byzantine Empire. Legend has it that monks working for the emperor Justinian I smuggled silkworm eggs to Constantinople in hollow canes from China. All top-quality looms and weavers were located inside the Palace complex in Constantinople and the cloth produced was used in imperial robes or in diplomacy, as gifts to foreign dignitaries. The remainder was sold at very high prices.

Islamic world

In Islamic teachings, Muslim men are forbidden to wear silk.

Many religious jurists believe the reasoning behind the prohibition lies in avoiding clothing for men that can be considered feminine or extravagant. Despite injunctions against silk for men, silk has retained its popularity in the Islamic world because of its permissibility for women. The Muslim Moors brought silk with them to Spain during their conquest of the Iberian Peninsula.

Medieval and modern Europe

Venetian merchants traded extensively in silk and encouraged silk growers to settle in Italy. By the 13th century, Italian silk was a significant source of trade. Since that period, the silk worked in the province of Como has been the most valuable silk in the world. The wealth of Florence was largely built on textiles, both wool and silk, and other cities like Lucca also grew rich on the trade. Italian silk was so popular in Europe that Francis I of France invited Italian silk makers to France to create a French silk industry, especially in Lyon. Mass emigration (especially of Huguenots) during periods of religious dispute had seriously damaged French industry and introduced these various textile industries, including silk, to other countries.

James I attempted to establish silk production in England, purchasing and planting 100,000 mulberry trees, some on land adjacent to Hampton Court Palace, but they were of a species unsuited to the silk worms, and the attempt failed. British enterprise also established silk filature in Cyprus in 1928. In England in the mid 20th Century, silk was produced at Lullingstone Castle in Kent. Silkworms were raised and reeled under the direction of Zoe Lady Hart Dyke. Production started elsewhere later. In Italy, the Stazione Bacologica Sperimentale was founded in Padua in 1871 to research sericulture. In the late 19th century, China, Japan, and Italy were the major producers of silk. The most important cities for silk production in Italy were Como and Meldola (Forlì). In medieval times, it was common for silk to be used to make elaborate casings for bananas and other fruits.

Silk was expensive in Medieval Europe and used only by the rich. Italian merchants like Giovanni Arnolfini became hugely wealthy trading it to the Courts of Northern Europe.

North America

James I of England introduced silk-growing to the American colonies around 1619, ostensibly to discourage tobacco planting. Only the Shakers in Kentucky adopted the practice. In the 1800s a new attempt at a silk industry began with European-born workers in Paterson, New Jersey, and the city became a US silk center, although Japanese imports were still more important.

World War II interrupted the silk trade from Japan. Silk prices increased dramatically, and US industry began to look for substitutes, which led to the use of synthetics such as nylon. Synthetic silks have also been made from lyocell, a type of cellulose fiber, and are often difficult to distinguish from real silk.

Silk Production

The Making of Silk Fabric : The process of making silk is delicate and involves a number of steps.

- The first stage is called sericulture. This is the cultivation of the silk worms. The most popular species for obtaining mulberry silk is Bombyx mori. The worms are raised in a controlled environment and are fed mulberry leaves. The worms form a cocoon around themselves by secreting a protein from the top of their head.
- The farmers collect these cocoons and deliver them to the factory, where they are subject to filature operations.
- The first step is to sort the cocoons according to color, size, shape and texture.
- Then, the cocoons are made to go through a serious of hot and cold immersions. In this way, the sericin (the gummy substance that holds the fibroin strands in the silk filament together) is softened.
- Once this is done, the filament is unwound from the cocoon and combined to produce a thread of raw silk. This is the process of reeling. Usually, three to ten strands are reeled at a time.
- Finally the skeins into which the filament was reeled, are packed into bundles called books which are then put into bales to be exported to the mill.

- In the mill, the silk fiber is woven into silk fabric, using either a hand loom or a power loom.

Sericulture or silk production has a long and colorful history unknown to most people. For centuries the West knew very little about silk and the people who made it. The Roman historian, wrote in his Natural History in 70 BC "Silk was obtained by removing the down from the leaves with the help of water…". For more than two thousand years the Chinese kept the secret of silk altogether to themselves. It was the most zealously guarded secret in history.

A Secret out to the World

In spite of their secrecy, however, the Chinese were destined to lose their monopoly on silk production. Sericulture reached Korea around 200 BC, when waves of Chinese immigrants arrived there. Silk reached the West through a number of different channels. Shortly after AD 300, sericulture traveled westward and the cultivation of the silkworm was established in India.

It is also said that in AD 440, a prince of Khotan (today's Hetian)—a kingdom on the rim of Taklamakan desert — courted and won a Chinese princess. The princess smuggled out silkworm eggs by hiding them in her voluminous hairpiece. This was scant solace to the silk-hungry people of the West, for Khotan kept the secret too. Why share it with the westerners and kill a good market?

Then around AD 550, two Nestorian monks appeared at the Byzantine Emperor Justinian's court with silkworm eggs hid in their hollow bamboo staves. Under their supervision the eggs hatched into worms, and the worms spun cocoons. Byzantium was in the silk business at last. The Byzantine church and state created imperial workshops, monopolizing production and keeping the secret to themselves. This allowed a silk industry to be established in the Middle East, undercutting the market for ordinary-grade Chinese silk. However high-quality silk textiles, woven in China especially for the Middle Eastern market, continued to bring high prices in the West, and trade along the Silk Road therefore continued as before. By the sixth century the Persians, too, had mastered the art of silk weaving, developing their own rich patterns and techniques. It was only in the 13th century—the time of the Second Crusades—that Italy began silk production with the introduction of 2000 skilled silk weavers from Constantinople. Eventually silk production became widespread in Europe.

The Secret of Sericulture

Producing silk is a lengthy process and demands constant close attention. To produce high quality silk, there are two conditions which need to be fulfilled – preventing the moth from hatching out and perfecting the diet on which the silkworms should feed. Chinese developed secret ways for both.

* The eggs must be kept at 65 degrees F, increasing gradually to 77 degrees at which point they hatch. After the eggs hatch, the baby worms feed day and night every half hour on fresh, hand-picked and chopped mulberry leaves until they are very fat. Also a fixed temperature has to be maintained throughout. Thousands of feeding worms are kept on trays that are stacked one on top of another. A roomful of munching worms sounds like heavy rain falling on the roof. The newly hatched silkworm multiplies its weight 10,000 times within a month, changing color and shedding its whitish-gray skin several times.
* The silkworms feed until they have stored up enough energy to enter the cocoon stage. While they are growing they have to be protected from loud noises, drafts, strong smells such as those of fish and meat and even the odor of sweat. When it is time to build their cocoons, the worms produce a jelly-like substance in their silk glands, which hardens when it comes into contact with air. Silkworms spend three or four days spinning a cocoon around themselves until they look like puffy, white balls.
* After eight or nine days in a warm, dry place the cocoons are ready to be unwound. First they are steamed or baked to kill the worms, or pupas. The cocoons are then dipped into hot water to loosen the tightly woven filaments. These filaments are unwound onto a spool. Each cocoon is made up of a filament between 600 and 900 meters long! Between five and eight of

these super-fine filaments are twisted together to make one thread.

* Finally the silk threads are woven into cloth or used for embroidery work. Clothes made from silk are not only beautiful and lightweight, they are also warm in cool weather and cool in hot weather.

Literary sources such as The Book of History, and The Book of Rites give further information about sericulture. Reeling silk and spinning were always considered household duties for women, while weaving and embroidery were carried out in workshops as well as the home. In every silk-producing province the daughters, mothers and grandmothers of every family devoted a large part of the day for six months in a year to the feeding; tending and supervision of silkworms and to the unraveling, spinning, weaving, dyeing and embroidering of silk. By the fifth century BC, at least six Chinese provinces were producing silk. Each spring, the empress herself inaugurated the silk-raising season, for silk production was the work of women all over China. The technique and process of sericulture were guarded secrets and closely controlled by Chinese authorities. Anyone who revealed the secrets or smuggled the silkworm eggs or cocoons outside of China would be punished by death.

Silk Development in China

When silk was first discovered, it was reserved exclusively for the use of the ruler. It was permitted only to the emperor, his close relations and the very highest of his dignitaries. Within the palace, the emperor is believed to have worn a robe of white silk; outside, he, his principal wife, and the heir to the throne wore yellow, the color of the earth.

Gradually the various classes of society began wearing tunics of silk, and silk came into more general use. As well as being used for clothing and decoration, silk was quite quickly put to industrial use by the Chinese. This was something which happened in the West only in modern times. Silk, indeed, rapidly became one of the principal elements of the Chinese economy. Silk was used for musical instruments, fishing-lines, bowstrings, bonds of all kinds, and even rag paper, the word's first luxury paper. Eventually even the common people were able to wear garments of silk.

During the Han Dynasty, silk ceased to be a mere industrial material and became an absolute value in itself. Farmers paid their taxes in grain and silk. Silk began to be used for paying civil servants and rewarding subjects for outstanding services. Values were calculated in lengths of silk as they had been calculated in pounds of gold. Before long it was to become a currency used in trade with foreign countries. This use of silk continued during the Tang as well. It is possible that this added importance was the result of a major increase in production. It found its way so thoroughly into the Chinese language that 230 of the 5,000 most common characters of the mandarin "alphabet" have silk as their "key".

Silk and its Trade

Silk became a precious commodity highly sought by other countries at a very early time, and it is believed that the silk trade was actually started before the Silk Road was officially opened in the second century BC. An Egyptian female mummy with silk has been discovered in the village of Deir el Medina near Thebes and the Valley of the Kings, dated 1070 BC, which is probably the earliest evidence of the silk trade. During the second century BC, the Chinese emperor, Han Wu Di's ambassadors traveled as far west as Persia and Mesopotamia, bearing gifts including silks. A Han embassy reached Baghdad in AD 97, and important finds of Han silks have been made along the Silk Road. One of the most dramatic finds of Tang silks along the Silk Road was made in 1907 by Aurel Stein. Some time around 1015, Buddhist monks, possibly alarmed by the threat of invasion by a Tibetan people, the Tanguts, sealed more than ten thousand manuscripts and silk paintings, silk banners, and textiles into a room at the Caves of the Thousand Buddhas near Dunhuang, a station on the Silk Road in north-west Gansu.

From about the fourth century BC, the Greeks and Romans began talking of Seres, the Kingdom of Silk. Some historians believe the first Romans to set eyes upon the fabulous fabric were the legions of Marcus Licinius Crassus, Governor of Syria. At the fateful battle of Carrhae near the Euphrates River in 53 BC, the soldiers were so startled by the bright silken banners of the Parthian troops that they fled in panic. Within decades Chinese silks became widely worn by the rich and noble families of Rome. The Roman Emperor Heliogabalus (AD 218 - 222) wore nothing but silk. By 380 AD, Marcellinus Ammianus reported, "The use of silk which was once confined to the nobility has now spread to all classes without distinction, even to the lowest." The craving of silk continued to increase over the centuries. The price of silk was very hight in Rome. The best Chinese bark (a particular kind of silk) cost as much as 300 denarii (a Roman soldier's salary for an entire year!). Many sources quote that Roman citizens' demand for imported silks was so great as to be damaging to the Roman economy.

Silk was even beginning to have a civilizing effect on the barbarians. In 408 AD when Alaric, a Goth, besieged Rome, his price for sparing the city included 5000 pounds of gold, 3000 pounds of pepper, 30,000 pounds of silver and 4000 tunics of silk.

Today's Silk

World silk production has approximately doubled during the last 30 years in spite of man-made fibers replacing silk for some uses. China and Japan during this period have been the two main producers, together manufacturing more than 50% of the world production each year. During the late 1970's China, the country that first developed sericulture thousands years ago dramatically increased its silk production and has again become the world's leading producer of silk.

Indian Silk Fabric : India is the second largest producer of silk after China and the largest consumer of silk in the world. As per the 2001-02 records, India produced 17550 MT of silk.

Types of Silk Fabric : There are innumerable varieties of silk moths, but only four main types of commercially valuable natural silk :

- **Mulberry silk**

- **Tasar silk** : This is a copperish colored silk. It is coarse and is used mainly for furnishings. It is produced by the silkworm *Antheraea mylitta* , which mainly thrives on the plants Asan and Arjun. It is reared on trees in the open.
- **Muga silk** : This is a golden yellow colored silk that is produced in Assam. It is obtained from the semi-domesticated silkworm, *Antheraea assamensis* which feeds on the aromatic leaves of Som and Soalu plants.
- **Eri silk** : This is got from the domesticated silkworm, *Philosamia ricini* that feeds mainly on castor leaves. The eri cocoons are open-mouthed.

In India, mulberry silk is produced in many states such as Karnataka, Andhra Pradesh, Tamil Nadu, Jammu & Kashmir and West Bengal. The other types of silk are produced in Jharkhand, Chattisgarh, Orissa and the north-eastern states.

There are a wide variety of silk textiles made from these four kinds of natural silk. These may be handwoven or woven in power looms. In the mulberry silk variety, some of these silk fabrics are:

- **Plain silk** : This variety of silk textile may be produced on both the hand loom and the powerloom. Available in various shades and patterns, and an entire range of qualities.
- **Organza** : This is a very thin silk cloth that is made of highly twisted yarn.
- **Crepe** : This silk textile is woven from‘s’ and ‘z’ twisted yarn. The crepe sarees of Mysore are very beautiful.
- **Satin** : An extremely elegant type of mulberry silk fabric. Banarasi satin sarees are very popular.
- **Matka silk** : A thick kind of silk fabric, used for furnishing. By varying the amount of yarn used, the texture and thickness may be modified. It is produced in Bhagalpur in India.
- **Murshidabad silk** : Produced in the Murshidabad district of West Bengal, this type of silk cloth is used to make sarees and scarves. It is available in varying qualities.
- **Dupion** : This type of Indian silk fabric, is a specialty of the handlooms in Bangalore, India. It is available in a number of shades; and used for both garments as well as soft furnishings.

- **Charka silk** : This is a thick variety of silk from India that is used to make *zari* sarees. It is woven on a handloom.
- **Chiffon** : A very soft and light variety of silk fabric, it is made of highly twisted yarn that is woven on a power loom. It is a very thin, but strong fabric.
- **Chinnon** : This is a very soft and crimped silk textile. It is woven of twisted yarn on a power loom.
- **Tabby silk** : This variety is produced in Kashmir and is used to make sarees and scarves.

9

Glossary of Terms

Apparel Wool Wool suitable for manufacture into clothing products.

Belly Fibre shorn from the belly of the animal, usually heavy in condition and often containing vegetation. In the case of male animals the portion around the pizzle is stained with urine.

Blow Each sweep of the hand piece or shears in the shearing process.

Board That part of the shearing shed where the sheep and goats are shorn.

Brand :

- A temporary colouring agent applied to a small area of an animal for identification purposes.
- The identifying marks on a bale of fibre.

Bulk Line The sale lot from a clip into which the majority of fibre has been placed.

Burr Particular varieties of seed heads found in wool and other fibres such as clover burr.

Catching Pen The pen from which the shearer catches an animal for shearing.

Classing The grading of wool or other animal fibres into similar categories, taking into consideration such factors as type, fineness, length, style and fault.

Clip Quantity of shorn wool from a defined area (farm or locality) or group of sheep.

Coloured Wool A term used to describe wool with melanin pigmentation.

Comb :

- Stationary unit of shearing handpiece which enters and holds the fibre as it is cut.
- A machine which removes short fibre (noils), neps and vegetable matter and further aligns the fibres.

Condition Refers to the amount of non-wool constituents, such as yolk, sand, earth etc. present in greasy wool.

Cortex Dense fibrous central region of a fibre.

Cotts Matted fleeces which require an additional opening operation prior to the normal opening at the start of the scouring chain.

Cotted Portions Matted parts of a fleece, usually around the points, which require an additional opening process.

Crutchings Wool removed from around the tail end of sheep usually in the autumn/winter to prevent flystrike and to also make it easier for lambs to feed from the udder.

Cuticle Surface layer of wool and hair fibres consisting of overlapping scales.

Cutter Reciprocating unit of shearing handpiece which cuts the fibre against the stationary comb.

Dags Animal fibre contaminated with hard clumps of dried faeces, which is either adhering to, or has been clipped from, the anal area.

Down Tube Jointed tube containing a flexible drive shaft connecting a shearing handpiece to an individual electric motor or overhead gear.

Ewe Female sheep.

Expert Australian term for the person who grinds the shearing gear and keeps the handpieces and plant in order.

Eye Clip or Wiggings Wool shorn from the face and head of sheep to prevent wool blindness and which contains a high proportion of kemps.

Fault Any factor which limits a fibres end use or incurs extra processing cost.

Fellmonger Person who removes the wool from sheep skins, and treats pelts.

Fellmongery The premises where wool is removed from sheep-skins to produce slipe wool and treated pelts.

Fibre Diameter (Mean) The average thickness of fibres in any parcel expressed in micrometers (or microns).

Fine Fibre assessed to be the thinner diameter within a breed, flock or clip.

Fleece The coat of an animal.

Follicle Tubular depression in the skin from which a hair or wool fibre grows.

Free :

- Fibre free from vegetable matter.
- Sometimes used to mean that the fleece is free grown i.e., not cotted.

Free or nearly free (FNF) Free or nearly free of vegetable matter (VM). A term used to describe wool containing 1% or less V.M.

Full wool Wool shorn annually.

Greasy Wool Wool in its natural state as shorn off the sheep.

Hair Fibre similar in chemical composition to wool but containing a medulla.

Halfbred Wool Broadly used to describe wools of half Merino and half long wool breeding.

Hand-knotted carpet A carpet made by knotting tufts of pile yarn onto the warp threads as the fabric is woven by hand.

Hogget :

- A sheep from 7 to 18 months of age.
- The fleece of a hogget which was shorn as a lamb.

IWS The International Wool Secretariat. A partnership body funded by woolgrowers from Australia, South Africa, New Zealand, and Uruguay, for wool promotion and research world-wide.

IWTO The International Wool Textile Organisation - a body representing the interest of the world's wool-textile trade and industry with membership on a national basis. IWTO covers standards for wool testing, terms of contract and arbitration and is a forum for the international wool-textile trade and industry.

Kemps Short, straight, brittle, hairy fibres that are shed and remain in the fleece.

Keratin Chemical substance of which animal fibre is composed.

Lambs Wool Wool shorn from lambs. It is characterised by a curly tip and soft handle and is generally finer and higher yielding than full length fleece wool from mature sheep of the same breed.

Lanolin A product from the refining of wool grease (wax) recovered during scouring and which is used in cosmetics, ointments and a range of other products.

Liming The use of lime and sodium sulphide solution to dissolve all remaining wool from pulled sheep skins or to remove hair from cattle skins.

Line Several bales of fibre of a similar type.

Locks Very short staples of fibre and second cuts, which fall from the fleece during shearing and skirting.

Lot One or more bales of similar dimensions and weight within commercial limits and of similar fibre type, individually identified by number and marks of origin and put together for the purpose of sale.

Lustre The manner in which fibres reflects light. A characteristic of most strong wools and mohair.

Medium The middle fibre diameter range within a clip.

Medulla Core of large air-filled pockets between collapsed cells which occur in the centre of hair fibres. Fibres containing a medulla are called medullated and have a different appearance to unmedullated fibres. In kemp, the medulla forms the greatest portion of the fibre and is surrounded by a comparatively thin layer of cortex.

Medullated Fibres Fibres containing a medulla, or hollow core, which makes it stiff and hairy. Meduallated fibres appear chalky because light is reflected from the inner wall.

Merino Wool Fine apparel wool grown by sheep with more than three-quarters Merino blood.

Micron The standard unit of fibre diameter measurement being one millionth of a metre.

Neck The collar of fibre from under the animal's neck which is often matted and contains vegetable matter.

New Wool Wool which has not previously been manufactured.

Oddments Lines of fibre other than the main body section, eg. necks, pieces, bellies, crutchings, locks and eyeclips.

Off-Type Fleeces which do not match the main lines of a clip and which should be kept separate. These could include fleeces with different breeding to the bulk of the clip, very fine or very strong and badly faulted wools.

Painting The application of a chemical depilatory to facilitate the removal of the wool from sheep skins, with the wool remaining in good order.

Pen Stain Green excreta contamination on wool caused by close contact with daggy or defecating sheep. Causes shading problems in dyed product.

Pendulum A magnetic holder used to hold shearing combs and cutters for sharpening.

Permanently Discoloured Wool which shows yellow discolouration which cannot be removed during the scouring process. Such fibre should not be used for a pastel shade product and a dark shade is advisable.

Pie wool Wool traditionally recovered from the head and shanks of skin pieces of slaughtered sheep after decomposition of the skin tissue. Process now replaced with slipemaster process using hot water.

Pieces Poorer coloured, shorter heavy conditioned portions, skirted from the perimeter of the fleece.

Pigmentation Black or coloured fibres formed by malanocyte cells producing minute pigment granules, which evolve in the follicle.

Pizzle Stain Urine stained fibres from the bellies of male animals or crutch of female animals.

Porthole Opening or doorway through which sheep leave the shearing board after shearing.

Pressing Compressing loose fibre into bales in either a shearing shed or store.

Processing Faults Faults which when present in animal fibres are of a permanent nature eg. canary yellow, or which will need addtional work by the processor in order to rectify or remove eg. cotts, vegetable matter.

Quality Number System A subjective system of assessing the fineness of wool using an arbitrary number. Originally the number indicated potential spinning ability. With this system, the finer the wool the higher the quality number

Raw Wool Greasy wool; wool which has been scoured, carbonised, washed or solvent degreased; scoured skin wools; washed skin wools; and slipe wools. It consists of wool fibre together with variable amounts of vegetable matter and extraneous alkali insoluble impurities, mineral matter, wool waxes, suint and moisture. Raw wool has not entered yarn or felt making process.

Scoured Wool Greasy or slipe wools that have been commercially scoured, carbonised, or solvent degreased, excluding washed and partly washed wools.

Scouring Washing wool to remove the natural impurities of wax. suint, and dirt.

Sebaceous glands Glands attached to all primary and some secondary follicles and which secretes wool wax. Merinos with a higher ratio of secondary follicles produce greater quantities of wax than coarse-woolled sheep.

Second cut A staple of animal fibre which has been cut twice.

Second shear wool Wool from sheep shorn more frequently than once every eight months.

Seed Ovules from plants (other than burr producers) which adhere to the wool and other animal fibres to cause vegetable contamination i.e. bidi-bidi, grass seeds, etc.

Semi-Worsted Processing A comparatively modern system developed to provide an alternative route to produce yarns with similar characteristics to worsted spun yarn but in a shorter, more economic way. Because there is no combing step, the wool used in this process must be of good uniform length and free from vegetable matter.

Shearing The operation of removing the fleece from animals by machine or blades. Frequency of shearing may be once a year, twice a year, or three times over two years.

Shearing board Area in shearing shed where animals are shorn.

Shearing shed Synonymous with woolshed. Building in which sheep and goats are shorn. Commonly abbreviated to shed.

Shed Hand Synonymous with woolhandler. Persons, other than shearers, employed to handle and usually prepare the shorn fibre in the shearing shed.

Shive Vegetable matter, usually that contained in the back wool, such as leaves, grass etc. . Does not refer to burrs or seed.

Shorn Hogget Fleece off a hogget shorn as a lamb.

Skin Pieces Clumps of wool attached to pieces of skin removed inadvertently during shearing and which, if not removed prior to manufacture, will cause problems in processing.

Slipe Wool Wool removed from the skins of slaughtered animals, by a chemical depilatory which loosens the wool fibres.

Slipemaster Machine used to remove wool from pelt trimmings and head pieces in a fellmongery, and with the aid of scalding water.

Sound Evenly grown fibre, of good tensile strength throughout the staple length.

Stand Area immediately surrounding an individual shearing machine.

Staples A mass of fibres growing in bunches, or clusters and also known as locks, each of which is held to the adjoining locks by binders or fibres running obliquely from one staple to another.

Strong Wool with a large fibre diameter for its type.

Style The degree of excellence or fault in a line. A subjective term broadly used to embrace character, colour, condition, soundness, freedom from seed and other faults.

Suint Natural water soluble impurity present in wool and some other animal fibres, secreted from the sudoriferous or sweat gland attached to the follicle.

Sweating Method of dewoolling skins dependent on induced bacterial degradation to loosen the wool within the skin.

Tare The weight of packaging material enclosing the fibre in the bale.

Tender Fibre with a tensile weakness along a portion of the staple length.

Unsound Fibres which are weak or tender in tensile strength.

Wool grease Natural impurities of wool (wax and suint) secreted by glands attached to the wool follicle. Also called yolk.

Woollen Processing The yarn produced by woollen carding and spinning (condenser spun), and which is bulkier and fuzzy compared to other yarns. These characteristics carry through to the texture of the fabrics and knitted wares.

Woolmark Registered IWS trade mark denoting products made from pure new wool, which also meet strict performance criteria.

Wool table Slatted table on which fleeces are skirted and may be classed.

Worsted Processing The branch of the textile trade which uses mainly the longer stapled fibres which are gilled to align the fibres and combed to remove the noils and vegetable matter and gilled to straighten the fibres. The yarn produced is very smooth and level and the fabric clear and smooth handling.

Yield The amount of clean fibre, at a standard regain expressed as a percentage of the weight of greasy fibre.

Bibliography

Wools of New Zealand (formerly the New Zealand Wool Board) for the information on shearing from "The Shearing Handbook".

Mr A Marshall, Wools of New Zealand, for background information on the Llama.

Mr B Morrison, R D 3, Eketahuna, for assistance with shearing.

Mr R Dunick, Christchurch, for assistance with shearing the Alpaca.

Mr J Woodward, Mohair Fibres Ltd, for assistance with Mohair and Cashmere fibres.

Mr W R Regnault, Director of Wool Diploma Studies, Massey University, Palmerston North, for assistance with slipe wool production.

Mrs T Reeve, Box 32, Horitu, Waikato, for assistance with Angora Rabbits.

Mrs G Absolon, Box 1681, Palmerston North, for assistance with Angora Rabbits.

Mr R Johnson of Kingston Morrison, Wellington, for assistance with the Yak.

International Mohair Association for assistance with Mohair Production.

MAF (Ministry of Agriculture & Fisheries) for assistance with Angora Goats and Cashmere Goats.

NZ Society of Animal Production, 1992, Vol. 52, for assistance with Shearing the Alpaca.

The Economist Intelligence Unit Report, "Luxury Fibres" for assistance with background information on the Angora Goat, Cashmere Goat, Camel, Angora Rabbit, Llama and the Yak.

Index

A

B

C